CW01660411

# THE KEY TO STUDY SKILLS

***SIMPLE STRATEGIES TO DOUBLE YOUR READING, MEMORY, AND FOCUS***

**Lev and Anna Goldentouch**

**With Suraj Sharma**

**www.KeyToStudy.com**

**Goldentouch Consulting Ltd.**

info@KeyToStudy.com



The Key to Study Skills: Simple Strategies to Double Your Reading, Memory, and Focus

ISBN 978-965-7732-00-7

To our students from whom we learn daily
and
To the course graduates: each of you is a hero capable of changing the world.

# CONTENTS

# FOREWORD

The ability to learn and retain new information is a skill many people desperately desire. And yet, their desire shrivels up at the thought of effort, and they simply give up and never go on to acquire advanced learning skills including speedreading and memorization they desperately need to succeed.

I can sympathize. I used to be the world champion when it came to using excuses about dealing with my memory.

However, you do not have to wait as long as I did. And starting right now, you can go beyond dreaming about improving the quality of your mind. Instead of being like those who learn only a handful of words and phrases when studying a language, you can leap towards holding a decent conversation in a fortnight.

And unlike so many who cave into procrastination when faced with learning a new skillset for a new career, you need not let fear set in, nor must you do as they do and simply give up.

Why?

Because now you hold a powerful book in your hands. A tool that will not only help you overcome the fear that cripples so many, on that will teach you the skills you need to gain mastery over how you read and what you remember. These are the skills that will melt away any angst you have felt and make any worries or concerns about learning irrelevant.

Dr. Lev and Anna Goldentouch have the ability to make difficult concepts clear in an easy to follow, well laid out and organized manner. One of the main techniques they teach is speedreading. Speedreading is a scientifically verifiable art, and only the likes of Lev and Anna could convince me to try it. Plus, they have taught me new things about the art of memory that I will cherish and share for the rest of my life. Together, their instantly applicable lessons in learning make *The Key To Study Skills* invaluable.

Listen: The ability to learn is a skill by which practice and patience are the stepping-stones to a fuller and richer life. But ask yourself as you read ...

Is patience really necessary?

Not necessarily.

Within the pages of this book, you will learn the skills necessary to help you achieve your goal of learning and remembering what you learn at speeds so blazing hot, you will be amazed by just how much you can achieve in record time.

So, whether you are studying in school or immersed in autodidacticism, get reading *The Key To Study Skills* and brace yourself for a whole new and improved you.

Anthony Metivier, Ph.D.
www.MagneticMemoryMethod.com
August 2015
Berlin, Germany

# PREFACE

Albert Einstein once said, "Insanity is doing the same thing over and over and expecting a different result."

For years, I learned as I was taught in school. The techniques I learned worked, I was getting excellent marks, and I even finished a Ph.D. in a good university. I believed I had a good set of techniques and skills for learning. However, there was only one problem. I did not enjoy the process of learning.

When I married Anna, after a short courtship, the truth became apparent. The amount of content I consumed was well below my potential. My brain was starving for stimulation.

Anna taught me how to get out of my comfort zone. She taught me to read faster, remember more and help others. After ten wonderful years with Anna, her mission is also my mission – to help people to learn FAST, remember what they learn and achieve their creative potential. We decided to name our techniques and teaching the KeyToStudy System.

In 2013 with help of Jonathan Levi, we mass-produced our method on Udemy:

https://www.udemy.com/superlearning-speed-reading-memory-techniques

Through the Udemy course, tens of thousands of students have learned the skills Anna and I teach. The course is also available as a book:

http://www.amazon.com/Become-SuperLearner-Reading-Advanced-Memorization-ebook/dp/B00VI7ZBUS

With the success of the Udemy course and the book, since each student was different, I had to answer thousands of questions. To help as many people as possible, I posted the answers to the questions on my blog:

www.KeyToStudy.com.

Another key advantage of the blog was and is the ability to provide free training exercises:

http://www.KeyToStudy.com/examplary-training-schedule/

Our students ask some great questions, and I answer those questions on the blog. With time, however, I decided to consolidate many of the questions and answers from the blog into a practical book. The purpose is to:

- Encourage our students to continue improving their skills.
- Answer questions.
- Spur new thoughts and ideas to encourage growth.
- Explain more in depth the concepts taught in our course and book.

This book is for those who have tried using other books or courses teaching speedreading techniques, creative learning skills, and memory techniques but failed. If the reader has never previously tried any other method, then you have before you a tested and successful method of improvement. Anna and I do not promise greatness; however, our goal and heartfelt mission is to help remove some of the obstacles on your way to improving your learning speed, retention and reaching your creative potential.

This book was created by our great community of students who were willing to share their difficulties and successes. Anna and I have spent countless hours researching the methods we present. Thorough research backs each method. I honestly believe the methods, skills and techniques presented (along with diligent practice) will help you unlock your learning potential, increase your reading speed, improve your retention, and skyrocket your memorization skills.

# INTRODUCTION

*What information consumes is rather obvious: it consumes the attention of its recipients.* - Herbert Simon

## Read Faster And Remember More

Who wouldn't like to be able to read faster and remember more? In this knowledge and data-driven world, your overall productivity as a professional, student, or businessperson depends on how efficiently you can ingest, digest and process the information and data coming at you from every possible direction. During the last two decades, an adequate means to deal with the overwhelming incoming information and data has not been developed. Neither has there been any serious development or attention devoted to the idea of how learning styles must evolve with the changing circumstances of the digital age.

Enter the KeyToStudy System, a new path-breaking methodology for faster learning, better retention and efficient information processing for everyone.

## Results On Two Levels

The KeyToStudy System works and produces results on two different levels.

**Level 1**: The first level is the ***framework***, which is the foundation of the overall philosophy of attention appropriation.

**Level 2:** The second level is a collection of ***techniques, practices, and exercises*** built on the foundation of the *framework.*

It is imperative our students understand the difference between the Level 1 foundation of the framework/philosophy, and the Level 2 technique/practice/exercise of the system. A clear grasp of the concepts in Level 1 will shorten the time needed to learn the methodology itself, and Level 2 will expedite the acquisition of the method.

## Efficiency In Reading

Efficiency in reading boils down to two fundamental parameters:

1. **Reading speed**: The number of words per minute read; and
2. **Retention**: Retention is measured in the percentage of text recalled.

The philosophy behind both parameters is based on several principles: clarity, intention, and mindfulness. Without truly understanding these principles, the techniques explained in this book will only produce shallow and temporary results at best.

## KeyToStudy Principles

The KeyToStudy principles are:

- **Clarity**: Clarity is the simple act of determining the purpose of the text from its title and deriving certainty from it.
- **Intention**: Intention is reading with a purpose and ensuring the reading is conscious, intentional and not careless.
- **Mindfulness**: Mindfulness is keeping the title of the text in mind and reading with a certain presence of mind.

When the student understands:

- That 80% of all reading is simply a matter of purposefully looking at the text; and
- An equally big chunk of remembering is simply a matter of connecting new information to previously known information,
- Then *a transformative change occurs in both reading speed and retention capacity.*

## Structure Of Chapters

Some chapters have a section called "For Further Research," which contains links to material within the chapter. These links provide each student with the ability to do independent research. By placing the links at the end of the chapter, the student will not become distracted from the text and can choose the proper time for extra research.

You will also note there are links within the text of the chapters. These links are imperative to the subject being discussed.

Finally, throughout the text you will find our email address: info@KeyToStudy.com as a reminder we want to hear from our students.

## Our Goal

Our goal is to build a community of SuperLearners who exchange ideas and help each other grow. We delight in helping each of our students fulfill their potential and in turn become mentors to those who cross their path.

Again, our hope is you will persevere and experience for yourself a new joy in learning. We wish the student good luck on their journey to becoming a SuperLearner. Our expectation for each of our students is to **READ WITH CONFIDENCE!**

## Books, Courses And Resources

For discounts on our books and courses, as well as other learning resources, please visit:

http://www.KeyToStudy.com/learning-resources-cheatsheet/

# PART 1: WHO NEEDS THE KEYTOSTUDY SYSTEM

# Chapter 1: My Story: How I Developed My Reading Strategy

## Holes In My Education

When I was a kid, my parents wanted me to become a chess champion or a math professor and did not allow me to read the books I loved like science fiction and the classics. This produced significant holes in my education, which became apparent when I was 19 years old. As a straight-A student in a prestigious university, I expected myself to know things; yet, I failed simple trivia questions my less distinguished friends could answer from psychology and history. I desperately needed to do something. I addressed the issue in my typical head-on fashion. After getting my first degree, I found I had too much time on my hands and extra money to buy any book I wanted. I bought books and started reading – seriously reading.

Since the holes in my education included literature, history, and philosophy, I decided to fill the holes. Eventually, as I began to read and learn more, my questions became more focused. The method I had developed (buying books and reading) could no longer satisfy me.

I started to work on my Ph.D., and I was required to read complicated articles that were just too boring to handle. I was required to look for information using this new search engine called Google (the year was 1999). I needed a new method. The method required basic principles that could explain and systematize the abundance of seemingly unconnected information I was learning. At this point, my method consisted of reviewing articles I had already read, and when an article interested me sufficiently, I would "dive in" and reread the entire article.

## Meeting Anna

I met Anna the year I finished my Ph.D. She taught speedreading and comprehension. I told her I had tried to learn speedreading myself, but it did not work, and I did not believe in what she was doing. Needless to say, she had other assets that caught my attention, and it was not very long before we were married.

Anna explained with the new method she was teaching I would read much faster and remember EVERYTHING no matter how boring or outdated it was and for as long as I needed to remember the information. After approximately ten weeks of training with Anna, I graduated from the course with a reading sped of 1000 words per minute (wpm) with 80% retention.

To keep up with the people around me, I needed to digest a massive amount of articles. I began focusing on materials and details I could reuse in my future work. I still felt I read very slowly so I decided I should increase my reading speed. I continued to practice what Anna taught me, and currently I am reading at approximately 3000 wpm with 80% retention using several proprietary methods.

## What I Learned

Here is what I learned from years of training:

1. Each period of life comes with **unique challenges**. As an effective tool to address these challenges, reading strategies need to be adapted.
2. How we learn is a matter of **motivation** and not merely an issue of the methods we use.
3. It is okay to leave gaps or even huge holes in our education, as long as we **come back and fix the gaps** when we are ready.

The moral of the story is I was able to fill in the gaps and marry a wonderful woman. Together we continue to help others become SuperLearners. With the above principles in mind, the KeyToStudy System continues to grow and be refined to meet the challenges of an ever-changing society.

# Chapter 2: Getting Better At Getting Better

## Kaizen

We would like to introduce the Japanese concept of kaizen for those who may not be familiar with the concept. Kaizen is the Japanese word for "change for better" and can be translated loosely as "good change." The idea is not searching for the biggest challenge and focusing all attention on it, but rather handing small challenges one by one, day by day until the sum of small improvements generates an enormous impact.

By improving standardized activities and processes, kaizen aims to eliminate waste. While kaizen usually delivers small improvements, the culture of continual aligned minor improvements and standardized approach yields substantial results in terms of overall improvement in productivity.

Kaizen includes the idea of "getting better at getting better" as an essential ingredient to productivity. For a SuperLearner, the *constant improvement is a continuous process*. For the KeyToStudy student, implementing the continual improvements and standardized approaches presented within this book will produce a cycle of questioning, learning, and implementation.

## Continuous Improvement Steps

This kind of continuous improvement can be broken down into six steps:

1. **Standardize**: Come up with a process for a particular activity that is repeatable and organized.

2. **Measure**: Examine whether the process is efficient using quantifiable data, e.g., time to complete, hours spent, etc.

3. **Compare**: Compare your measurements against your requirements. Does this process save time? Does it take too much time? Does it accomplish the desired result?

4. **Innovate**: Search for new, better ways to do the same work or achieve the same result. Look for smarter, more efficient routes to the same end-goal that boosts productivity.

5. **Repeat**: Go back to Step 1 and start again.

## Our Training

Our training follows the same methodology of continuous improvement. We generate measurable, repeatable and reusable steps.

1. We start with **visualization**.
2. Then, we reuse visualization for creativity and **memory improvement**.
3. We **build speedreading** upon a stronger memory enhanced by improved visualization skills.
4. Our improved reading abilities are the basis for **better learning skills**.

In this book, we try to dedicate particular attention to these steps. There are two additional steps, which are crucial for learning. We do not spend a lot of time on them in our course; however, these steps should be recognized and implemented:

5. Before you begin the learning process, **identify the need for change**.
6. **Implement the lessons** learned after you complete a learning process.

## Need For Change

The need for change is required as a driving motivation for learning. Ask yourself:

What skill or knowledge will make the **maximum change** in my well-being/understanding/contribution with **minimal effort investment**?

Once an answer emerges, *overcoming the minimal obstacles* is easy on your way to knowledge. On the other hand, an unfocused search for knowledge may cause you to lose interest, retreat and lose confidence.

## Is It Worth The Effort?

The *implementation* part is harder. Before implementation is undertaken (and at each step of the implementation process), we should ask ourselves, "Is it worth the effort?"

If the answer is "no go," maybe it is better to limit the losses. If the answer is "go," we have an obligation to ourselves to implement what we learned in practice, even if it is hard.

Many people do not follow the "go / no go" logic when deciding if something is "too much work" at the crucial moment. However, this logic is probably the best opportunity to invest your energy and benefit from the results.

If you have not been progressing, be honest with yourself and understand the true reason for not advancing. In my experience, a good schedule induces active preparation and reduces negative procrastination.

Asking the right question, finding a good answer and acting upon the new understanding generates positive change in our world. Let us get better at getting better!

## For Further Research:

http://en.wikipedia.org/wiki/Kaizen

http://lifehacker.com/get-better-at-getting-better-the-kaizen-productivity-p-1672205148

# Chapter 3: What Is The KeyToStudy System

With the recent success of our "*Become a SuperLearner*" Udemy class and book with the same name, I often remind myself of our humble beginnings, and the fundamental principles of our methodology. The KeyToStudy System has improved and expanded because of the many years of research by Anna and myself.

## KeyToStudy System

The KeyToStudy System builds upon the following ideas:

1. **Getting things done:** We ask our students:

   - to have **clear goals**,
   - to **use their skills** while learning to achieve meaningful results, and
   - to find time and motivation to **practice**.

*We consider hands-on experience more important than theoretical understanding.* Unlike many other methodologies, we build several skills gradually in a mutually complementary form to produce the best results. Focusing on one particular skill may render the whole system ineffective.

2. **Visualization:** Our visual processing is much faster than our audio processing; much like a GPU (graphics processor unit) is typically stronger than a CPU (central processing unit). However, *to use information correctly, encoding of the information must occur in a format our visual cortex can process.* We use visualization to achieve just the encoding process. There are several useful ways to visualize concepts: creatively, logically and otherwise. Occasionally, some of our students may not be able to visualize consciously, yet are still capable of great speed, which may occur subconsciously.

3. **Memorization:** A strong memory is a key to effective learning. Please note we are <u>*not*</u> focusing on the memory

athlete skill set. However, we are focusing on the tasks students, teachers, business professionals, lawyers, programmers, engineers, doctors, and linguists perform in their personal and professional life. Therefore, we adapt the memorization techniques to remember textbooks and functional elements, not endless numbers or stacks of cards associated with modern memory championships.

4. **Speedreading:** Once the brain is trained to process large amounts of data, speedreading becomes a handy and necessary skill. Currently, speedreading is probably the best way to learn a large quantity of data in most subjects. When we started to develop the methodology in the early 2000s, books were still the primary modality of reading. Today, we consume most of our information in digital format; therefore, we have adapted our methodology accordingly.

5. **Analysis:** Trying to remember more information than can be used is unreasonable. It is counter-productive if fictions of our imagination mix with the information we learn. An advanced skill set always includes:

- adaptation to the material,
- use of prior knowledge,
- prioritization of what we read, and
- developing the best strategy for our personal style and particular need.

6. **Community:** One of our most important priorities is building and maintaining a strong and active community of SuperLearners. People are different individuals, and we can help each other become better. By working with Jonathan Levi, Suraj Sharma, and many others, we are building a strong and flexible community capable of learning, helping and developing each other to become SuperLearners.

Your success is our success. Please do not hesitate to contact us:

info@KeyToStudy.com

# Chapter 4: The Science Behind The KeyToStudy System

Anna and I have conducted statistical research with thousands of students; however, we could never afford a "control" group receiving a "placebo" method. Therefore, instead of focusing on success statistics, I concentrate on the other methods that inspired us. Below are the methods we discuss/explain in this book, and are listed here for a preview of the upcoming chapters.

| | |
|---|---|
| Visualization | Dual coding, Yoga visualization exercises |
| Reading stages | Metacognition, SQ3R methodology, skimming, and scanning |
| Perspectives | 5WH, Attribute listing |
| Colors | Thinking hats, synesthesia |
| Visual angle, saccades, subvocalization suppression | Shultz tables, Meta-guiding, "The Speed Reading Book" by Tony Buzan |
| Mind maps | General semantics popularized by Tony Buzan, Tree data structure |
| Memorization | Chunking, Memory Palace, PAO (Person-Action-Object), Major System |
| Analysis | Information theory, Socratic method, Content analysis, Critical thinking, Ontology |

## For Further Research:

**Visualization:**

http://en.wikipedia.org/wiki/Dual-coding_theory

**Reading stages:**

http://en.wikipedia.org/wiki/SQ3R

http://en.wikipedia.org/wiki/Speed_reading

**Perspectives:**

http://en.wikipedia.org/wiki/Five_Ws

**Colors:**

http://en.wikipedia.org/wiki/Six_Thinking_Hats

http://en.wikipedia.org/wiki/Synesthesia

**Mind Maps**

http://en.wikipedia.org/wiki/Tree_%28data_structure%29

**Memorization:**

http://en.wikipedia.org/wiki/Chunking_(psychology)

**Analysis:**

https://en.wikipedia.org/wiki/Information_theory

http://en.wikipedia.org/wiki/Socratic_method

http://en.wikipedia.org/wiki/Content_analysis

http://en.wikipedia.org/wiki/Critical_thinking

http://en.wikipedia.org/wiki/Ontology_(information_science)

# Chapter 5: This Course Is For You!

Our perfect audience consists of people of every age and degree who find a need or satisfaction in reading and learning daily. The training described in this book is hard; it requires motivation, dedication, and wisdom. Fortunately, we have a great community of SuperLearners who strive to achieve the same goals and will support you through each and every step. However, there are common questions we would like to address.

## Age

The KeyToStudy System as presented in this book is fine-tuned for people between 13 and 65 years old who need to read and learn daily. Younger students should put more emphasis on creativity, and older students should focus more on memorization and analysis. Effort should be distributed based on personal abilities in such a way there will be no stagnation and no burnout - please make sure your schedule is adjusted according to your individual capabilities.

## ADHD And Dyslexia

While some of our students claim our methodology "cured" their ADHD and dyslexia (see Further Research below), ***we do not make such claims***.

If you have dyslexia, you will need to train much harder; however, the result of training may AMAZE you. If you have ADHD, you will need to get extra creative in generating interest in your training; however, you will start to enjoy texts you could not focus on prior to training.

Some people do have rare health issues and learning disorders and do need specific personalization. You can ask us free of charge at info@KeyToStudy.com. We have trained tens of thousands of students and may have some suggestions just for you.

## Bilingual

Many people know more than one language. When a person is bilingual, speedreading skills do not transfer between languages without training. For example, Lev Goldentouch learned to speedread Russian within 10 weeks; however, English speedreading took 8 more weeks, and Hebrew speedreading came 6 weeks afterward. Some languages, like Spanish and Portuguese, are more closely related, and the skills may be transferred between them virtually effortlessly. It makes sense to acquire skills in the language you are most familiar with and then retrain for the second and third language.

## Professional Adaptation

Some people do not believe this book is useful for their profession. If you are a knowledge worker and read daily, you will definitely benefit from this course. Our students include programmers and engineers, lawyers, and business professionals, medical doctors, and psychologists. On www.KeyToStudy.com, we provide specific examples of how the methods we teach can be applied to some common professional challenges. If you cannot find a solution for your particular material, you can challenge us on info@KeyToStudy.com. We may write an article especially for you!

## Good Books For Speedreading

Not every book is suitable for speedreading. **Overview articles** and **textbooks** are typically great for speedreading; however, there are some exceptions.

Do not try speedreading advanced math. Wikipedia is excellent for training memorization, but perhaps a bit too dense for speedreading. When attempting to speedread legal and medical information, you may need to reread the text several times: first for the general idea, then for the specific terminology and finally for particular examples.

**Most blog articles** are great for speedreading, as long as they are at least four paragraphs long.

Occasionally articles do not contain enough information to justify more than scanning. For example, "Politician Talked and Reaffirmed His Positions" is typically not interesting. Try to scan where there is not enough information and to read otherwise.

**Novels** are great for speedreading. Modern works are more suitable than older literature. Personally, I love to speedread French existentialists and Russian classics. You may want to reread occasional descriptions to understand the particular scenery described within.

## Chinese Connection

We Westerners need to learn visualization skills. Fortunately, Chinese characters provide a very natural visualization system for those who can read them. Two-time World Memory Champion Wang Feng uses a combination of Chinese characters and rhymes with amazing results. It is possible his training more than 7 hours a day for 1½ years before his first memory competition made the difference. He can remember 500 digits and/or 500 words in 5 minutes, which is slightly short of 2 words per second. This is faster than he can say the word. In fact, he chunks words and numbers in 2x2 structures and remembers the whole structure at once. He says, *"My life is easier now that I know mnemonics. It's really helpful for remembering names and details – and things from books I read. I don't need a pen anymore."*

## Memory Championships

The World Memory Championships is an organized competition of mental sports in which competitors memorize as much information as possible within a given time period. The Championships have occurred annually since 1991 and hosted by various organizations.

The first winner was Dominic O'Brien, who combined memory palaces and the Major System of memorization into a single Dominic method. Dominic O'Brien has been a champion for 8 years until the new millennium brought new champions.

An accountant, Ben Pridmore (so far three-time world champion), was the first man to remember a randomly shuffled pack of cards in under 30 seconds. His technique, he claims was old-fashioned storytelling.

A young math teacher, Jonas Von Essen, held the championship in 2013 and 2014, probably using a two-digit PAO (person-action-object) system.

In this book, we explain some of these systems. To ensure progress, it is important to choose a system that comes naturally to ***YOU*** and then practice it extensively. If you practice for two weeks on a memory skill set (i.e., memory palace, PAO, mind mapping, etc.) and cannot identify what works better for you, please contact us at info@KeyToStudy.com and we will help.

## Misconceptions

One common, often-repeated question we are asked is, **"Can anyone master speedreading and memorization?"** Our experience shows the biggest limitation to mastering the skill of speedreading and memorization is simply laziness and a lack of motivation. Even students who suffer from dyslexia and brain damage have completed the course and improved their results significantly. Here are some of more common questions and comments:

### "This is a con; it is scientifically impossible."

Every scientific theory is based on assumptions. Some scientists assume a wrong learning strategy and evaluate the effort required to reach results using a particular strategy. The results show no one can read and memorize as much as we claim. Same scientists figure bees cannot fly due to some aerodynamic limitations...

### "I do not read. Why do I make no progress?"

A simple strategy is not enough. You do need to practice systematically to train your brain to use its new skills. If you do not read for a long time, you will eventually degrade to your most comfortable reading method. This is not surprising: if you do not walk for a long time, you cannot actually run and need physiotherapy. Why should the brain be any different?

**"The faster you read the less you understand."**

This is probably a true statement for reading speeds above 1000 wpm. An average person reads 250 wpm. You probably can quadruple your reading speed and improve comprehension since your mind will stop wandering off.

**"I took three other speedreading courses and none worked."**

You need to train memory *before* you can train reading. Your biggest limitation is not how fast you can read, but how quickly you can process what you read in your working memory. Train your memorization, and speedreading will follow.

**"I understand why I will read better, but will I work better?"**

Working memory capabilities are linked closely with measured IQ results. The primary tools we use to develop our skills are visualization and creativity. Einstein used to make many "mental experiments" as a way to visualize complex physical phenomena. Data scientists always look for new ways to visualize data. When you analyze financial data, you display visualization for various implicit information (like Bollinger bands). Visualization is a great way to address complex issues. If you speed up the way you get information, widen the range of versions you analyze and improve the quality in which you view the results - it is an ENORMOUS competitive advantage.

## Good / Bad Training Schedules

We recommend several good training schedules, like http://www.KeyToStudy.com/exemplary-training-schedule/

However, many people use bad schedules which result in discouragement and failure to accomplish their goal of learning to speedread and improve their memory. Here are some examples:

**1. Read the whole book, watch all the videos, play each game for 10 minutes**

While this generates a feeling of knowing the subject, it does not actually improve any skill.

**2. Deciding to train 8 hours a day and finish the course within a week**

Some activities require brain adaptation and rest. If the student does not rest and the brain does not adapt, the results will be suboptimal. In the best-case scenario, you will need much more effort; in the worst-case scenario, you will suffer a burnout.

**3. Try to memorize 1 year of learning within 2 days**

Again, this is an extremely unlikely scenario. Generally, we build strong memories, and, over time, add further memories to them. For example, we develop strong concepts/skills and slowly add examples for each concept/skill. Trying to squeeze too much material into too short a time will generate a mess causing various concepts/skills to mix with each other.

**4. Read something into one memory structure / reread into another / continue until happy**

When memorizing, typically the first reasonable memory structure is good enough. Unlearning and relearning something once may generate dual coding. However, if you complete this process too many times, you once again create a mess. Our brains process information in many different ways. The act of perceiving information through several cognitive avenues, i.e. audio or visual, mind maps or memory palaces, enables us to retrieve information when needed. The ability to process information in multiple ways and retrieve the information when needed is what we call dual coding.

**5. Training twenty different skills in parallel**

If you train speedreading and yoga, this will probably work great. However, if you train speedreading, three foreign languages and anatomy, you may generate too much pressure on your memory. Nothing bad will happen; you will simply be inefficient.

**6. Speedread while sleep hacking**

This is probably something you should not do because you may end up very confused.

**7. Combining five methods from five different sources**

Not all methods work well with each other. If you combine our methods with (say) subliminal reading, you will start losing retention.

**8. Fixating on one exercise**

You need to take several steps to become a proficient speedreader. There are several ways to proceed with each step. Either being unable to complete a particular exercise or being exceptionally good at a specific exercise is not sufficiently important to fixate on the exercise.

**9. Learn the course for 2 weeks; take a month off and repeat**

It takes some time for the brain to adapt. If you do not give your brain enough time for this adaptation, you will make no progress.

**10. Play all the games; read no books**

Reading books or articles is probably more important than playing the games. Do not ignore reading, or you will make no progress.

## The Fastest Reader In The World

While the fastest talking speed is around 600 words per minute (637 words per minute record was set by a British salesman Steve Woodmore back in 1990), the reading speed is much higher. The World Championship Speed Reading Competition stresses reading comprehension as critical. The top contestants typically read around 1,000 to 2,000 words per minute with approximately 50% comprehension or above. The world champion is Anne Jones with 4,700 words per minute with 67% comprehension. Those who claim 10,000 words per minute have yet to reach a satisfactory comprehension level. In fact, Anne Jones has won the World Speed Reading Championship six times! She finished Dan Brown's book *Inferno* in 41 minutes, 48 seconds.

### The Rain Man

Most people know "mega savant" Kim Peek best by the movie character he inspired (*Rain Man)* played by Dustin Hoffman in the 1988 film of the same name. Fast absorption was no problem for Peek, who could just as easily read and memorize a telephone book as a compendium of Shakespearean plays.

Kim could take in 10,000 words per minute reading two pages at a time; the left page with his left eye and the right page with his right eye. Kim Peek used synesthesia to reach his goals. For him, numbers appeared to have colors.

### Richard Feynman/Synesthesia

Richard Feynman, winner of the 1965 Nobel Prize in Physics, had colored letters and numbers mixed. In his words,

> *"When I see equations, I see the letters in colors – I don't know why. As I'm talking, I see vague pictures of Bessel functions from Jahnke and Emde's book, with light-tan j's, slightly violet-bluish n's, and dark brown x's flying around. And I wonder what the hell it must look like to the students."*

Only recently, scientists discovered by performing daily exercises ANYONE can develop synesthesia. Synesthetes see characters just as others do (in whichever color actually displayed, yet simultaneously perceive colors as associated to each one.). Play the accuracy and synesthesia game every day at http://www.KeyToStudy.com/accuracy-synesthesia, and you will see letters and numbers in color!

## For Further Research

### ADHD and Dyslexia

http://www.KeyToStudy.com/SuperLearning-cure-addadhddyslexia/

### Memory

https://en.wikipedia.org/wiki/World_Memory_Championships

http://en.wikipedia.org/wiki/Memory_sport

http://en.wikipedia.org/wiki/Memory

http://en.wikipedia.org/wiki/Dominic_O%27Brien

# PART 2: MINDSET AND MOTIVATION

# Chapter 6: Know Yourself

We are different people, with specific strengths and weaknesses. By understanding your personal style, you can understand what difficulties you may have. Each of us has a bit of every style although some styles are more predominate.

## Technocrat

This is a typical style for engineers and programmers. People with this style are very logical and have excellent control of logical markers and mind maps, processes and flows. It is not uncommon for technocrats to have difficulty with visualization; however, this should not stop a technocrat. The speed and efficiency with which technocrats operate mind maps is unmatched. Technocrats adapt reading speed to content density much more than other styles.

## Artist

This style is the opposite of a technocrat. Artists create visualizations very easily, maybe even too easily. Occasionally the visualizations get a life of their own and start generating details not supported by the text. Artists are usually great with memory palaces. Artists need to monitor their speed carefully when speedreading and not allow themselves too much time for marker creation. The majority of memory champions are very creative.

## Sportsman

Some students push themselves very hard. They need very clear goals, and they work very hard to achieve those objectives. Typically, the laconic structure of PAO memory technique resonates well with sportive speed and accuracy. Sportsmen tend to push themselves too hard and make several critical mistakes:

- Skipping critical steps of training assuming they are "less important" or "trivial."
- Ignoring rest and becoming burned out.

- Pushing speed faster than comprehension allows, resulting in poor understanding at high speeds.

For this type of personality, training with Anna is very helpful. When trained correctly, this kind of student generates the best overall speed and comprehension.

## Perfectionist

Many lawyers and doctors read slower than average speed because they feel each word is important. When memorizing, perfectionists tend to create great visualizations, but tend to forget to connect them with equally good links. Perfectionists may often try to remember EVERYTHING resulting in extremely high retention at a price of creative edge and speed:

- Perfectionists try to memorize physical definitions and mathematical rules, instead of attempting to understand them. This results in word-by-word recitation instead of ability to solve mathematical tasks.
- Perfectionists focus either on speed or on quality, and often fail to balance. By working on speed SLOWLY without allowing quality to degrade, perfectionists can overcome this limitation.
- Perfectionists always work harder and are most likely to persevere in creating lifelong skill sets.

## Personal goals

Since you are reading this book, you have your own agenda. You want to learn something you could not learn before, handle some formidable challenge, and/or become better at doing something we cannot anticipate. Write down these additional personal goals below.

**ADDITIONAL PERSONAL GOALS**

1. ______________________________

2. ______________________________

3. ____________________________

4. ____________________________

As an additional exercise, identify your style from the styles above.

What is major your style?

__________________________________________________

What are your minor or complimentary styles?

__________________________________________________

Do you need to make any adaptive plans for your major skill (i.e., as a perfectionist I need to ________) or minor/complimentary skills?

## The Discontinuity Principle

The more you are used to something, the less stimulating it is for our thinking. When you disrupt your thought patterns, those ideas that create the greatest stimulus to our thinking do so because they force us to make new connections to comprehend the situation. Roger von Oech calls this a "Whack on the Side of the Head," and Edward de Bono coined a new word, PO, which stands for "Provocative Operation."

Try programming interruptions into your day. For example:

- Change your working hours,
- Get to work using a different route,
- Listen to a different radio station,
- Read some magazines or books you would not normally read,
- Try a different recipe, and/or
- Watch a TV program or film you would not normally watch.

Provocative ideas are often stepping-stones helping us to think about other ideas. Abutting ideas next to each other, such that their friction creates new thought paths is a technique that flourishes in the east but causes discomfort in Western thinking.

## Obstacles To Creativity

If our goal is to be creative in making and linking markers, it is useful to take note of barriers to creativity. Take your time as you go through the following section. Take note of your own natural barriers and make a plan to overcome those obstacles. Also, take note of obstacles you may not believe will affect you. Just keep those in the back of your mind so if they do "pop up," you have an awareness of the obstacle and a means of creating a plan to overcome the obstacle.

- **Being too busy** and getting too involved with a problem
- Having **conflicting goals** and objectives
- **Not** allowing yourself **enough time to relax**
- **Competition** in the present environment can hamper motives for creative output. Concerns with job advancement or opportunities as opposed to job stability or security may affect incentives to be creative at work.
- Most of the **obstacles** to creativity can be found **within yourself**.
    - Fear of criticism
    - Lack of confidence
    - State of mind/body (for example experiencing negative stress)

**Dehumanizing mass media** can contribute to limitations on creativity. Spend less time immersed in the popular culture (television or listening to pop music), or take conscious breaks from the everyday world to practice creative thinking.

Other factors that limit creative behavior include:

- **Stress:** Stress is not only a distraction that drains energy, which could otherwise be used creatively; it is not good for one's health.
- **Routines:** Routines or set ways of performing tasks have their uses. However, allowing those routines to become too entrenched in your life causes you to limit the range of responses available to you. Set routines can lead to the development of the anathema of creativity, the "bureaucratic mind."
- **Beliefs:** Having a strong belief in something not only limits our response options but also causes us to restrict the way in which we perceive and process information from the outside world. We may "filter out" information which contradicts our belief, and end up in our own "reality tunnel" in which we remain blissfully unaware of much that occurs in front of our very eyes.
- **Ego:** Having a strong ego identity with a particular belief exacerbates this situation and can lead to us aggressively defending it to the detriment of creativity, our society, and ourselves. This is not to imply one must have no beliefs; merely you need to be very aware of your beliefs and consequent limitations.
- **Fear:** Fear of self-expression and of the judgment of others can severely limit one's creativity.
- **Self-criticism:** Negative thinking and self-criticism are also limiting factors of an individual's creativity.

## Blockages

Blockages that keep creative ideas from fully developing:

- Tradition
- Control
- Overspecialization
- Negativism
- Prejudice
- Fear of failure

- Impatience
- Uniformity
- Fear of Ridicule
- Conceit
- Lack of Funding
- Confusion
- Insecurity
- Jealousy
- Group Pressure
- Laziness
- Apathy
- Lack of Commitment
- Lack of Support
- Intolerance
- Tenseness
- Fear of Change
- Toxic Nostalgia

## Positive Environmental Factors

- Business corporations have found the creativeness of their employees are promoted when the structure of their organization is less hierarchical and more democratic and free flowing.
- The clearest example of environmental influence is when one is creative in virtue of serendipity. These are instances when the environment facilitates creativity by affording stimulating observations. One study suggested that cues in the environment while completing one task can facilitate insight on a later task, without the subject's awareness. Moreover, there have been many historical accounts that claim the Zeitgeist or cohort at a particular point in time has influenced events.

## Negative Environmental Factors

- A **too-hectic** environment that does not provide quiet time for reflection and introspection hampers creativity. Creativity is also hindered by:
- A **sterile** environment that does not feed the senses

- **Demands** for quick production of results
- **Harsh words** (from others or from ourselves)
- **Rigid rules** and barriers that prevent us from gathering information and/or from connecting with others

## Believing You Are Not Creative

The main thing hindering creative thinking is our belief we are not creative. Look at it this way. If you tell yourself, "I am a creative person," then you must have feelings about yourself to support that identity. If you tell yourself, "I am just an ordinary human being," then you will have a different set of beliefs. Once you have a particular identity and set of beliefs about yourself, you will become interested in seeking out the skills needed to express your identity and beliefs. If you believe you are "uncreative," then there is no need to learn how to become creative.

Affirmations can be used to create a suitable self-image.

## Sleep Hacking

We need to discuss sleep hacking. For some reasons I do not fully understand, many students think sleep is a waste of time. There are two ways of sleep hacking:

1. Healthy ways to benefit from healthy sleep, and
2. Controversial ways to reduce sleep time.

## Order Out Of The Sleep Hacking Mess

Why do we sleep? Science does not have a full answer. We know only approximately 2% of people can sleep much less than 6 to 7 hours per day without significant damage to their wellbeing.

The damage may include depression or other moods swings including temporary dementia. The damage is typically temporary, and can often be treated by getting a good night's sleep and possibly simple pills. Some of our eating disorders may originate from not getting enough sleep and looking for alternative sources of energy. Therefore, if you do not sleep 7 hours per night, suffer from eating disorders and have unexplainable mood swings, prepare to hack your sleep.

## REM Sleep Cycle

The most important part of the sleep cycle is apparently REM. By accurate timing of your short naps or siesta, you can increase the amount of REM in your sleep. As a result, for the same amount of sleeping, you will improve memory and creativity, problem-solving and visualization.

If you meditate twice a day for 15 minutes or more, you can further increase the benefit you get from your sleep. While you meditate, you can learn and test several tricks that may later help you sleep. You will be able to fight nightmares and recurring dreams, reduce sleep apnea and breathe deeper when you sleep.

Some try to remember their dreams by setting up an alarm clock or psychological alarm trigger during their REM cycle of sleep. If you really need to remember your dreams, it is better to keep a steady schedule and a habit of writing down your first thoughts when you wake up. From there, you can try to reverse engineer the dreams. The skill is hard to learn, and the benefit of it is not apparent. Morning and evening meditation definitely help. In any case, breaking the REM sleep cycle reduces the efficiency of your sleep. Breaking the REM sleep cycle should be avoided if possible.

## How Much Sleep?

Now that we know how to improve the efficiency our sleep, it is reasonable to ask, **do we need that much sleep at all**? A few lucky people (about 2%) do not need to sleep more than 2 hours. However, if you are not Thomas Edison or Benjamin Franklin (and probably you are not), you should get approximately 6 hours of sleep at night, and a short siesta nap (approximately 20 minutes). The alternative is to sleep approximately 8 good hours at night. Choose whatever works best for you.

During the years of teaching this course, we have had complaints from students who try to practice the so-called Uberman sleep hack. They complained of a reduced ability to memorize, a drop in reading speed and other issues that can be attributed to the efficiency of the working memory processes. If you ask me, we get a much higher efficiency boost by learning to use our working memory efficiently than we get by reducing sleep.

To summarize, **for maximal efficiency you should:**

- **Sleep 6 hours per day**,
- Take a small **20-minute siesta nap** and
- Do **two 15-minute meditations** – one before you go to sleep and one after you wake up.

**IF YOUR MEMORY DROPS<br>OR<br>YOU HAVE STRANGE MOOD SWINGS,<br>TRY TO SLEEP MORE.**

## For Further Research

### Sleep Hacking

https://www.psychologytoday.com/blog/your-genetic-destiny/201505/sleep-apnea-may-raise-risk-depression-in-men

https://www.psychologytoday.com/blog/dream-factory/201504/6-ways-you-can-put-your-dreams-work-you

https://www.psychologytoday.com/blog/dream-factory/201505/how-direct-your-dreams

http://health.howstuffworks.com/mental-health/sleep/dreams/5-tricks-for-remembering-dreams.htm

https://mindfuldreamer.com/how-to-remember-your-dreams-10-tips-for-better-dream-recall/

https://en.wikipedia.org/wiki/Power_nap

http://www.supermemo.com/articles/polyphasic.htm

# Chapter 7: Know Your Texts

Before you set up your goals, it is important to understand what kind of texts you will be dealing with. Many texts will include elements of each text type below; however, some text types will be more common.

## Facts And Anecdotes

The most common type of text we encounter is a collection of facts and anecdotes. They are abundant in technological and business blogs, self-development, history books, political journalism, and psychology.

On average, people read 250 words per minute. When we claim "1000 words per minute at 80% retention," we mean within a minute we can read three pages of A4 journalistic text and recollect 80% of the facts and anecdotes within.

## Data Crunching

Do not even try to speedread content with five numbers per sentence. When presented with some financial data, poetry or statistics it is sufficient to be able to retain what we see at a reasonable speed. If you can recreate a company balance sheet after looking at it for 2 minutes, you should be happy. When we claim "95% retention of dense texts," we mean the ability to recreate the company balance sheet after 2 minutes.

## Deep Understanding

Science and engineering require understanding rather than retention. When reading a complex scientific text, it makes sense to reread it several times until understanding of all elements can be achieved, and the elements make sense. In this instance, learning a reading strategy makes more sense than a particular focus on speed or retention.

## Web Search

Occasionally we just need to overview a document very fast and zoom in on the area we need. When we claim to "preread at 3000 words per minute," we mean an ability to focus on specific area of a particular document fitting our search criteria with a speed of 3000 words per minute.

Many of us need to achieve the ability to reach each of the goals below. It is okay to generate several sets of goals. Make sure you train until you accomplish all goals; however, with multiple goals, you will need to train longer.

## Now Set Up Your Goals

**For what type of text are you training?**

_________________________

**Reading speed at 80% retention 1000 wpm**

Yes / No / Other _____________

**Preread at 3000 wpm**

Yes / No / Other _____________

**Retention of dense texts**

Yes / No / Other _____________

**Deep understanding**

Yes / No / Other _____________

# Chapter 8: Intensity And Duration

The training process will be anything but short and easy. You need to learn a new set of skills, which will help you for the rest of your life. You are supposed to achieve the ambitious goals you set for yourself. The following questions will help you set reasonably ambitious goals.

## Length Of Study

How long are you willing to study? Even if you do not have a one, you should **set a deadline** for yourself. Typically 3-4 months will do. Do yourself a favor and do not start learning speedreading if you do not have enough time to accomplish the goal.

Memorization and reading strategy will be very helpful for most purposes and will require much less effort. Warning: If you allocate more than 4 months to complete this study, you will probably take longer breaks and recovering from these breaks will be challenging for your willpower.

## Time Devoted To Reading

How much time are you going to devote to reading per week?

**Daily reading** is crucial for your goals. Reading is the skill you are learning; therefore, time set aside for reading is of vital importance. You will need to read in a way suitable for the current state of your training:

- Visualizing what you read,
- Memorizing details,
- Speeding up the process, and
- Analyzing the discrepancies.

Try to read at least 1 hour per day if you can, and at least 3 times a week. The more you read, the better you will progress.

## Time Devoted to Training Games

How much time are you going to spend with training games per week?

In the KeyToStudy System, we use many **training games**, which are *complementary* to reading. You need to play a broad range of games to cover a wide variety of skills. If you forget to train some skills, you may develop bad habits. It is hard to change bad habits. It is much easier to avoid them in the first place.

It is probably best not to train with any particular game for more than 15 minutes per day, and you can train with as many games as you want. Try to see where within your schedule you can fit 15 minutes of gaming sessions and how many of such sessions you need.

## Plan Your Rest Sessions

You will need short **5-minute rest breaks** between 15-minute sessions of work. Place these work sessions and breaks strategically within your calendar. Try not to train more than 3 hours per day, as it is excessive and not effective. Do train when your brain is susceptible to training. If you combine the KeyToStudy System with learning foreign languages, you are generating excessive pressure on the same areas of your brain. Have at least 2 days per week where you can learn nothing and simply rest. Also, do not train if you did not get enough sleep. Your results will be lower, and you will get frustrated.

## Generate A Schedule

Try to pledge how time much you will learn.

**I plan to learn for _____ weeks.**

**Monday:**

reading _____ minutes

training____ minutes

rest ____ minutes

**Tuesday:**

reading _____ minutes

training____ minutes

rest ____ minutes

**Wednesday:**

reading _____ minutes

training____ minutes

rest ____ minutes

**Thursday:**

reading _____ minutes

training____ minutes

rest ____ minutes

**Friday:**

reading _____ minutes

training____ minutes

rest ____ minutes

## Keep A Diary

It is important to **keep a diary** of your reading, training and rest sessions each day. Some prefer to manage their activities in Google Spreadsheets. The tool you use is less important than documenting your progress. If you become stuck for some reason, you will be able to review where things went wrong and will be able to fix your mistakes.

## Start Your Diary

Date:

Day _____

Rest ____ minutes

1. Start time: __:__:___

Exercise ___________________

Setting ____________________

Goal ______________________

Result _____________________

Took ___ minutes

Rest ___ minutes

2. Start time: __:__:___

Text ____________________

Setting ____________________

Goal ______________________

Result _____________________

Took ___ minutes

Rest ___ minutes

etc.

## Brain Games And IQ

Many brain gyms and brain games of various sorts claim they can make you smarter. This is hardly scientifically sound. If you play some game, the practice will eventually increase the specific skills required to succeed in the game. After playing the game for a while, the specific skills for the game will improve. Typically, this does not mean that other skills related to intelligence improve. If you play several games, you may enhance several related skills. In theory, by choosing the right combination of games, you could improve a broad range of cognitive functions. Does this theory work? Nobody actually knows.

## Measuring Intelligence

How do you measure intelligence? You ask several people to play some cognitive games and measure distribution of scores. Now each person plays the same games, that person may be positioned with respect to people who played the game before. There are a limited number of intelligence-measuring games since the development of such games requires significant research. A person is not allowed to take the same test repeatedly as this will change the performance scores of that person. There is a funny fact that if a person passes a standardized test several times, a higher score may be achieved. On average the best score is made the second time, but students that failed the second test will often pass a third one. Therefore playing the right games allows achieving a higher score on the intelligence test.

Now you play a game to improve your intelligence, and you score higher on the intelligence test. Does this mean you became smarter? Not really, it only means you developed some measurable skills. Moreover, if you do not practice the same games for a while, your relevant skills will decrease. I read very fast. I remember almost everything. Yet, I believe I will score lower in the training exercises than half of you in the KeyToStudy course simply because I do not need to play the games. Some students will get excellent scores in the training games but will not read. Other students will not play games but will read. Who will be a better reader over time?

## Training Exercises And Reading

When we built the training schedule for the course, we assumed that training exercises and reading will be used in a certain sequence, and each training exercise will be incorporated as a reading skill. Now, some students focus solely on passing the training exercises without integrating them in their reading skillset. The "speedreading IQ" test will be very high, but reading speed and retention will not match.

Playing brain games and going to brain gyms is better than not playing games at all, but the actual effect is probably much less than what you see in game statistics. Unless you can integrate the new skills into your everyday life and routine, the games' effect is probably transient and not very effective. Do play the games that develop the skills you actually need, or better yet develop new skills that require you to read new books, to play new games and generate new experiences. New books and new experiences boost creativity, intelligence and common knowledge probably more than most brain games.

## For Further Research

https://www.psychologytoday.com/blog/finding-the-next-einstein/201501/irony-brain-games-don-t-increase-iq-measure-iq

http://www.lsac.org/docs/default-source/research-(lsac-resources)/tr-14-01.pdf

# Chapter 9: Raising The Bar

## Starting Small

When learning a new SuperLearning skill set (and each skill set involves many different skills), it is crucial to practice the new skill and transform the skill into a habit. The first 2 weeks or 20 hours are especially important. During this time, there is a need for instant gratification. Do not try to do the hard tasks head-on.

Start by:

- Viewing TED links,
- Read a couple of blog posts, and
- Play a couple of games as long as you gain levels.

Visualization is very rewarding and an immediate skill to master. Start with the fun tasks to give yourself a boost in confidence. Do not allow self-doubt to kick in.

We have had many students. Whether you realize it or not, you are in better shape than most of them. How? You are beginning to understand the methodology and reasoning behind the method. In the introduction, we discussed the KeyToStudy System in terms of a framework and the techniques built upon the framework. By taking the time to set goals and motivate yourself to learn the new skills, you are setting a proper framework to learn the techniques.

## Building A Ritual

Try to ritualize the way you complete the exercises each day. It is important to note the exercises change quite often so ritualize the routine and not a specific exercise:

- time of the day,
- location,
- mindset,
- the order in which you do a reading exercise,
- play a game and
- read theoretical posts.

You need to add SuperLearning to your comfort zone. This will reduce the stress and excitement, but increase your persistence, and persistence is the key to success.

## Stack Up Skills

We build the SuperLearning path so that each skill builds upon others. It is best to have a solid foundation. If you feel you continually fail with some skill, there is a great likelihood some other student has already reported a similar experience and received a workaround answer.

Try to avoid using too many workarounds; however, but do not be shy to use one or two workarounds if needed. We do not believe this is cheating. The skill set stack looks a bit unclear at first, because of its complexity. Please do not worry as the skillset has been thoroughly tested, and, if you persist, it will become crystal clear.

## Habits First/Results Later

We do measure almost everything. The training results can be plotted; however, do not expect it to be a solidly rising graph. When you build up a new skill, all older skills get some beating for a short period. You will have good days and bad days. There are many dimensions to the KeyToStudy System and with time, you will achieve greater mastery in each skillset.

**Priority Caution**: If you message me after getting a bad score on a training quiz (scores are for your eyes only), I will understand your priorities are wrong. The priority is not the score. ***The priority is the skill***.

- Was the skill easier today than yesterday?
- Did you remember more than yesterday?
- Were you tired when you started your training session?
- Have you missed several training sessions in a row?
- Are you playing "catch up" from missing training?

The point is there are many reasons for a low score. High scores are not the goal at this point – *the habit is the point.*

## Progressive Overload

In our Udemy course, *Become a SuperLearner*, Jonathan covered this topic extensively. The complexity of the tasks you complete increases as you progress in the course. Occasionally the new tasks will seem impossible to you. Please, allow your brain to adapt and do not become alarmed. Brain adaptation may require several hours stretched out over several days. Be patient.

## Healthy Environment

If you are maintaining a healthy lifestyle by eating good food, walking at least 20 minutes a day, working out and meditating, you will have a greater gain because your body and brain will function better. You do not need to do all of these to succeed; however, you need to take regular breaks.

It is important to have people around you support your goal. You can use our Facebook page as a support group. I do suggest you become an active participant.

https://www.facebook.com/groups/superlearner

We all come from many different countries. Some have better English skills than others do. Even if you are somewhat embarrassed by your language skills (the typical reaction is to not want to look stupid) the goal is to have like-minded people support you in your goal. As far as I know, not a single individual in the group will make fun of another person. Our purpose is to grow and become SuperLearners.

## Reward Yourself

Each time you reach your personal goal, reward yourself. Find a reward suitable to the situation – maybe a funny website. For me, coffee and an energy bar work. You can shout your achievement on our Facebook page (at least until we have a dedicated area). You can show off with your friends, just remember nobody loves a conceited showoff (try to be humble).

## 10 Tips For Speedreading

Reading is a common way to acquire knowledge. The sad truth is most of us cannot read efficiently. *What is efficient reading?* We can measure reading efficiency in terms of reading speed and retention, where retention is the number of details we remember correctly after reading.

In our Udemy course, we provide a training routine that allows our students to increase efficiency significantly in terms of speed and retention. Generating benefit from what you read is your responsibility, so do choose what you read. Below we provide some tips that will help you become a more effective and efficient reader.

1. **Commit to self-improvement**: The human mind is more powerful than most of us imagine. We do use more than 10% of our brain, but we seldom use it efficiently. To use your brain effectively, you need to exercise it in the same way you exercise your muscles. Starting from a small success, we generate momentum, and then we build a skill set that can change our lives.

2. **No excuses**: Perhaps you have seen a popular TED Talk, where Joshua Foer describes how he went from what he calls a "lousy memory" to the US National Memory Champion in just one year. Most of our students have some sort of "problem" – ADHD, dyslexia, head trauma, lack of imagination, poor creativity – you name it. By rigorous training and with some help from other students and teachers, all of them reach their goals. The brain is amazingly versatile at correcting its own fallacies – something called neuroplasticity. When faced with a real challenge, the brain adapts.

3. **Trust yourself:** Do not read the same word over and over again. Do not read slower than you need to figure out the details. Do not occupy yourself with self-doubts. Do not give up. By trusting in your own skills and removing the mental crutches that were useful

when we were 6 years old, we can generate significant improvements in our reading efficiency.

4. **Do not progress blindly:** Measure everything. It is very easy to read very fast and loose comprehension or to understand everything but read very slow. Some people do not remember numbers, names or facts. It is very easy to lose interest in the information we do not retain anyway.
5. **Visualize everything:** Our visual perception is faster and more accurate than any other perception at our disposal 60% of neurons in our brain deal with some aspect of visual perception. By integrating visualization in our reading experience, we double our efficiency.
6. **Train your memory before you train your reading:** By relying on computers and mobile devices, we do not have the proper motivation to train memory. However, we need a quick, flexible and versatile memory to remember what we read. All of our students are asked to master memorization before training speedreading.
7. **Do not underestimate skimming:** You do not need to remember everything you read entirely. Skimming is very easy to learn. Proper skimming allows you to filter what you want to read and prepares you for in-depth reading. Skimming does not substitute for speedreading, but it is a significant step in the speedreading process.
8. **Some skills are hard:** Training subvocalization suppression or increasing visual angle requires a lot of hard work. Do not start with these skills unless you have mastered the basics. If you decide to practice these skills, do take regular breaks. Many people hear about speedreading, Google subvocalization and start training without consulting qualified teachers. After a while they develop eye spasms, stop understanding what they read and claim there is no such thing as

speedreading. *Thousands of our students on Udemy and on KeyToStudy.com mastered speedreading with subvocalization suppression and high retention by working progressively from simpler skills to harder skills.*

9. **Start reading now:** It is easy to delay reading. It is easy to play the training video games. It is easy to be busy. We are busy all the time. If we do not prioritize time for reading, we will not read. If we do not decide we really want to know more about something, we will not read. Finding sufficient time, focus, and motivation is crucial for effective reading.
10. **Relax and enjoy:** Reading is fun. Breathe deeply, sit comfortably, imagine how you will read the book, and how its content will make your life better. Celebrate your reading. Share your insights with friends.

We start to read when we are 6 years old and not yet ready to read effectively and efficiently. When we grow up and are ready to learn, it is hard to change the old habits. However, if you do learn to speedread correctly, you will enjoy an entirely new world of knowledge, understanding and fun.

## Nature Versus Nurture

Some of our students are curious regarding the "nature versus nurture" controversy. The subject is very much open for conversation and debate. I will try to share some of my own experience.

Back in 2008 an amazing book entitled *Outliers* was written, which claimed to determine some of the factors that contribute to high levels of success. The book was very well written, widely believed and accepted. *The only problem was there was no factual connection between the book's thesis and reality.*

The most stunning example was the 10,000 hours rule. The rule proposed you needed to study for 10,000 hours to reach outstanding success. This proved to be a cruel myth. In fact, there are some areas where 10,000 hours of training account for 10% of performance, while in other areas you can triple your performance in 100 hours. In some areas, a person's natural talent or even mutation is responsible for their ultimate success while another person requires 100% perspiration and hard work to achieve their ultimate success.

## Similarity In Memory Champions

Let us take for example memory sports. I have talked with many top-level memory champions, and they are remarkably similar. I generalize their similarities below, and, of course, there are exceptions.

The top memory sportsmen do not appear to be any different from any random selection of people, except for their remarkable memory. They had not been different from anyone else until about 20 plus years old when they had some unremarkable job and too much spare time.

During their entire life they were daydreaming, and could do nothing about it. At some point, they have discovered memory palaces, mainly by mistake, and their daydreaming was channeled into memorization/visualization. Their markers became hilarious and exciting. They created markers very fast. So fast, in fact, they enjoyed making markers 5 hours per day every day. After 3 years of practice, they won a memory championship, wrote a book and started to talk to the public about their remarkable skill and fun they have using it.

## Students Versus Memory Champions

Now let us examine the details.

| My Students | Memory Champions |
|---|---|
| Many have trouble visualizing | Have been visualizing (daydreaming) well before learning a thing about memory |
| Many come up with pretty boring markers, which, by the way, is perfectly okay to remember things | Come with some amazingly cool markers and can do so for hours each day |

Frankly, I do not think memory champions' markers are so amazingly fun. However, they are fun when compared to the champions' quite boring existence prior to the discovery of memory skills.

It is clear not everyone can or wants to become a memory champion. I do not think I could ever become a memory champion. I love to do other things much more than memorizing random numbers and decks of cards.

## Memory Challenges

The top ranking memory champion recommends the web site www.ArtofMemory.com for anyone who is willing to become a memory sportsman. One of the coolest features of the site is a list of memory challenges. Unlike technical memory exercises, these mental challenges are packed with useful information. If you are a premed student or a want-to-be memory sportsman, and you want to check to see if your memory is up for the task, then go no further!

## Creativity And Writing For Me

Creativity and writing are amazingly natural for me. I can come up with 30 ways to use something stupid in less than a minute (divergent thinking test), and write a 1000-word essay in less than an hour. I learned things, trained occasionally, but not merely enough to justify the ease with which I create.

However, when I need to design a logo, an app or a site it is totally an uphill struggle. I have a lot of experience, yet I usually fail and frankly have no idea why. Maybe I am somehow too different, and being different has its perks and its price.

Speedreading is a unique story. I have no talent for speedreading whatsoever. I did not think I could speedread until I met Anna. The practice did not come easy; in fact, I struggled *A LOT*.

## My Struggle/My Answers

I had an issue with *each and every step* of Anna's method. Overcoming my struggle is why I have answers for so many students. I was there. I did that. I failed time after time miserably. It took me 20 weeks to graduate the basic 8-week course. Ultimately, after 10 *years* of hard work, Anna considers me her best student. I think **the key to success**

**was motivation**. Not reading was simply not a viable option, and since I need to read for HOURS each day, I had an excellent incentive to improve.

## In Speedreading Nurture Wins

I am not sure regarding memorization, but in speedreading, nurture probably wins over nature. There are so many different books, so many ways to read and comprehend; everyone is probably talented in one style or another.

Discovering your personal style is a lot of hard work. Is it worth it? Definitely! Also, I think some help from Anna can reduce the effort 10-fold, maybe more.

## Reading Coaching

Sometimes our training just does not work. I recognize such cases and just ask, "How many hours did you read last week?" If the answer is below 2 hours, there is little chance that you will learn speedreading. There is an enormous value in the adage of simply "stop thinking and start practicing." Practice focuses energy, builds motivation, generates personal insights, and reduces procrastination.

It is not enough to read a speedreading book. *If you do not read varied and challenging material relevant to your everyday life, you will not be able to train your skills in action.* Playing the appropriate games also does not generate a sufficient result by itself. Reading skills are:

- Specific for the language you are reading,
- Specific for the sort of materials you are reading, and
- Specific for the medium (computer/book) you are reading.

To adapt to a new reading scenario takes time. By reading a balanced portfolio of materials while learning speedreading methods, we produce a balanced and correct skill development.

There are some additional reasons so many people report they could not learn speedreading.

1. **Some people are misinformed**. There is no "magic trick" for speedreading. Speedreading is not a

hoax and not a genetic mutation. Speedreading is expensive in terms of the time and effort required to acquire the skill.

2. **It is important to train your brain to process massive amounts of information BEFORE training your eyes to acquire the information very fast.** Otherwise, the retention will drop below a reasonable level. If this happens, you will be forced to unlearn your training and relearn from zero with an emphasis on retention. *Relearning is very frustrating!*
3. **Not only the reading method but also the whole approach to the reading process needs to be modified.** If there is no separation of reading stages, no Pomodoro rests, or no analysis after reading, it is very hard to maintain the reading speed for long texts.
4. **Your brain will resist the changes.** Very often, your brain may trick you into thinking that a change happened well before it actually happens. Do not believe your inner intuition, and test everything with a timer in your hand.

## Why Are We Sure Anyone Can Learn?

1. **Brain plasticity**: The brain regularly regenerates, builds new skills, and creates new relations.
2. **Frequency**: By persistent learning, say 1 hour a day, 5 times a week for 10 weeks, we generate new habits. This new habit will have an energy of its own to push you beyond your current limitation.
3. **Intensity**: The high-speed visualization required for speedreading is mind-blowingly intense. Once you start using it, you will get positively addicted.
4. **Shaping**: Progressively building and personalizing the skill, you will ensure that it fits your capabilities and you have fun using it.

Just as you learn to go to a gym until you cannot imagine your routine without it, you can learn to speedread. One of the significant advantages of the KeyToStudy System is you can receive reading coaching. You can use our online community to share your progress, ask questions, and find answers and encouragement. Alternatively, you can schedule a one-to-one with Anna, who is the best speedreading teacher and trainer alive. Write info@KeyToStudy.com to schedule a session with Anna.

## Train Like A Navy Seal

Train yourself like a navy seal using visualization and goal setting. Since we learn to master vivid visualization, we can use this wonderful tool for goal setting.

The first time I encountered visualization as a tool for achieving goals was when I studied some military-grade methods. The methodology of mental toughness for reaching goals and confronting obstacles looks incredibly simple:

- **Set clear goals**: Set long-term, mid-term and short-term goals, so you can focus on one thing at a time. The goals should be very detailed and include all possible situations and what can trigger them. If there are no special reasons, do not deviate from the set tactics during the implementation stage. The imagery at this point is a tree of possible scenarios, triggers, actions, and reactions. Create a marker per scenario with many details.
- **Mental visualization**: During the goal-setting stage, we define various scenarios. During the visualization stage, we simulate each scenario in our mind in great detail.

  1. Make a vision board. Imagine every element in the situation.
  2. Generate mental movies of each imaginable scenario.
  3. Try to create an environment you will face and see how you perform.

  Visualization practice prepares you for any reasonable scenario, so no emergency can pose a surprise (emergency conditioning method).

- **Control of arousal**: Sometimes everything goes wrong. In this case, it is imperative to calm down and act logically. Something needs to protect you against a "fight or flight" response. This calming trigger is usually some deep breathing and visualization of a relaxing environment. The visualization should be very specific, vivid enough to generate a proper response, but not too vivid to lose awareness. This sort of visualization requires a lot of practice.
- **Positive thinking**: The focus should be on a positive outcome. The motivation is not to quit no matter what. There should be an unyielding motivation for why you proceed doing the hard things and not to avoid the confrontation. Believe, make others believe in success and seek out role models. Visualization of people who count on you to succeed actually helps here.

As you can see, there are several different kinds of visualization, each handling a particular aspect of a mission. Once again, it is important to point out you do need a mission before you start generating goals. Proper visualization increases the chances of success by at least 10%. Procrastination helps when you need to consider creative solutions and visualize scenarios.

Once the goals have been set and all scenarios visualized it is time to **ACT**. If you do not act, all the goal-setting effort has been for nothing, and we will do a lot to avert losses.

## For Further Research

**The First 20 Hours -- How To Learn Anything:**

https://www.youtube.com/watch?v=5MgBikgcWnY

**Nurture versus Nature:**

http://lifehacker.com/talent-does-not-decide-whether-you-succeed-1687427688

http://www.brainpickings.org/index.php/2014/07/15/leonard-cohen-paul-zollo-creativity/

http://en.wikipedia.org/wiki/Outliers_%28book%29

http://www.brainpickings.org/2014/01/22/daniel-goleman-focus-10000-hours-myth/

http://www.slate.com/articles/health_and_science/science/2014/09/malcolm_gladwell_s_10_000_hour_rule_for_deliberate_practice_is_wrong_genes.html

http://www.bbc.com/future/story/20121114-gladwells-10000-hour-rule-myth

**Memory Champions**

http://mt.artofmemory.com/

http://mt.artofmemory.com/challenges

**Goal Setting Visualization**

http://www.smart-goals-guide.com/goal-setting-strategies.html

http://www.jonathanfields.com/the-truth-about-vizualization-and-goal-achievement/

**Reading Coaching**

http://lifehacker.com/stop-thinking-and-start-doing-the-power-of-practicing-1694073303

http://www.selfgrowth.com/articles/speed-reading-tactics-5-proven-reasons-why-speed-reading-doesnt-work

http://www.selfgrowth.com/articles/4-secrets-to-succcssful-speed-reading-mastery-revealed

http://www.selfgrowth.com/articles/speed_reading_tactics__6_essential_ideas_you_need_understand

# Chapter 10: Your First Training

Ready! Set! Go! After a brief introduction to the Tachistoscope principle, you will find several training exercises you can start right away! You can begin learning to speedread without further delay! Remember to work the training exercises into your training schedule.

## Tachistoscope Principle

Tachistoscope is the device that launched the speedreading training in the late 1930s. The word *tachistoscope* is derived from the Greek words '*tachys*' meaning swift and '*skopion*' meaning instrument for viewing or observing.

The device projects a series of images onto a screen at rapid speed to test visual perception, memory, and learning. Visual recall is enhanced as the flashed images are increased in number or complexity as exposure duration times are decreased.

Often numbers are used as the visual targets. Research has shown humans have the capability of recalling correctly, and in the proper sequence, eleven numbers exposed for a 0.5-second flash duration. Tachistoscopes were used during the late 1960s in public schools as an aid to increase reading comprehension for speedreading.

There were two types. In the first type, the student would look through a lens similar to an aircraft bombsight viewfinder and read letters, words and phrases using manually advanced slide film. The second type projected words and phrases on a screen in sequence. Both types were followed up with comprehension and vocabulary testing.

While the device produces high improvement after some training, the skill level decreases rapidly. The rapid decline occurs when practice is not continued at the baseline level (before exposure). Only very few professions (i.e., law enforcement) may require continuous training of visual recall. The tachistoscope is not used outside of a small circle of professionals.

## Training Similar To Tachistoscope

As you can surmise, the KeyToStudy System includes several training exercises, which by their nature are very similar to the Tachistoscope. This is one of the reasons our training ALWAYS works, but it is also one of the reasons the training should focus on a comprehensive set of skills.

The protocol I use involves a grading system, which provides feedback to the trainee concerning the accuracy of the responses. When at least 70 percent accuracy is achieved, the next level of difficulty is displayed for recall and response. **The goal of the training is to increase the number and/or complexity of the visual targets while maintaining accurate recall.**

While some of the training exercises require a high level of skill, other exercises may be started as soon as you want. Below are some skills you can begin to train right away.

## Linking Markers

Creating short stories that include given words is a very simple way to remember things. Practice the linking markers exercise in several ways.

http://www.KeyToStudy.com/linking-markers-exercise/

**Level 1**: Create stories with words

**Level 2**: Make visual animations. Try to make them extremely fast

**Level 3**: Make the first and last words incredibly vivid. Then, travel the visualization backward.

**Level 4**: Train with chunking 4 words per chunk. Improve memorization speed times 4!

## Short-Term Visual Memory

The more letters you can see and remember at once, the faster you will read. This exercise trains both working memory and eye speed.

http://www.KeyToStudy.com/short-term-visual-memory-training/

**Level 1**: Two letters, deduce one letter from other

**Level 2**: Try to remember all letters at once and then recreate them from memory

**Level 3**: Now use 4 letters. You cannot deduce anymore, need to remember everything

**Level 4**: Same thing, but with saccades and chunking. Divide the screen into quadrants

## Sliding Words

This exercise enhances visual angle and teaches saccades. When the speed increases you can no longer subvocalize and vocalization is suppressed.

http://www.KeyToStudy.com/sliding-words/

**Level 1**: 5 words per line, 250 wpm

**Level 2**: 5 words per line, 500 wpm

**Level 3**: 7 words per line, 700 wpm

**Level 4**: 11 words per line, 1000 wpm

## Find The Differences

The fundamental quality of accuracy is the ability to notice minute differences at high speed. Rather than one exercise, we have several exercises here.

**Level 1**: Find mimicry in nature

**Level 2**: Find differences between images

**Level 3**: Find differences between texts

**Level 4**: Find differences between character strings (fast)!

~~~~~

These four exercises you can do at any level of the course. You will not be bored or disappointed!

~~~~~

## STVM Example

Go to:
http://www.KeyToStudy.com/short-term-visual-memory-training/

Choose S/T/U (intermediate) with 12 symbols

You can both increase and decrease difficulty, but this is the primary training mode after you get proficient.

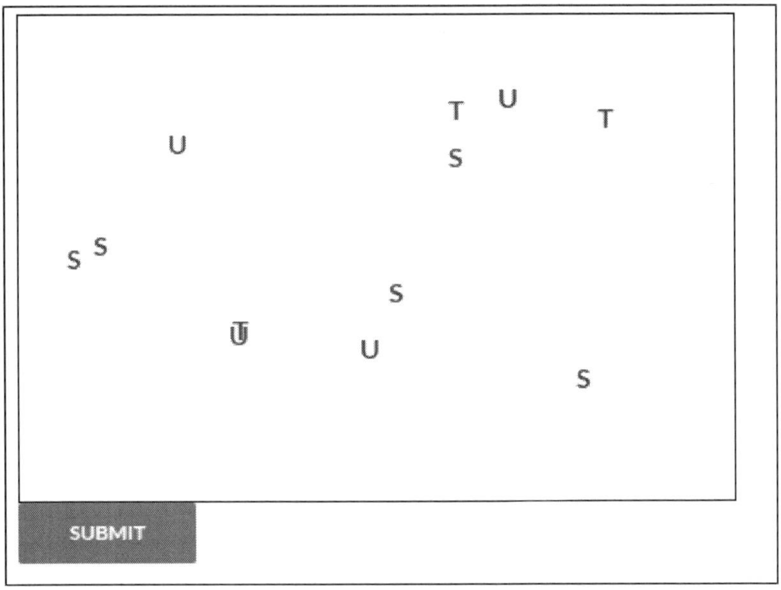


Try to divide the screen into four quadrants since quadrants are quite easy to remember.

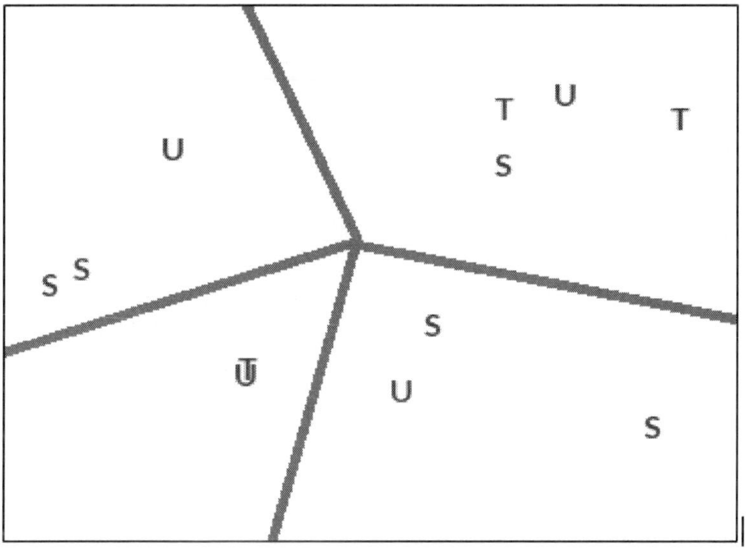


If a beginner, scan the quadrants one by one. If advanced, look at the middle of the visual field try to get the quadrants using peripheral vision.

Try to remember each quadrant in visual working memory noticing geometry. It is OK to reorder the objects a bit to remember better.

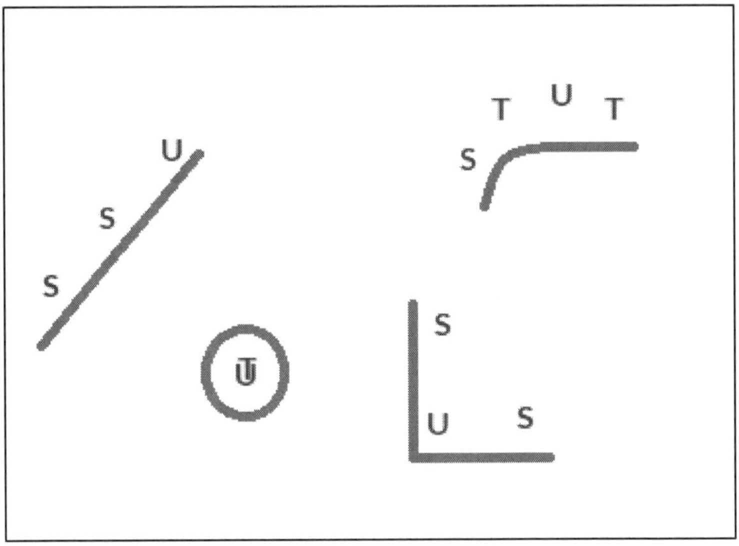


At this point, the objects disappear and you need to recollect them.

SSU diagonal

UT merged

STUT rounded corner

SUS quad corner

Sometimes we have enough time to subvocalize each. This improves retention. Other times we do not subvocalize and improve speed.

Now count each letter. For example:

4*S

4*U

2*T

You get 10 letters, but you know you need 12 letters!

Count again....

5*S

3*T

4*U

Now this is 12...

Using *a priori* knowledge to check yourself is not cheating!

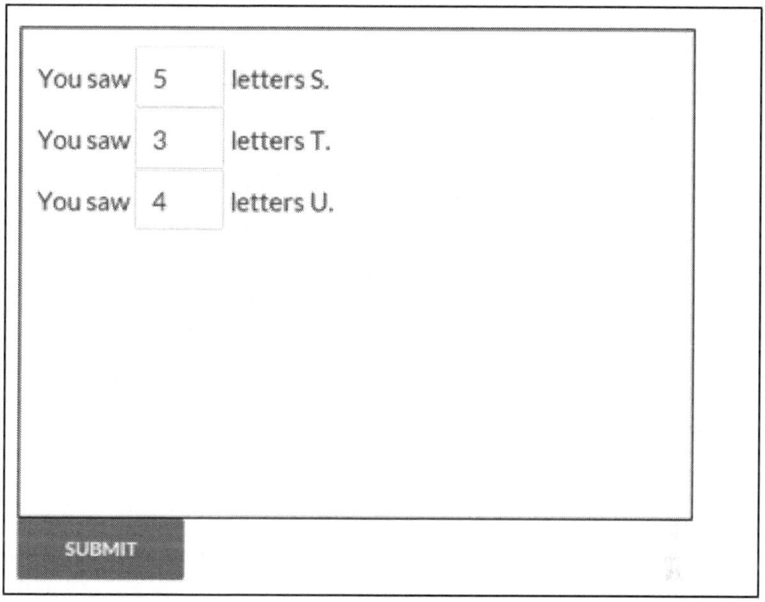


Accuracy in S: (5/5),
Accuracy in T: (3/3),
Accuracy in U: (4/4),
Total accuracy: 100%

OKAY!
Now repeat the exercise.

~~~~~

An excellent working memory is required for great speedreading. If you do not train your working memory, you will not be able to process what you read.
~~~~~

## Skill Degradation

How can you resist gradual skill degradation?

1. **Speedread every day at least 20 minutes**. You do not have to train anything special, just read any book or blog you like.
2. **Focus on strategies**, rather than specific exercises. The specific exercises are just crutches that support you until the strategies become your second nature.
3. **Understand the principles**. If your reading speed decreases for some reason, you can ramp it up quickly using the correct principles.
4. **Use the community to support your training**. Others will provide you motivation to read further and better.

## For Further Research

**Tachistoscope:**

http://www.oepf.org/sites/default/files/journals/jbo-volume-14-issue-2/14-2%20Godnig.pdf

https://en.wikipedia.org/wiki/Tachistoscope

# PART 3: VISUALIZATION AND CREATIVITY

# Chapter 11: Introduction To Markers

Most texts are divided into paragraphs. Memidex Dictionary defines a paragraph as:

> *a distinct section of a piece of writing, usually dealing with a single theme and indicated by a new line, indentation, or numbering.*

Since a paragraph is dealing with a single theme, its main theme can be highlighted within the paragraph using a simple marker.

**The goal of this chapter is to introduce you to finding markers and visualizing them.** You will go through several steps, and, after you complete the steps, you will have a good idea of how to find, mark, and visualize markers.

## Marking Up Your Text

**Simple exercise:** Before we continue the explanation of the visual marker concept, please choose a simple printed text. Use a **simple, old-fashioned hold-in-your-hand marker/highlighter to underline 2 to 3-word clusters of meaningful words** within each paragraph. The concept of this exercise is to bring out the keywords/markers in each paragraph.

**Hint:** When you finish you should probably have no more than 3 to 5 keywords/markers highlighted. As you will see, these keywords will become the markers we link together.

~~~~~

**Example:** Below is a paragraph from the following Wikipedia article: *Syntax Highlighting* (http://en.wikipedia.org/wiki/Syntax_highlighting).

It has three markers highlighted:

> Syntax **highlighting** is a **feature** of text editors that are used for programming, scripting, or
~~~~~

> markup languages, such as HTML. The feature **displays text**, especially source code, in different colors and fonts according to the category of terms. This feature facilitates writing in a structured language such as a programming language or a markup language as both **structures** and syntax errors are visually **distinct**. Highlighting does not affect the meaning of the text itself; it is intended only for human readers.

As you can see, the paragraph may be summarized by three markers:

1. **highlighting feature**
2. **displays text (in)**
3. **distinct structures**

## Visualizing Markers

The human brain is superb at processing visual objects, much more so than words. Since we have identified our markers in the preceding example, we can visualize them as icons.

**highlighting feature**

**displays text**

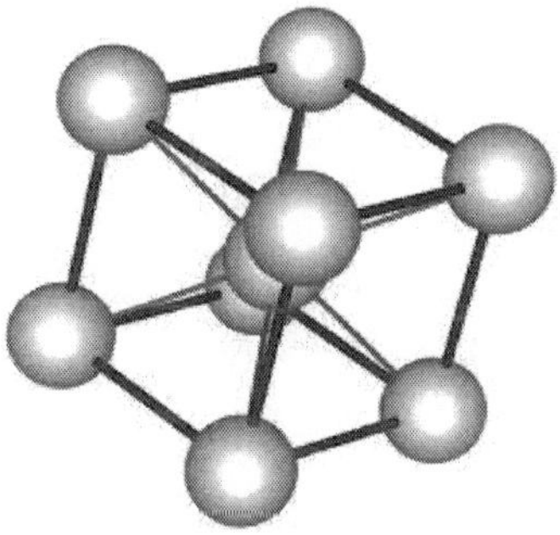

**distinct structures**

Put this visual marker in a 2x2 structure called a chunk. Think of it as IKEA shelving unit.

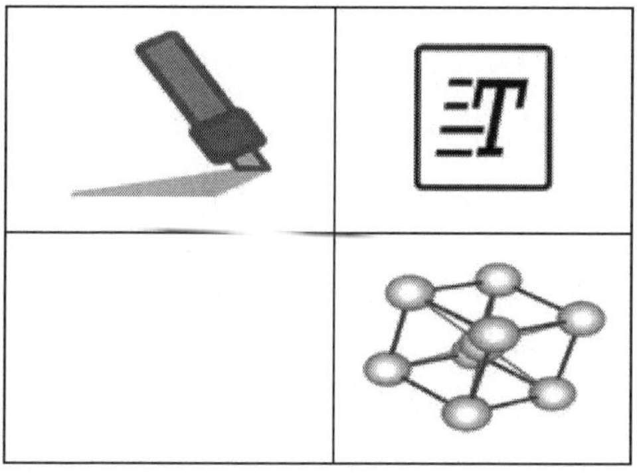

Some students prefer more complex honeycomb shelves since they hold more items

Now you can visualize the whole structure as if it is on a wall in your living room or in any other room in your house.

This is, in a nutshell, the full memorization process end-to-end:

- analyze text,
- create visual markers,
- generate compartments,
- place these compartments into your memory palace.

~~~~~

**Next Step:** The next step is to practice by marking and visualizing the markers in your own texts.

If you absolutely cannot come up with visualizations on your own, try using Google Image Search. For me, the best setting is as follows:

If you do not come up with a good image, you may have chosen a bad or complex word to mark. Try to look for synonyms or alternatives within the text.

## Markers Versus Details

Typically, we generate about two markers per paragraph with approximately five details per marker. Creating markers takes time, and we need details to make the marker
~~~~~

memorable. If we add too many details per marker, we will start forgetting details. If we add too many markers, we will read slower and we may start adding details that are not supported by the text.

~~~~~

**Digital Highlighter:** For example, if you use the Chrome browser you can install and use the DIIGO plugin to underline words.

To get the computer's idea of what possible markers could be, try using Wordle or my application http://www.KeyToStudy.com/tag-cloud-generation/ in which case you get "Highlighting language markup feature text syntax." There is more than one way to generate markers.

~~~~~

**Goal:** Try to reach the point where you no longer need to think about which words to mark, but the words "magically" catch your attention. This means you are "getting" markers automatically.

## Question About Markers

**IA**

*Hi, I have been doing the proposed training Week 1 exercises for 12 days in a row now. I still struggle coming up with markers. The linking marker exercise 15x4 takes me anywhere from 20 to 35 minutes. Also, my visualization skill hasn't improved all that much. I also struggle with those exercises. Should I keep doing Week 1 exercises or move on to Week 2? Either way, I'll keep trying my best, thanks*

**Dr. Lev Goldentouch**

*Maybe you expect too much from your markers (perfectionism).*

1. *Limit your time STRONGLY when coming up with markers, e.g. take one minute and max your result within that minute.*
2. *Continue to Week 2.*

**IA**

*You sure know your stuff Dr. G. I started Week 2 training today. Also went back to the linking markers exercise in Week 1 and timed myself one minute for each. Afterward, I did all of them. I spent like 2 minutes on quickly playing back all the images. Then I did the exercise and did great! I must say, I'm really happy because I was getting really frustrated. Thank you!*

## For Further Research

http://www.memidex.com/paragraph

## Digital Highlighters

https://www.diigo.com/tools

http://www.wordle.net/

# Chapter 12: Two Sorts Of Markers

## Convergent Versus Divergent Thinking

**Convergent** thinking is oriented towards deriving the single best (or correct) answer to a well-defined question. Convergent thinking emphasizes:

- speed,
- accuracy,
- logic, and the like, and
- focuses on accumulating information,
- recognizing the familiar,
- reapplying set techniques, and
- preserving the already known

Convergent thinking is based on **familiarity with what is already known** (i.e., knowledge). It is most effective in situations where a ready-made answer exists and needs to be recalled from stored information. The answer may need to be worked out from what is already known by applying conventional and logical search, recognition and decision-making strategies. One of the most important aspects of convergent thinking is it **leads to a single "best" answer**, and thus leaves no room for ambiguity. Answers are either right or wrong. IQ tests are frequently regarded as epitomizing convergent thinking.

***Divergent thinking****, by contrast, involves* ***producing multiple or alternative answers from available information***. Divergent thinking requires:

- making unexpected combinations,
- recognizing links among remote associates,
- transforming information into unexpected forms, and the like

Answers to the same question arrived at via divergent thinking may vary substantially from person to person but be of equal value. They may never have existed before, and are often thus novel, unusual or "surprising."

Sometimes this is true merely in the experience of the person producing the variability in question, or for the particular setting, but it may also be true in an absolute sense. However, contrary to what is sometimes assumed **both convergent and divergent thinking lead to the production of ideas**.

Nonetheless, there is a **significant qualitative difference**:

- **convergent** thinking usually generates ***orthodoxy***, whereas
- **divergent** thinking always generates ***variability*** otherwise it would not be divergent

This seems at first glance to confirm divergent thinking is indeed synonymous with creativity. However, variability alone does not mean creativity. It may cause "surprise" in the beholder. However, this is not enough since surprise can be produced through "blind" variability. Mere unregulated self-expression such as daubing paint on paper, writing text in any way that pleases the writer, picking out notes at random on the piano, or doing things differently from the usual regardless of accuracy, meaning, sense, significance, or interestingness does not indicate creativity.

## Logical Visual Markers

**Logical visual markers** are the default sort of markers you should use. These logical visual markers follow convergent thinking. In fact, logical markers are often so trivial we do not even notice them. The idea is very simple:

***If you understand the text, then you can learn something significant from the text.***
***The information you learned is a marker.***

## Verify The Marker

To **verify the marker is strong** check the following:

1. **What is your opinion** regarding this new find? Is it expected or surprising? Is it well proven or controversial?

2. **Is the subject of interest**? Neurons work in clusters. Do you have enough related information stored in your brain?
3. **Does it create further links**? Do you have action items based on this find? Can you actively use it in your life?

## Higher Level Logical Marker

A **higher level of logical marker** is a logical template or scheme, which can be applied in all situations like a **mind map** or programming UML.

1. **How do different markers relate to each other?** Causation, contradiction, generalization, corollaries, etc. work great.
2. If you were to put the relevant markers in space, **which data structure would it be?** If tree/mind map, can you imagine each branch of the tree?
3. **How do the markers relate to other ideas we have?**

If you are ready for an even more complex logic, go to the article entitled *My Personal Hyperlinking Format* at http://www.KeyToStudy.com/personal-hyperlinking-format/.

## Creative Visual Markers

We cannot always analyze what we read. Foreign languages, medical and biological details, names and dates, are the sort of information that avoids direct analysis. To remember these markers you need to be creative.

In our Udemy course, Jonathan teaches to imagine each of these markers in very clear almost tangible detail, add senses, etc. This works great for 80% of our students, for the other 20% of students we recommend to focus not on the objects but focus on the way they interact with each other.

We create fast-speed animations where objects morph into each other or break each other, and so on. Animations are like fast-speed stories. Since they are visual, they are potentially 10 times faster than stories.

To see if the markers are strong, we can ask the following questions:

1. **To which extent does each object lead to another?** Notice good linking here is as important as good markers.
2. **How unique is the resulting animation?** If we reuse the same animation too many times, we risk mixing up details from various fields. If we have something too unique, we may have trouble recreating it.
3. **How does the animation make us feel?** Creative animations should make us experience strong feelings: laughter, disgust, fear, greed, joy.

~~~~~

A higher level of creative markers needs a common setup such as a memory palace.

## Comics Method

Alternatively, I occasionally mention my own "comics" method." The typical questions I ask:

1. **What is the common theme?**
   Is it past/present/future?
   Is the theme heroic/comic/childish?
2. **What colors prevail?**
3. **How do different storylines interact with each other?** Notice you will have some animations ending and other animations starting as you progress in the article.
4. **How is this creative marker built into the larger logical setup?**

You may want to dedicate "anchor" markers connecting to the common ideas. If you have a story, you may wish to have the first and the last frame of the story to have some logical connection. If it is a memory palace, you need to know how and why you opened the door.
~~~~~

# Chapter 13: Etymology Method

As an example of logical markers creation, I present my "etymology method." Before you train using this method, please do the following simple exercise:

~~~~~

1. Open the Mnemonic Dictionary: (http://mnemonicdictionary.com/)
2. Think of an abstract word and a way of remembering the word. If no words come to your mind, choose randomly from the GRE word list: http://mnemonicdictionary.com/wordlist/GREwordlist
3. Now search the word in the dictionary.
4. Try to pick up new tricks. Add your own tricks to the dictionary to help the community.

Often we need to learn new professional terms or words that are new to us. When we encounter this need in a real-life situation, we have very little time to respond. Often we have little time and dozens of terms to learn. It helps to train just in case.

~~~~~

## The Method:

Very often, I ask students to understand the meaning of what they are trying to learn and use very accurate markers. Note this conversation with the following student:

**EY:**

*I can create images for the words in the dictionary (some easier than others), but my main problem is I can't link the word to the visual marker I created. For example taking the word you explained 3 months ago: Aberrant. 'Aberrant is not normal, like something very big or something very small, the image is of a giant marrying a dwarf or someone taking a "road less traveled by" '*

*Now I have the image in my mind vividly, but how do I link it to the word itself "Aberrant?"*

**Dr. Lev Goldentouch:**

1. *Search Google "aberrant etymology"*
2. *ab=away, errare=stray*
3. *ab sounds like "Abe," errare sounds like "error"*
4. *"Honest Abe was so tall he made errors large and small"*

**EY:**

*So, just to be clear I have to connect the image (i.e., visual marker) to the word by some kind of a phrase that contains the word itself – so when I read the word I remember the phrase with the marker. BTW, I tried the "etymology technique" (yeah, that's what I'll call it) and it is really easier to create visual markers now.*

~~~~~

The basic idea I use is very simple: rather than trying to create visual markers from scratch, **use the actual factual details of the subjects you are learning to create a stronger marker**. Not only will such a marker be more accurate and memorable, but you will also learn a thing or two. The question of new definitions comes up very often.

**EAY:**

*Is there an easy to way to memorize definitions?*

*This is a problem I stumbled upon. I'm just starting Section 3 in this course, and the way you guys propose to memorize is to make a story or an image and link it. And I tried it. It helped me in some things. But, how does this work for scientific definitions, especially word-by-word.*

*For example, if we take the word hypothesis. Hypothesis is a proposed explanation for a phenomenon. How may I take the definition and turn it into an image or a story?*

**Dr. Lev Goldentouch:**

*Step 1: Go to the* ***etymology****. From Greek hupothesis 'foundation,' from hupo 'under' +thesis 'placing'*

*Step 2:* ***Learn each part****. Hippo loves water and is always under it. Thesis is your place in science.*
~~~~~

*Step 3:* ***Rationalize****. Hypothesis is the foundation under your scientific theory.*

*Step 4:* ***Reread the accurate definition*** *to see what you missed. Hypothesis is a supposition or proposed explanation made on the basis of limited evidence as a starting point for further investigation*

*Step 5:* ***Synthesize your own understanding****. Hypothesis is a foundation placed under a scientific theory that is a starting point of theory construction. This foundation is based on limited evidence.*

~~~~~

Please notice after learning the exact details of the concept I can still encode the details as fun and creative imagery. I just make this imagery extra accurate. This accuracy may make you come up with some absurd ideas. However, as long as the absurdity leads back to the actual meaning, you have understood and applied the concept.

~~~~~

For example:

***IG***

*I am a little confused on connecting my markers to the words. For example, the word "argument" for which I came up with an image of two people yelling at each other. However, when I am going from the image back to words, I mix it up with words like disagreement? I had similar trouble with words like photography and photograph. Should I be coming up with separate markers for every word or do some words have the same marker?*

***Dr. Lev Goldentouch***

*You cannot distinguish between things you visualize in the same way. You need markers that are more accurate. See etymology: argument from Latin argumentum "evidence, ground, support, proof; a logical argument," – means than in an argument one person tries to prove something to another. Disagreement from the noun of action agreer "to please" – feeling unpleasant with what is happening around. Now you can use some disambiguation typecasting like men argue and women disagree, or whatever makes sense in your mind.*

~~~~~

The most powerful methods are also the simplest to use. With the etymology method, you can create markers for some very complex concepts, and then each time you meet these concepts you will have readily available markers. Please do use these very strong markers carefully, with detailed links and context: **if you ignore context too many times, you will start to become confused and will need a new set of markers.**
~~~~~

# Chapter 14: Training Visualization

You cannot rely on Google image search to come up with markers. Visualization skills can be learned quite easily using several methods.

These initial exercises will help you develop visualization capabilities. They are also useful for controlling your focus and mindfulness.

Many students initially fail when starting learn visualization techniques. Do not give up. You can continue with the training even though you have not aced visualization. With time, your visualization skills will become as good as your other skills, or you will learn how to modify your personal style to use the visualizations that are easy for you.

## 1. Photograph

- Find a photograph.
- Take your time to analyze it.
- Memorize every detail you can.

Then:

- Simply close your eyes
- Try to recreate it in your mind
- Bring in as much detail as you can:
  - the colors,
  - the birds in the sky,
  - the freckles on the skin
  - whatever is there.
- Open your eyes to get more detail if you have to.

Remember, this is not a test. Do this exercise until you can easily recreate a photograph in your mind.

## 2. Object

For the second exercise, we are going three-dimensional. This time, pick up a small object perhaps your pen or your keys.

- Again, analyze all the details and memorize it.
- Take your time.

- Now, close your eyes
- See the object mentally
- The challenge here is to start rotating it.
- See every detail but from all angles.
- If you feel comfortable, begin to bring in some surroundings.
- Place it on an imaginary table.
- Shine a few lights on it and imagine the shadows flickering.

## 3. Focus

This method may not work for some of you. If you are unable to do this exercise after several attempts, *do not worry about it* and just continue practicing other exercises.

- Start with a point.
- A black point on a white background is very precise and holds your focus.
- When your focus is fully attracted to the point, you start to increase it into a circle.
- The circle encompasses several things
- You can bring shapes into and out of it with the power of your mind.
- Increase the circle as much as you can without losing the intensity of your focus.
- Bring in a simple inanimate object such as a flower, a statuette, a candle.
- Make the object rotate and dance in your imagination.
- Try to experience it with all senses.
- When the object becomes lively, try to transform it into a specific person.
- Visualize the person in all details.
- Generate a conversation with the person, to the point where you are drawn into the conversation.
- At some point both the circle and the person disappear, and you drift into magical landscapes created by your imagination as the result of your conversation.

## 4. Online

- Open Google Search
- Choose a random image
- Look at the image for 10 seconds.
- Close your eyes.
- Try to visualize the image.
- Be accurate regarding number and position of details.
- Remember as many details as possible.
- Try to visualize the entire image.

There are several levels in this exercise:

1. **Simple** objects, like office supplies
2. **Larger** objects, like cars
3. **Complex ideas** expressed in clipart
4. **Optical illusions**
5. **Fantastic landscapes**

Each level of detail enables visualization that is more complex. The complexity of visualization typically matches the complexity of the text. *A fantastic landscape is about as complex as an average Wikipedia article.*

## Getting Stuck With Visualization

About 1% of our students become stuck with visualization. They either cannot get into the visualization mode and see pitch black, or they cannot get out of visualization mode and experience vivid hallucinations.

## Trouble Visualizing

**If you have trouble getting into visualization**, this may mean your visual processing is just too fast. What other people experience as images and objects, you may experience as logic and connections. You may get an inexplicable subliminal "feel" of the image without getting the image itself.

Guess what? This is exactly what the top speedreaders feel like. They need to process the information so fast that no images are formed. Instead, they improve their subliminal perception and use pauses between paragraphs to connect the new subliminal information to other things they know.

Try to focus on how various things connect to each other, and you will get the feeling of the marker without even seeing it. Practically, you will be jumping several steps, so expect a bumpy ride, but eventually a high pay-off.

## Trouble Getting Out Of Visualization

**If you have trouble getting out of visualization**, this may mean your visual processing is too rich. What other people experience as images, you experience as vivid objects, maybe even with touch and smell. Most of the memory champions are like this. To overcome the speed limit, try not to add to the object details beyond the bare minimum, and pace yourself. Limiting your time to do things has amazing influence on people with vivid visualization, enabling very fast and very accurate reading.

# Chapter 15: Playful Aspects Of Creative Markers

Some of our students are extremely driven and focused. Generally, these are excellent qualities for SuperLearners. Unfortunately, some of the playful aspects of creative marker creation require "letting go." You cannot afford perfectionism when you read at 1000 wpm.

You should not remake markers when you use high-level visualization or the "comic" method (see Chapter 12). You do need crazy stunts to link some markers together in a memorable form. The sooner you "let go" and "fool around" with imagery the better. The following discussion from our Udemy course explores this point.

~~~~~

**ASKF:**

*I have been thinking about this course and reading the discussions and it seems some people have difficulties in creating markers or coming up with images, or generally visualizing things. I was wondering why and from my own experience while starting to create markers.*

*I concluded that it might spring from the fear of doing something wrong, silly or embarrassing. The difference between this style of learning and what people often associate with learning is that this is more creative – in German we have a term for learning: "sich das Lernmaterial aneignen" which means something like "**making the material your own**" and that seems what is happening here.*

*But by coming up with my own images for markers I am choosing almost randomly from the text (like Jonathan with the name "Ebenezer") instead of trying to pick seemingly important terms and trying to remember them by their exact name, the very serious process of learning seems to be turned into something more anarchic and funny. Cartoon like and sometimes downright silly markers start dancing around in my head.*
~~~~~

*I can see how that could scare people – it definitively scares me a bit. I start wondering whether it makes sense to conjure up armies of ice cubes while trying to memorize an article about the Cold War. It seems so far off from what I thought learning was. When I heard about these techniques the first time, I couldn't believe they were of any use. Only now, I realize this actually works – so I would like to encourage people who experience problems to have the courage to be silly and let their brain come up with whatever it wants to come up with and not try to shape or control that process too much.* ***There are no unacceptable images in our heads!***

~~~~~

**KC**

*I can vouch for this. You really need to LET GO and allow your brain to think ANYTHING. My personality is naturally like this, so it has made it easy for me to come up with markers (my only struggle is retaining markers and linking them). We live in a world where we're not "allowed" to say certain things and think certain things, but your deep subconscious mind doesn't "understand" or "interpret" those boundaries. If you have any thoughts and visualizations that would be considered taboo, just let them express themselves. They will only benefit you, as they will stick out a lot more and make things memorable.*

~~~~~

**Dr. Lev Goldentouch**

*This is an interesting discussion. I was not thinking along the lines of cultural differences and conscientious mindset when suggesting possible remedies to visualization blocks. I will try to put more emphasis on openness and creativity in the future. Thank you for the insights!*

~~~~~
~~~~~

**UG**

*For me, creating markers is, fortunately, easy. However, the thing is I have to stop and think about my marker, create a detailed image in my head and store it.*

*The problem starts when I'm trying to read very fast and I don't have time to create a marker. I can actually create a simple marker, but as I still read the text, I only think about the marker and my eyes just move in saccades and solely forget that I have to create a new one.*

*In the beginning of the course, Jonathan showed how he creates markers, but he moves slowly to show us in which details he makes them. I still don't understand how to create that much of a detailed marker at that speed.*

**Dr. Lev Goldentouch**

*Try reading:*

*http://www.KeyToStudy.com/cant-visualize-fast-enough-reading-speed*

*and*

*http://www.KeyToStudy.com/markers-on-the-fly*

*Tell us if it helped.*

~~~~~

**DSL**

*Dr. Goldentouch, from the second link you provided you wrote, "In our private one-on-one course we often ask students to remember 20 objects within 60 seconds, which includes analyzing 20 objects, building 20 mental markers and building 20 links between markers and running the full end-to-end loop at least once or twice – all of that within 60 seconds." On average, how long does it take a student to achieve that level of mastery with markers?*

***Dr. Lev Goldentouch***

*Every person is different. Everybody has some sort of challenges mastering speedreading, but these challenges may be very personal. On average, it takes 3-4 weeks to master this skill. If it goes harder for you, do not give up and continue practicing. If you see no progress in a week, you are*
~~~~~

*doing something wrong. Contact us info@KeyToStudy.com and we will do our best to help.*

## Creativity Training Example

Assume a simple object. Now take 1 minute and try to get as many uses for it as you can.

~~~~~

To improve the results, try shifting perspectives.

### A Pen

1. **Writing tool**: write, doodle, marker
2. **Stylus**: draw on a computer, leave invisible marks, carve on wood
3. **Sharp object**: make holes on paper, office weapon, use as a nail in clay
4. **Prolong object**: fix door axis, use as a ruler, axis of scales, drum-stick
5. **Materials**: money laundry
6. **Container**: a small bomb, ink spritz
7. **Combinations**: flashlight, telescopic pointer, concealed arrow launcher
8. **Historical**: memorabilia, sign declarations, sign peace treaties, sign checks, invisible ink
9. **Body**: juggle with pen, put pen in mouth, clean ears, clean nose, measure depth of...

~~~~~

Now let us go from goals to ways to achieve goals.

### 30 Ways To Draw Attention

1. **Body**: Cry, wave your hands, jump
2. **Social conventions**: Drop your pants, roll on the ground moaning, point somewhere and cry, insinuate a crime (robbery, terror act)
3. **Money**: start dropping money, take a purse of an old lady
4. **Special people**: call for police/firemen/medics, try to appear choking

5. **Art**: sing with a voice of an angel, draw a circle around yourself and start chanting
6. **Politics**: burn a flag of some country
7. **Outsourcing**: hire a PR company
8. **History**: burn a temple, burn yourself, start sitting protest/hunger
9. **Container**: throw garbage cans
10. **Material**: hold a box with a sign of radioactive material, wear biohazard suit

# Chapter 16: Little Details Make A Big Difference

Since you can now generate markers, we will try to add details. Details are the small creative modifications making each visualization unique.

One of the things that limit our reading speed is the speed of creating markers. If we were required to create a marker per each detail within a text, we would end up with a choice between 250 wpm at 80% retention and 1000 wpm at 20% retention. In fact, one of the reasons other speedreading courses do not work is the fact students do generate a marker per detail.

Instead, **we urge our students to generate approximately two markers per paragraph and approximately five details per marker.** This way our students can read 1250 wpm at 80% retention.

## Details Generated Per Marker

What are the details we generate per marker?

1. We **base all details on information readily available in the text**, either directly or contextually.
2. We can **generate the color and size** of the marker according to:
   - **type of content**: emotional/factual/innovative, etc.
   - **importance** of the paragraph for us.
3. We can **add texture** according to materials mentioned in the text (money=metallic, energy=oily, document=paper, etc.).
4. Then we add some sort of **animation**: pulsating, growing, shining, contracting, etc., according to the type of modifications the marker is subjected to.

5. Next, we **choose** if the marker should be of **something new or something old**, **something familiar or exotic**, etc.

***All of the above transform a generic marker into a specific one.***

In fact, the process of adding details should be fast, intuitive and specific to the text we are reading. Consider the conversation below.

~~~~~

***SL:***

*Just to make sure I'm creating and linking my markers right, I'll paste an excerpt from a book I'm currently reading.*

> *"Similar questions have been asked by visionaries throughout history, and many techniques have been developed to explore and develop our potentials. One of the most* ***effective methods*** *is also one of the most ancient—**yoga**.*
>
> *The word yoga is a cognate of **yoke**, meaning **"to combine, connect, or unify."** What is said to **be unified is the personal self and the universal Self**. This rarified state is a goal of nearly all esoteric practices. It is also known as **achieving a state of illumination**, or to be awakened or enlightened. The shift from everyday awareness to an ecstatic form of consciousness gives one direct access to knowledge of unmediated Reality."*

*The bold and italicized phrases are what I'd consider important concepts. For example, for yoga, I conjure up an image of an old man wearing a white loincloth practicing yoga underneath a tree. The word yoga is a cognate of yoke, which I imagine as an egg yoke. For the unification of the personal self and universal Self, I imagine the egg yoke transforming into a big silhouette of the old man. For illumination, I imagine the old man becomes a bright white light.*

*So to link these markers, I imagine the old man practising yoga underneath a tree, then, an egg yoke falls*
~~~~~

*from the sky and transforms into a big silhouette of the old man who then lights up in a bright white light. Any suggestions to improve?*

***Dr. Lev Goldentouch:***

*ADD DETAILS*

*"Unity" – egg is a symbol of unity, see e.g. golden egg http://en.wikipedia.org/wiki/Brahma*

*"throughout history/ancient" may be easily incorporated in man's age*

*"Potential" is some sort of height at which the yoke is positioned*

*The sentence "The shift from everyday awareness to an ecstatic form of consciousness gives one direct access to knowledge of unmediated Reality." is important and dense.*

*"The light causes the man to open eyes and his insight is like a secondary explosion of light..."*

~~~~~

If we **need more than five details**, it is better to add another marker. For example, we may need specific markers to encode people and dates. If, inside a paragraph, we need a name, date, and place, we will need much more than two markers.

Fortunately, markers for dates are easy to create after some practice with the PAO technique (see Chapter 20). Markers for names and places are hard to create, but once we create them, we can reuse them in all the text we read. By creating a personal marker dictionary, we do not need to recreate the name and place markers each time we see them. We just reuse readily available imagery from our personally created dictionary.

These additional markers need to connect to the current marker within some sort of linking system. Typically, I just put stickers on the original paragraph's marker and link the stickers to the auxiliary markers.

The links we use to bind the markers may also hold additional information. We can imagine the links as some sort of physical strings. These strings could hold metadata (color, strength, elasticity, new/old) and the logical basis (what
~~~~~

forces are applied to the string: pull/push, symmetric/asymmetric) of the nature of the association.

Usually, we are highly competent professionals in one area or another. This means we learned several prerequisite courses or acquired some knowledge from personal experience. The knowledge we acquired that is relevant to what we are learning may be called "domain knowledge." We can build our new understandings on top of what we already know.

Advanced students can process some details in parallel, further increasing the reading speed and comprehension. For example, we can generate a compartment (with a door) within the main marker and put within the compartment four to five auxiliary markers already available from the domain knowledge. This way we encode examples to some rule within the rule and without paying the penalty of creating extra markers.

When creating markers we are supposed to generate approximately two markers per paragraph, but our texts are much denser. What do we do? We add details and auxiliary markers!

## Analogies

You use an analogy when you say something is like something else (in some respects but not in others). For example, a jumbo jet is like an albatross because:

- they both fly,
- they both have wings,
- they can both travel a long way without landing, and
- both can sense where they are going;

But they are unlike because:

- they have different means of propulsion,
- are made of different materials, etc.

Analogies are key for many approaches to creativity. The term *bionics* has been used to describe the systematic use of biological and botanical analogies to solve novel engineering problems.

Often analogies are used very informally: 'This problem makes me think of X (analogy) – that suggests to me maybe we could try Y (idea drawn from analogy X).' However, the underlying logic will be along these lines:

1. **Identify** what it is you want ideas for, and try to **find a core verb phrase** that captures the essential functional nature of what you are looking for – e.g., 'How to make X.' 'How to prevent Y.' 'How to speed up Z.' 'How to become better at A.'
2. For each verb phrase **generate a list of items** (people, situations, objects, processes, actions, places, etc.) that is *'like'* it in some way – e.g. analogies to 'making X' (having a baby, making a pudding, the Genesis creation story, a robot car factory, etc.).
3. **Pick one of these analogies** that seem interesting – preferably, where the verb phrase and analogy are from different domains – e.g. a biological analogy for a mechanical problem.
4. **Describe the analogy**, including active aspects (such as how it works, what it does, what effects it has, how it is used) as well as passive aspects (size, position, etc.).
5. **Use this description to suggest ideas** relevant to your problem. Does the analogy have features you can use directly? Do the differences suggest other ways of looking at your problem?

**Analogies can be:**

- **Close/direct**: A straight functional parallel, e.g., selling science is like selling baked beans or the human arm is like an angle pose lamp.
- **Fantasy**: What is the image that comes into your mind if you were to solve it in your wildest fantasy or within some other cartoon/fantasy world?

- **Remote and/or surprising**: 'Selling widgets' is like 'steering an elephant'. These analogies are more likely to challenge assumptions and lead to new insights and ideas – but the parallels they suggest are unlikely to have much 'rational' status. In the extreme, they merge into the use of random stimuli.
- **Personal/component**: Here you become a component in the system, e.g., if you are looking at how to get shells to more accurately hit the target, think of yourself as the tip of the shell.

## Osborne's Checklist

Use Osborn's Checklist when working with markers. This is an excellent list of questions to stimulate your imagination to create markers.

- **Put to other uses**? As it is? If modified?
- **Adapt**? Is there anything else like this? What does this tell you? Is the past comparable?
- **Modify**? Give it a new angle? Alter the color, sound, odor, meaning, motion, and shape?
- **Magnify**? Can anything be added, time, frequency, height, length, strength? Can it be duplicated, multiplied or exaggerated?
- **Minify**? Can anything be taken away? Made smaller? Lowered? Shortened? Lightened? Omitted? Broken up?
- **Substitute**? Different ingredients used? Other material? Other processes? Other place? Other approach? Other tone of voice? Someone else?
- **Rearrange**? Swap components? Alter the pattern, sequence or layout? Change the pace or schedule? Transpose cause and effect?
- **Reverse**? Opposites? Backwards? Reverse roles? Change shoes? Turn tables? Turn other cheek? Transpose '+/-'?

- **Combine**? Combine units, purposes, appeals or ideas? A blend, alloy, or an ensemble?

## Exaggerations

From Osborn's original checklist (above), magnify and minify are two idea generating transformations, both of which are forms of exaggeration. The table below shows a selection of exaggerations to illustrate the problem:

'I need a lot of capacity in my Reprographics Department to cope with a few key peak loads, but this means that for much of the time much of it is idle.'

| Forms of Exaggeration | Type | Examples |
|---|---|---|
| Exaggerate upwards | Magnify | I have photocopiers standing idle |
| Exaggerate downwards | Minify | My photocopiers are barely used at all |
| Exaggerate scope | Invade context | The whole organization is underused |
| Exaggerate significance | Aggrandize | Our over-capacity is a national scandal |
| Exaggerate selectively | Caricature | Reprographics Rest Home! |

Why does exaggeration appear to work? Because many times our mindset is related to the scale of a problem and while there might be a form of action that is acceptable in a crisis, it is not acceptable with a lesser problem.

To test your unspoken assumptions about the scale of the problem, you should think about what would be appropriate if the problem were of a different order of magnitude. Exaggerated solutions can often be applied directly, although the more likely scenario is you will find they are inappropriate as they stand, but may suggest other ideas that would be acceptable.

Similar principles can also be useful when building on ideas for solutions. Imagine you are in search of a way to prevent vandalism by youngsters and someone suggests, "Keep them in after school." You could build on this idea by exaggerating it in various ways. For example, magnify the idea to "Keep them in permanently" suggesting giving them a permanent role (e.g., school monitor) or minimize it to "Gentle restraint after school" suggesting ideas such as an after school club that they may actually enjoy.

**Structured Version**

1. **Define the problem** to be addressed or the idea you need to develop
2. Make a **list** of all the **component parts** of the idea or if a problem, its objectives, and constraints.
3. **Choose one component** from the list in No. 2.
4. **Develop ways of exaggerating** it and note them on a separate sheet.
5. **Note down all ideas** you have from No. 4.
6. **Repeat** ad lib from Step 3.

## Simple Way To Get Abstract Markers

***AZ***

*I am having so much trouble coming up with markers for abstract stuff. I just do not know what picture to come up with. I just cannot find a symbol or icon standing for a complex, abstract idea. Can you give some specific guidelines on where to look?*

***Dr. Lev Goldentouch***

*Try Google Image Search, Shutterstock is even better. In image search go to search tools and choose image type "clipart." Eventually, you will get it without computer aid.*

*Please notice once you come up with a marker, you can reuse it any time you encounter the same concept.*

## Slow Markers Versus Fast Markers

Fast visual markers are like free associations, they come fast, they are personal, and you have little control of what they look like. While you train with slow visual markers, you can only hope your brain's automatic mechanisms improve accordingly. Probably some of the markers you currently discard are perfectly legit as fast markers and only need some more details from the text. The "slow" markers should be built deliberately and should be used for long-term memorization.

## Generate Visual Markers On The Fly

Generating markers slowly is not good enough for speedreading. Generating markers fast requires a certain level of skill. Our beginner-level students do not know how to overcome the controlled visualization speed limitations. When the students are ready, we teach them to reduce the level of control and enjoy free associations. Below are some discussions from our Udemy course.

**Question:**

*How do you make markers on the fly while speedreading? I'm just wondering, because it takes a lot of time to make the markers but speedreading goes so fast... Do you just need enough to go markers that you can actually assign them at this speed?*

**Dr. Lev Goldentouch**

*It is like free associations. Once your mind is trained sufficiently, the first association you get is your marker. Free associations are extremely fast, but you need some practice to make good associations.*

*Your brain should create markers/images, which should in turn be related to each other like comics or a website, etc. When I was training, I was asked to create an image per page, per paragraph, per sentence, per detail I want to remember and to draw these images on a page near the titles I give to the article, the sections, the paragraphs, etc. Eventually I stopped drawing, but the brain continued marker generation.*

*Everything is slow at first, but if it does not improve with training, you need to change something. After some training mental markers should appear very fast (approximately 100 msec per marker). It is like looking at clouds and saying, "this cloud looks like a dog" or looking at a person and think "with this prolonged face and low personal hygiene he looks like a rat."*

*There are people who cannot generate visual association and need to use different methods. Usually this is quite rare, less than 1% of the students. If this is your case, you will need to schedule a Skype meeting with Anna to handpick the methodology (email to info@KeyToStudy.com).*

*You need to generate markers as fast as you get free associations. We do not measure the speed or the time it takes you to get there as long as you can generate markers FAST. In our private one-on-one course we often ask students to remember 20 objects within 60 seconds; the process includes analyzing 20 objects, building 20 mental markers and building 20 links between markers and running the full end-to-end loop at least once or twice – all of that within 60 seconds.*

## Remove Unwanted Imagery

### Ways of Stopping Compulsive Trains of Unwanted Images

- **Switch attention**: Open your eyes, switch your attention to thinking about something very mundane like what you had for lunch, and discontinue the fantasy.
- **Stop! Method**: Try putting the images into words, then snapping your fingers and ordering them to 'Stop!' or getting someone to shout 'Stop!' for you, or even just saying it to yourself, though that is not so effective. Take a deep breath and then let it out slowly, relaxing your face, neck, shoulders and arms as you do so. Take a second deep breath and let it out slowly, relaxing your front and back and legs right down to the ground as you do so. Then take two normal breaths, shorter and shallower.
- **Flooding method**: Attempt creation of more images of a similar kind – flooding yourself with them, to reduce the demand, e.g., move closer and further from

the imagery, examining it in detail and from every angle, until the mind is exhausted. If going close feels uncomfortable, imagine a telescope, so that you can see the detail from a safe distance.

- **Reversal method**: To eliminate a passive worry, imagine its pleasurable opposite. If you are distressed about a deadline, fantasize about the enjoyable experience of meeting it!

## Learning Words

www.Vocabulary.com would be a good place for this exercise. You can try thinking of markers for all of the random words while learning them. Specifically I like http://www.vocabulary.com/articles/chooseyourwords/.

Not only can you learn new words, but you can also learn to notice small differences that change the meaning.

For example:

***assure/ensure/insure***

Although these three often show up at the same party, giving hugs, they are not the same, thank you very much. To *assure* is to tell someone everything is okay, to *ensure* is to make certain, and to *insure* is to protect financially. Have it straight now? Are you sure?

Consider a small story to remember the difference in the words.

Be sure (confident) when you can enter a saloon:

Check your **ass** (donkey) is OK (healthy)... Assure he is fine.

The **ens**emble is playing: do you like the music? Ensure you will enjoy.

Cover **ins** and outs with dollar bills. Buy insurance.

## Learning Languages

When learning languages, the speed of your markers is not an issue. Try to have several representations for the same information so you will not forget.

1. Find two ways to encode the information

2. Generate small stories that are both visual and auditory. Do tell the story to yourself.
3. Do not jump contexts of your visualization
4. Consider additional markers to the number of items you need to remember

## Simple Memorization Of Numbers

There are many ways of remembering long numbers. It is easier to remember words than numbers, so most of the methods I know replace numbers by words. For example, remember texts where the length of each word is a number. It takes practice to generate such texts. Use http://www.rememberg.com/ when out of ideas. Enter a number into the search line and see what comes out.

## Remembering Formulas

Remembering formulas is typically a logical task. If you try to put formulas into PAO or Loci, you may memorize a specific formulation, but you will not be able to modify and reuse it sufficiently well.

~~~~~

Statistics is something almost everybody needs to use. Go to http://stattrek.com/statistics/formulas.aspx

Population correlation coefficient = $\rho = ( 1 / N ) * \Sigma \{ ( (X_i - \mu_X) / \sigma_x ) * ( (Y_i - \mu_Y) / \sigma_y ) \}$

Now let us start to analyze what it means:

**1.**

Population correlation coefficient = $\rho = ( 1 / N ) * \Sigma F(X_i, Y_i)$

This means we have some average of a function of two populations over all instances.

(We take average over smarts of all married pairs)

**2.**
~~~~~

The function is

$F(X_i,Y_i)=Nx(X_i)*Ny(Y_i)$

Product of normalized population instances.

(The relative smarts of a husband and the relative smarts of a wife generate smarts of a pair)

**3.**

$Ny(Y_i)= ( (Y_i - \mu_Y) / \sigma_y )$

We normalize each population by mean and standard deviation

(On average women are a bit smarter than men. We negate this by subtracting average. Smart men are smarter than smart women, stupid men more stupid than stupid women - negate that by dividing by standard deviation)

**4.**

Try to vocalize the process for dual coding

"We normalize X, and we normalize Y, their product on average is so co-related."

~~~~~

**The steps are typically the same**

1. Divide the formula into meaningful parts
2. Generate a story which explains why this is meaningful
3. Provide a cool example. The example does not have to be right, but it should be sufficiently simple to remember the rule.
4. Use common sense: if common sense negates the result, you need to update common sense. Otherwise, we have mathematical intuition at work!
5. Mathematicians often report synesthesia of math formulas sounding like music. Try to dual code what you understood.
~~~~~

There are plenty of formulas on:
http://stattrek.com/statistics/formulas.aspx
Try our method on them!

## SuperLearning For Writers

**TL**

*My goal is to be able to become a better writer this year. I also want to maximize my speedreading skills so I don't need to spend so much time reading books. I want to know if speedreading will help me write better.*

**Dr. Lev Goldentouch**

*Basically, when you speedread using our system (does not necessarily work for other systems) you become a better writer because:*

1. *You become acutely aware of the text structure and can build better structures yourself.*
2. *You hold a lot of knowledge and can easily come up with great examples and understandings.*
3. *The way you remembers things is very graphic which enables great analogies and metaphors, sometimes very unexpected.*
4. *If you practice synesthesia training, your texts get extra dimensions.*

## Working With Dreams And Images

To experience creative dreaming, it is essential to come into better contact with your dreams. Psychologists have revealed that each of us dreams every night. However, and unfortunately, most of our dreams are forgotten. Thus, keeping a dream diary helps retain the information longer. The building of the dream diary will demonstrate over a period of time that you recall more and more of your dreams by being more aware of them. Regular discussion of your dreams and diaries will also help in understanding them, any themes running through them and unconscious ideas.

- Before falling asleep, go over the following several times: 'Tonight I dream; when I awake I will remember my dreams.'

- On awakening in the morning, lie quietly, do not open your eyes and let your mind dwell on your initial thoughts. These initial thoughts could remind you of your last dream prior to awakening and with practice allow you to remember more and more of the dream's details.
- A notebook is essential alongside your bed, to record a diary of your dreams. You could try sketching your dreams or use a tape recorder to record middle of the night dreams. The following morning these tapes could be translated into the dream diary.
- Essential, keep the daily diary, try not to miss days out.

This technique was originally developed by Glouberman (1989) and takes for granted you have memorized a significant dream you have had and now wish to enhance it to allow it the opportunity to be of some function.

Possible suggestions for how you may go about this are:

- **Locate the dream** and get the feel of any atmosphere. Are you able to put a name to it? Is it familiar? Go into the dream, and experience the atmosphere. Identify feelings, relationships, and the situation. Is there anything familiar about them?
- **Discover the dream taking a 'birds eye view' of it,** flying high looking down on it, note what you see:
  - Do you notice anything significant?
  - Is there anything obvious you can do to improve the quality of the dream?
  - What would you like to whisper to the dream self?
  - Look at the dream from different angles, i.e. the left, the right, behind, in front, underneath, noticing what comes to mind about the dream and the dream self.

  - Envisage that the dream stage situated centrally in a room and physically walk around it.

- Developing the images can be achieved by **discovering the most striking feature of the dream,** the person, scene, building, object, event, and then move into it, either in your mind or by picturing it on a chair opposite and switching seats. Talk about yourself and your viewpoint, including your view of the dream itself. Transform into each important feature in turn. What does each feel and see? Have conversations between the dream self and any of these features, or between the various features. Every part of the dream, whether it is a person, a table or a movement, has a communication that you as the dreamer need to hear. Talk to the dream as a whole: 'Dream, what do you want to tell me?' Become the dream and answer.
- **Combine the viewpoints by returning** to the dream as the main dream character. Look intently at all the characters, features, perspectives, etc., and think about what each one has told you. Think about what you have learned from progressing through the dream and what you now understand about how you live in the dream world and how you might live? Invite your unconscious mind to take in and put together these various understandings and perspectives. Take the time to let them sink in. Try to put the lessons in words as clearly as you can.
- **Adapting and progressing the dream more successfully** by visualizing what new approach, attitude or personal quality you need to live this dream to feel especially enhanced at the end of it. Try reliving it with this new approach or personal quality. Should you find it too difficult to imagine acting differently, just say to yourself:
  - If I did have that quality ...

- If I were like that, what would I do?

- **If you get stuck anywhere, leave the dream** and reconsider whether you need anything else to go forward. Try to find a way to live the dream so that it feels good. Continue this reworked dream into the future. What happens next, and after that? Validate out the new approach you have just tried from the various perspectives you explored before. What do the other characters, features, etc. think? What does this new dream look like from the 'birds eye view', below and the various sides? If there are any further shifts that seem appropriate, try them out.
- **Understanding, re-examining, looking forward and surfacing occurs when you feel good about the dream,** thank your unconscious for giving you the dream, and thank your conscious self for working so hard. Request your unconscious to put together your new understandings, and to present you a new dream in the near future that will characterize your new state. Prior to and following emerging, think about the relevance of your understandings to your life. Where in your life are you relating to the world as you did in the dream? How could you operate differently? Write down your experience, paint the dream or express it in some other medium.

## Forgetting As A Way To Handle Traumas

Occasionally, we ask ourselves, "Why do we forget at all?" and/or "What if we could remember things forever?" Apparently forgetting things helps us to deal with traumas. One of the best ways to deal with traumatic experience is rewriting the traumatic memory.

**Some courage is required, so *do not attempt this if you do not have social support or are depressed.***

Focus on the traumatic memory you want to rewrite. Typically, you can reframe a negative experience into a positive one. Before you relive the experience, think of the best strategy to approach the negative experience and on how you want to feel with what happened.

Try to remember the traumatic experience. Now, in the middle of the experience, try to detach and look at the whole situation from an entirely different perspective.

- If the situation is humiliating and funny then laugh.
- If the experience is heroic, then experience a strong sense of pride and respect.
- If the situation motivated you to become stronger, then focus on the lessons you have learned and the person you are now.
- If you cannot find anything better, then focus on how all people suffer and need empathy of each other.

Feel the new experience in small details. It will not replace the old feelings all at once. You will need to build up from details to the core of what happened.

*"Our human compassion binds us the one to the other – not in pity or patronizingly, but as human beings who have learnt how to turn our common suffering into hope for the future."*
*Nelson Mandela*

Everyone has something to remember and something to forget. The things we want to forget do bind us together. As we learn new ways to remember new things, we should be thankful for the gift of forgetting.

## History Cheat Sheets

When learning history, you can always find a starting point with a good cheat sheet. In Google type: "XYZ history cheat sheet"

See for example http://www.dummies.com/how-to/content/world-history-for-dummies-cheat-sheet.html

or

http://www.dummies.com/how-to/content/us-history-for-dummies-cheat-sheet.html

## Structure Of A Cheat Sheet

1. **Year**. Use PAO to remember

2. **Place**. Try to position on the world map. Remember the name using the "sounds like" method.
3. **Person**. Use the "sounds like" technique to remember. Try to browse about the person on Wikipedia. If you can get an IMDB entry, even better
4. **Event**. This is something you actually need to understand. Try to generate a good marker, since you will return to it again and again. Try searching Google images for a classical representation. Typically, the event is the key for the construction of the relevant mental memory palace.
5. **Details**. Add details to the marker
6. **Consequences**. This is the context of the event. Each event makes a huge ripple. Typically a list. Remember using mental memory palace.
7. **Causes**. Another list, harder to obtain. Remember using mental memory palace.

Once you have everything, make sure it is in the same palace.

**For example:**

**1803:**
The U.S. buys 828,000 square miles of the Mississippi River from France. The "Louisiana Purchase" costs about $15 million, or 3 cents an acre.

**Event**: buying lands in Wild West.
**Memory palace**: buying Wild West carriage
**Details**: French salesman (Napoleon)
**Location**: sun going down (west) over a river with a steamer (Mississippi for me)
A poster from "*True Blood*" Louisiana location
**Price**: 15 bags with letter M (3x5 matrix) on a bench, a map with 3 bronze coins on a square, 69x12 squares. (69 love position, 12 hours)

**Time**: 1803=3 army drafts (army draft is 18 years old.)

**Consequences**: Stretching from the Mississippi River to the Rocky Mountains, the purchase doubled the size of the United States.

**Causes**: Before 1803, Louisiana had been under Spanish control for 40 years. Louisiana remained under Spanish control until a transfer of power three weeks before the formal cession to the United States. In November 1803, France withdrew its 7,000 surviving troops from Saint-Domingue (more than two-thirds of its troops died there) and gave up its ambitions in the Western Hemisphere. James Monroe and Robert R. Livingston had traveled to Paris to negotiate the purchase of New Orleans and did not anticipate the much larger acquisition, which would follow.

## For Further Research:

### Forgetting / Trauma

https://www.psychologytoday.com/blog/talking-about-trauma/201504/forgetting-ptsd-how-genes-affect-memory

### Cheat Sheet:

https://en.wikipedia.org/wiki/Louisiana_Purchase

http://en.wikipedia.org/wiki/Mississippi_River

http://en.wikipedia.org/wiki/Rocky_Mountains

http://en.wikipedia.org/wiki/United_States

http://en.wikipedia.org/wiki/Louisiana_(New_Spain)

http://en.wikipedia.org/wiki/Western_Hemisphere

http://en.wikipedia.org/wiki/James_Monroe

http://en.wikipedia.org/wiki/Robert_R._Livingston_(chancellor)

http://en.wikipedia.org/wiki/Paris

# PART 4: STRUCTURE AND MEMORIZATION

# Chapter 17: Linking Markers

It is not enough to remember details. **It is very important to connect the details with each other**. There are several levels of linking markers. We start with examples of low-level visualization and related linking, and end with high-level visualization and related linking of markers. We start from creating short and simple stories, build up associations and complex visualization, and end up with the creation of whole virtual worlds adapted for retention of hundreds and thousands of details.

## Anchors

We mark in the text the data we want to remember. However, how do we make sure we will be able to find our markers?

1. Generate special markers which we call anchors through which we remember all other markers.
2. Link all markers to each other and eventually to anchors.
3. Make sure that anchors answer a specific question we may ask later to retrieve other markers.
4. Anchors are "slow" markers: we make them very lively and easy to remember and try to connect them to our prior knowledge.

## Find Your Natural Markers

Some people use a highlighter, some write on page margins and some draw illustrations. We use different ways to mark what we read. When we visualize our marker, it works in the same way. Try to ask yourself:

1. Do you remember better the actual toys you played with as a child or comics you read when young?
2. Do you still remember the way home from your school, or do you remember funny stories with your schoolmates?

3. Is your own life more lively for you than the last blockbuster movie you saw?
4. Do you prefer nature or do you prefer high-quality rendering of a cool video game?
5. Do you effortlessly recall jokes, poems or equations?

Once you ask yourself the right questions you will understand what sort of markers work best for you. Check different sorts of visual associations with texts. What do you remember better? What comes to you effortlessly? What associations do you get for anything you read?

Do not be embarrassed by yourself. Some of my best associations are too obscene to be written in a book. So what? They are funny, they get me involved and they are very memorable.

## Follow Your Text

When creating structures to hold your text, try to follow the template in which the text is written. Typically, texts are hierarchical and open an idea into several subjects, and each subject into several statements. Some texts appear to have lists and pro/con tables. Do not try to force your own structure upon the text you read, follow the structure of the text instead.

## Markers Versus Details

Typically, we generate approximately two markers per paragraph with approximately five details per marker. Generating markers takes time, and we need details to make the markers memorable. If we add too many details per marker, we will start forgetting details. If we add too many markers, we will read slower and we may start adding details that are not supported by the text.

## Question: How Do I Link Markers?

**AD**

*The impression I am getting is that I have to read the text, choose out unusual words that stand out and turn them into images since that is what the brain likes the most and then go back and turn those images into a story or do I try to force myself to create the story at the same time?*

**NM**

*I can create markers pretty well now, still struggling in choosing what parts now and then. My problem is linking them together. I see you said the story method is too long to connect markers together effectively for speedreading, but I can't seem to find where you explain how you should link them.*

**Dr. Lev Goldentouch**

*You do sort of a story, but one that does not have to make sense. The story is more of a comic. You can see the flow visually, but you cannot actually vocalize the story behind it.*

*Most authors recommend placing the objects in a familiar environment, the loci or memory palace method. This way you can imagine a huge house or museum, and then you memorize your itinerary and the objects you see. I could not personally use the memory palace method since I am challenged this way (I cannot find food in my own refrigerator). Therefore, I developed my own strategies.*

*When I was training, Anna asked me to create an image per page, per paragraph, per sentence, per detail I want to remember and to draw these images on a page near the titles I give to the article, the sections, the paragraphs, etc. Eventually, I stopped drawing, but the brain continued marker generation.*

*The simplest way to link objects is to create some sort of funny physical interactions between them. I call it the "three stooges" style. It includes a lot of breaking through, sitting on, running into, etc., where you get a chance to memorize parts of objects meeting each other at various points. I initially used this method. It allows me to create links very fast with no effort, but the resulting imagery very soon loses all uniqueness.*

*The method I recommend to the students of this book is what I call* ***"cartoon" or "storyboarding."***

- *You start with creating the general mood of the storybook, during the preparation stage. Usually I go with some sort of 'dark' setting, maybe Steampunk or Iron Men environment.*

- *Then I start creating images one by one, giving each section/paragraph an image. Each detail of the paragraph is carefully planted in various active personages and the setting.*
- *Larger parts of content get more space than the smaller ones.*
- *Various sections are then linked by some sort of sinister plot. Maybe hugging bears or sitcoms are more suitable for your style.*
- *The storyboard method also boosts your creativity and encourages unique markers.*

*The third method I use I call* ***"hyperlinking."*** *It is inspired by website design. You can enjoy something similar on "Big History" (TV series):* http://en.wikipedia.org/wiki/Big_History_(TV_series).

*The method uses very simple markers but very complex links between them, where most of the information is carried by links. Using this method, I can learn whole disciplines and areas of knowledge, but I would not use it for a single article.*

## Linking Exercise

In the linking exercise, you have the first word open and you do not need to generate chunking. Many lists come in a form very similar to the linking exercise. All you need to do is remember how an object follows from another.

Go to http://www.KeyToStudy.com/linking-markers-exercise/. Choose 8x8 structure - I do not want this example to be too long.

hobby - easily - theatre - space - significantly - website - ambulance - between
muscle - knock - aloud - station - sadly - than - true - pause
certificate - mineral - emergency - proud - shortly - weather - release - govern
deposit - scheme - steer - excluding - anxiety - active - return - expert
movie - surround - onion - illustrate - birth - devote - earn - strip
cease - counter - population - satisfied - feature - crucial - arrive - alongside
according - afternoon - ruin - groceries - dishonestly - lose - detailed - necessarily
motion - disapproving - exhibit - terrible - climb - temporary - take - alarming

Once we generated all the links, we ask to complete the table using multiple-choice selection. The words come up as clues, which is very comfortable. However, as there are more words, the right word starts to hide in the long combo box. Finding the right word is good training for the scanning skill.

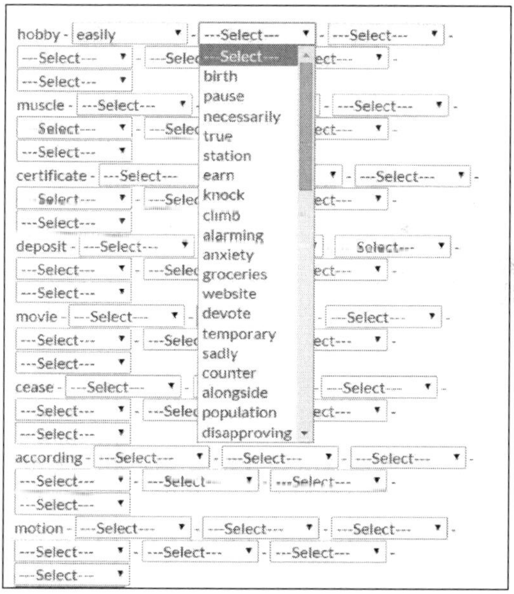


You can guess if you want, and when finished you get a score.

Now, how do we remember 64 associations? We create a comics/animation! It is imperative to keep the order right, so we add an artificial detail before each word. Try to add different colors for original and added words, like red of original and blue for added.

~~~~~

Association: hobby easily theatre space significantly website ambulance between

Comic Animation: (Gardening) hobby (makes growing flowers) easily (thrown on stage of) theater (where actor with flowers looks into) space (illuminated by stage light because he is) significant (his reviews crushed on a) website (so he needs an) ambulance (where he lies) between (sanitars.)

Very dramatic: an actor, scene, flowers, critics, heart attack.

~~~~~

Association: muscle knock aloud station sadly than true pause

Comic Animation: (Mafia) muscle (at a door) knocks (continues) aloud (from police) station (a siren sounds) sadly (much more) than (now. Not) true (this scene) pause (filming)

Here we have two motives within the same animation. We start within a film, but we do not know that, until we stop filming. Again, filming of a mafia story is easy to remember.

~~~~~

Association: certificate mineral emergency proud shortly weather release govern

Comic Animation: (Medical) certificate (approves) mineral (to be eaten in case of) emergency. (The scientist) proud (of the mineral, thanks) shortly (to the public, which retreats due to) weather (Mr Hyde is) released (and the city is his to) govern

I knew that this is Dr. Jekyll/Mr Hyde only when I came to the word "release" and it associated with a monster. Having Mr. Hyde is sufficiently horrific to remember the link.

~~~~~

Association: deposit scheme steer excluding anxiety active return expert

Comic Animation: (Safe) deposit (lock with electronic) scheme (and metal wheel to) steer. (Everyone bank owner) excluding (breath with) anxiety (as the mechanism becomes) active. (The deposit is) returned (and the bank owner thanks the) expert.

Try Oceans 11... TV offers an endless supply of stories to use.

~~~~~

Association: movie surround onion illustrate birth devote earn strip

Comic Animation: (Rapper watches a) movie (with huge boom box) surround (He eats) onion (and cries. He doodles to) illustrate (a demon's) birth (in satanic chamber with) devote (who sacrifice virgin) earn (the demon's favor as they) strip (the virgin.)

Occasionally we have a dream within dream scenario. With practice, we can easily handle it. It is much better than trying to recreate a link that became disrupted.

~~~~~

Association: cease counter populate satisfied feature crucial arrive alongside

Comic Animation: (The National Guard) ceased (the city as they) counter (zombies who) populate (the streets. Never) satisfied (the search for a) feature: (a crack or a door to break. It is) crucial (for human survivors to) arrive (to the guards with no zombie) alongside.

With practice, we can learn to visualize negations. Typically I place a burning red X sign in the scene where the negations happen for double coding.

~~~~~

Association: according afternoon ruin groceries dishonestly lose detailed necessary

Comic Animation: According (to the commander, this) afternoon (a group of zombies) ruined (a) grocery (store, killing thieves who) dishonestly (stole the army weapons.
~~~~~

They) lose (their life making) detailed (map of underground passes) necessary (for escape.)

Continue previous theme- easier than creating a new theme. It is hard not to mix added versus original words, like visualizing red details on a blue map. For "necessary" I use the exclamation point (!). I use similar punctuation symbols to emphasize/double code some other words.

~~~~~

Association: motion disapproving exhibit terrible climb temporary take alarming

Comic Animation: (Congress) motion (to impeach) disapproving (sexual behavior of the president, who) exhibit (a dress with a) terrible (stain. Demonstrators) climb (the Capitol stairs, blocking) temporarily (city center. The police) takes (no action, faced by) alarming (violence of the riots).

Here I chained president elections and riots - both of which you can find in the news. For temporarily, I visualized the day-and-night cut scene from "*House of Cards*." For alarm, I visualized police lights, etc.

~~~~~

A memory champion can encode a detail in 0.5 seconds. Typically, when faced with this exercise, students invest too much focus in each specific word, rather than following a theme where all the words are reasonable. It is very important to go with themes, and not create a different theme for every object, or the exercise may take forever to complete.

## Story Creation

### BM

*Is creating a story effective? Does it count as markers?*

*For the game you have posted for this chapter, I do the following. I feel it's not quite what you suggest but find it really hard to make markers for the objects in the game using one to two words.*

*My example... (the BOLD being the words to remember)*

> *I enter my kitchen, step on the floor covered in 10c **COINS**, I see a giant **PINEAPPLE** chopping up*

> *rotten **TOMATOES**, I hear this horrible yelping midget **DOG** spot a **LEMON** and throw it to shut it up but it breaks the Japanese Porcelain **FIGURINE** which was hopping around the lounge like a **RABBIT**, etc....*

*Is that sort of thing useful or is it too much work? Should I really be condensing it down? I have used this technique to memorize lists and lists of stuff in previous attempts at improving memory, but I am not sure if that will work for what we are doing here.*

**Dr. Lev Goldentouch**

*There are many methods for remembering things. The story method is very useful if you have a very high density of information; however, it is a bit slow. Try actually visualizing to remove vocalization and improve the speed of learning. For example, I often create visualized comics, e.g. quickly changing chains of images that have a certain story behind them.*

**Jonathan A. Levi**

*As Dr. Goldentouch mentioned, it is very effective, as you said it works well for lists and things you have to remember. However, for reading it will indeed prove way too slow. Still, if you have to remember a lecture and go on stage, this is a great way to remember the key points. In fact, one of the Ted talks we link to discusses this exact technique.*

**BM**

*OK cool, I guess my thoughts then are that I can create images for the different things such as dartboard, white cat, etc., good markers for them, but without that story I was creating I find it difficult to link them all together enough that one leads to the other.*

*If I can clarify the comic idea, that would be taking a marker, say for the dartboard, which for me would be a mate playing darts in my garage and him losing constantly and the despair in his voice. Taking that image and giving it a link to say a white dog, which my marker would be my pet dog, Max. I can link these two together as I lived with my mate before, but do I need to do that extra link? Are just the two markers I have described enough linkage to keep them all in the mind?*

*Thanks again.*

**Dr. Lev Goldentouch**

*Always link, if you have time make more than one link. The links allow navigation between markers, like between pages on a website.*

## Visualization Levels

**AB**

*Homework game, how to better use markers with the game?*

*I played the game and made markers for each image. This worked well until level 3. I felt this problem was coming from not having a connection between the clusters of images. They were all standalone for me.*

*So I made a story following chronologically to images and markers to each image. Example a 'can', 'bowling pin' and 'baseball glove' becomes: I saw a can and put a bowling pin in it, and then I proceeded to throw it with my baseball-gloved hand. This worked perfectly without a single mistake from level 3 to level 10, took me 30 minutes to do so.*

*I actually realized/wondered halfway (level 6) that I was actually using modified version of the memory palace. I feel that it's a good way for totally unconnected information. This story technique is ineffective for logical information. With practice, I hope I can use place markers and logically connect them to the big picture.*

*But with the unconnected images in this game how am I supposed to do that? Should I make up a big concept/marker to place all the images with markers in? Like I make individual markers for 'can', 'bowling pin' and 'baseball glove' then connect those markers with my image of a standard American dad in a movie who eats 'can' food and plays 'bowling' and 'plays throw ball'?*

**Dr. Lev Goldentouch**

*Depending on the level of visualization, you will get different results.*

*Low-level visualization: Put a pin into the can and then put the glove on the pin. Notice that putting the glove on the pin like you would put it on a hand is fun to visualize and creative, so easier to remember.*

*Middle-level visualization: Smash the can between the pin and the glove. Here all three objects interact with each other very graphically and in physical vicinity. Notice that taking one element out of the picture destroys the connection; therefore, the connection is strong.*

*High-level visualization: You are a knight, with a can on your head, a bowling pin as a sword and the glove on the hand holding the pin. Now each of the objects can interact with anything in the landscape around you and each other in multiple ways.*

**AB**

*Awesome! I think I get it.*

*So Low-level is simply objects 1-2-3-4 ... in order – basically the way I did it.*

*Middle-level is connecting multiple markers together in a cluster 3-3-3 and so on.*

*High-level is me being the starting point (Knight), my knightness I defined by a few items in my possession. I'd then use my items to interact with other object clusters. Like fighting a cat with sunglasses and a rose behind his ear with my pin.*

*Hmm, I notice there are multiple ways I can proceed if I visualize myself as a Knight. The most logical way as I see it is to connect an individual story to each of my possessions. So my markers would branch out like a tree. Me the Knight as the trunk of the tree and my possessions as big branches. From my big branches would extend small branches of marker clusters. That way it would be a clear way to move around the markers without messing up. I imagine this would be a strong and fast, but limited in speed. Because I don't use my possessions together.*

*There is another way that might be faster. But I wonder if this is harder to do. Instead of making branches, I'd make the entire environment in one go. Me as the knight and with my possessions. I would then interact with a cluster of items, each item having a cluster of items. Example: I'd fight a evil army, Evil cat, Evil Butterfly and Evil Lemon. The evil Butterfly would be carrying a weapon! An umbrella with a tomato on the end and so on.*

*When I think more about it, the latter I feel is what you meant by High-level visualization. The first I am limiting myself again to the system of markers. Well, actually in all fairness both systems are good in my opinion. The effectiveness depending on what you try to remember. Same at the different techniques the memory champion contests use. As we are trying to learn markers for remembering details in this course, I should go with the latter method?*

**Dr. Lev Goldentouch**

*High-level visualization may involve remembering hundreds or thousands of detail in the correct order by generating a whole virtual world. Typically, it is used for remembering very complex details with 100% retention level. The complexity of visualization required to remember thousands of details might be compared with creating the World of Warcraft game from scratch.*

## Speed Up Markers

Kids are great with visual associations. Ask a kid what a specific cloud looks like and you will get a story. Show a kid four stars and he will say it is a magic animal. You do not lose those skills as you get older. If you look at clouds and try to think what they look like, you will eventually succeed. By trying to find order in random patterns, you speed up your visual associations and marker generation process. Try to remember foreign words. What does this word sound like? The more you play with free associations, the better your markers will eventually become.

## How Do Neurons Fire Together?

Your brain contains circa 90 billion neurons that work together due to trillions of connections between them. Neurons prefer to connect over short distances with neurons close to them forming neighborhoods, islands, and archipelagos. When we do complex tasks, many neurons in the same neighborhood fire together. Each time neurons fire together, their connection grows faster and stronger. Only about 20% of neural connections are strong. Other connections are weaker and latent.

What does this mean to us? When we learn something new, we make sure to connect it to something we know quite well so that there will be strong connections into the new knowledge.

There is one foundational principle in the KeyToStudy System the student should understand: Within the brain, all information is interconnected. With each acquisition of new data/information, the key to retention is to connect the new data/information to information currently stored in the brain. Being able to recall the stored information easily and then attaching the new data/information, promotes recall and retention.

Reading with intention/purpose is fundamental in the KeyToStudy System. Eliminating noise (nonessential elements) in the text is essential for reading speed and retention. When a student is able to eliminate the noise, the effort that goes into learning anything is reduced considerably making reading and remembering effortless. By focusing on the key elements of the text and connecting those elements throughout the text, the "noise" or nonessential elements do not slow down the student.

As for practice, we urge the student to take the time to persevere and not give up on the practice exercises presented in this book. Some exercises you may be familiar with; however, a lot of the content presented here is new to most people.

These exercises require you to exert mental and physical energy towards your evolution into a SuperLearner. Do not be disheartened if the results are not immediately forthcoming. Perseverance in the replacement of old learning habits (ingrained through many years of schooling and/or study) with new learning habits of necessity requires persistence, perseverance, and practice. Consistency in the three Ps (persistence, perseverance, and practice) will ensure success will be yours.

A basic skill required by many of the exercises mentioned in this book is an active imagination and the ability to visualize. Some people may think they do not have an imagination or the ability to visualize. However, this is simply not true. It is impossible not to visualize. For example, imagine a beautiful red bird sitting on a snow-covered evergreen branch. What would you see in your mind? You would have some sort of an image occur in your mind. Visualization is nothing more than seeing an image in your mind. Improvement in visualization (which is nothing more than a skill) is accomplished through practice.

What about imagination? Imagination, much like visualization, is a natural occurrence. It is impossible not to imagine. Imagine putting your bare feet into a fresh snow. What happens? You immediately shiver and move your feet. Imagination is also a skill that can be developed.

Improving reading speed and retention simply requires creating a world in your mind where you visualize the parts of the text being read and imagine yourself interacting with those parts. Creating a world in your mind can help you become more imaginative, which in turn will help you come up with more visualizations for better retention.

Whatever your purpose may be for reading this book, **developing a better imagination is possible** and something a good memory requires. The fun part of developing an imagination is the best part of the KeyToStudy System, which is a better, more controlled and efficient imagination.

To conclude, we know these techniques will enable you to devour texts of any kind at a much higher speed, and to remember a much greater percentage of what you read. We know these techniques work because they have worked for multitudes of students from all walks of life and with different abilities. The ultimate goal of the training you are now embarking on is to ensure you read at least twice your present speed and remember twice your current retention score. However, like everything worth having in life, adopting the KeyToStudy System will take some time, some patience and a lot of practice.

# Chapter 18: Chunking And Sequencing

In time management, there is some simple advice stating to break a large task into smaller easily manageable tasks you can do one after another. If you can do several small and similar tasks together, if will reduce the total processing time. The first principle is called **sequencing**. We generate sequences of one marker following another as a long linked chain. The second principle is called **chunking**. We try to unite several similar markers in a group and handle all of them in one chunk. Chunking also deals with structuring the information in complex data structures.

## Simple Chunking

In low-level chunking, we detect similar markers and chunk them in groups of 3 to 5 markers per chunk. In this way, we effectively increase our working memory from 7 objects to 20 objects (5 chunks of 4 objects). Moreover, we can perform marker manipulation between the chunks and between markers within each chunk.

## Intermediate Chunking

In mid-level chunking, we work with data structures. These include linked lists, trees, and maps.

### Linked Lists

Linked lists are ordered chunks of markers connected by some sort of linking "animation" allowing us to effortlessly and accurately transverse forward and backward between them. A good example of a linked list is a task list, i.e., what to buy at the grocery store.

### Trees

An excellent way to remember texts are trees of markers. We have markers for articles, sections, paragraphs and sometimes sentences and terms within a sentence. The linking here is hierarchical from parent to children and similar to zoom-in animation on Prezi. Often we find it useful to connect the children of the same node as linked lists to increase accuracy. It is also a very natural way to follow the text logic.

**Maps**

Maps are fully associative ways to remember pairs of markers. We can use them to connect objects of seemingly unrelated trees. This is a great way to encode out-of-the-box thinking or interdisciplinary connections. References we see in any scientific article are examples of such maps.

~~~~

Below is a discussion from our Udemy course regarding these visualization manipulations.

## Chunking Mental Markers

**DM**

*I've developed a clear understanding of how mental markers work and am working toward making my markers more vivid and a bit more relatable to each other. Lately, I've been creating funny stories in order to chunk the mental markers (ex: "Crosby's Seafood on Highway 17 = David Crosby holding 17 sign while eating seafood"), but wonder if there are better ways to link those mental markers together. Could you provide other examples of mental marker chunking in action?*

**Dr. Lev Goldentouch**

*Try to check various approaches and see what works for you. Usually, there is a trade-off between speed of creating markers, accuracy in details and retention span (e.g., how well you remember the markers after a year). Therefore, advanced SuperLearners use more than one system of markers. Also, try to engage as many senses and association chains as you can if you need high-quality retention span, and for better accuracy try to create unique images.*

**Jonathan A. Levi**

*Just to add, I think you are definitely on the right track with your Crosby example, also because you've chunked 3-4*
~~~~

*details. Experimentation is key here, but I think you'll already observe really dramatic results just with the techniques you've already demonstrated. Great work!*

~~~~~

## Order Of Markers

**ATN**

*When recalling markers, should I be trying to recall them in the order I memorized them? This would seem logical especially when reading literature such as novels, which make sense in a particular order. If so, are there any techniques to achieve this?*

**Dr. Lev Goldentouch**

*Well, this is a very good question. When we compare the training required for handling complex data structures in one's brain versus the benefit, the mind-mapping methodology became compelling. Therefore, the short answer is use mind-mapping tools. Below is a long answer.*

*The most advanced structure I use is a directional graph, something like the Internet, where everything is linked to everything via some sort of hyperlinks, see e.g. https://www.bighistoryproject.com/home. This is equivalent to reading 2000 wpm in structural complexity.*

*The simplest approach is a linked list, like a story, the order in which the subjects are mentioned. This is equivalent to reading 400 wpm in structural complexity.*

*For the person who graduates from this course, I originally suggested a tree-like structure, where you have markers for each granularity (the whole article, per section in sequence of sections, per paragraph in section and per important fact within paragraph). The linking of the markers should be bi-directional on each level, so you can "walk through" the markers in the original and in the inverse order. This is equivalent to reading 1000 wpm in structural complexity. For a simple text, this method becomes very similar to mind mapping, and thus the short answer in the first paragraph.*
~~~~~

**Jonathan A. Levi**

*Just to add a personal testimony, as I said in the lectures I struggle a little bit with mind maps, and so I tend to replay markers back in logical strings. These are roughly in the order they were created, but sometimes, if the logic is clearer to me in another order, I'll change it up.*

*For example, in a scientific paper where they state assumptions, then methodology, then findings, I may playback assumptions and then replay the markers of findings, because, to me, this is more logical. Then I'll play back the methodologies.*

**ATN**

*But doesn't mind mapping by its geometrical definition involve adopting a top-down approach rather than the bottom-top (details -> concepts) approach that's been emphasized? Its starting point is a broad topic that then 'branches' out into details, right?*

**Dr. Lev Goldentouch**

*Basically, you need to be able to go both bottom-up and top-down. Here is an "ideal" approach expected at the end of the course:*

*First, you go top down when you prepare the structure of the document in your head. Then you add up details in a bottom-up fashion, correcting missing "branches" as you go. Finally, after reading the document you consolidate your knowledge by going top-down and verifying the details you remembered.*

*In real life, I work with connected graphs and Jonathan works with some personalized variation of linked lists, so the mind-mapping approach is not really a strong recommendation.*

~~~~~

## Remembering Markers

**KC**

*I'm really having trouble remembering the markers I'm making. For example, I would read a section in of an article, create 5 markers but only remember 2 of them. Any tips? The*
~~~~~

*way I do it is I pick a word that is a detail and then think of the first thing that comes to mind. For example, if I were picking a marker for your question, I would have picked the word "Marker" and I think of a blue plastic one the size of a highlighter where I can smell the chemical marker smell.*

**PICB**

*That sounds great, in that case, maybe the problem is your markers are not well connected, have you thought about that?*

**Jonathan A. Levi**

*If you have difficulty remembering markers, there are a couple things that could be happening.*

*One is like Pablo said, they don't link up nicely.*

*Another is you may just have to train your working memory to remember larger chunks of numbers. Try remembering 3 sequences of 3 numbers. Once you can get that, work on 3×4, etc.*

*In the meantime, you should try to review your markers more frequently. Perhaps a *very* quick review after each paragraph – just picturing the markers before going on to the next paragraph – will help you remember them when you get to the bottom of each page.*

*Keep us updated and let us know how it goes. I'll let Dr. Lev chime in as well with anything I missed.*

**KC**

*How are you linking the images? The way I do it is one image doing something to another image. For example, if my images are phone and chair I imagine the phone smashing the chair to pieces.*

**Dr. Lev Goldentouch**

*There are many ways of linking. The way you described above is a very simple one-way link.*

*Now consider a 2-way link:*

*You look at the phone and see an image of a chair. Where have you seen the chair? On your phone.*

*Consider nesting (Top level: phone, bottom level chair on the cover of 5S iPhone):*

*You see a movie on your phone's backside. In this movie, a fat clown with 5 balloons shaped like an S breaks a chair with his huge butt.*

*The same in the long chain (5s har 64G):*

*With the phone, you smash a chair, which transforms into 5 snakes which hide in a chess box (64 squares) of a grandmaster (G)*

*For hyperlinking, you need like 20 pieces of information....*

*What I am trying to say, if you use more pieces of information, you will be able to construct better data structures (fast creation, more stable, colorful, several ways of navigation within).*

## 20 Images Exercise

This exercise is one of the hardest we have. It simulates the situation where you see some complex math (or business) text with formulas, tables, visualizations, which at first appear to be meaningless and unconnected. Through the power of will, we generate meaning within this mess until everything falls within some templates.

Activate link http://www.KeyToStudy.com/random-images-generator/

You see 20 random abstract images

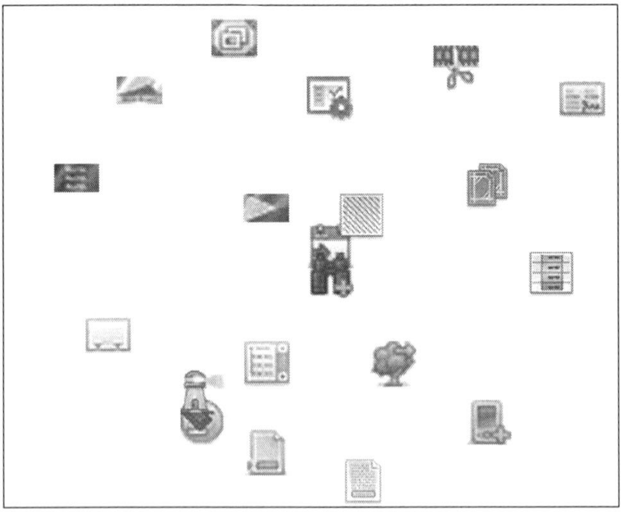

The first thing to do is chunk the images into groups of approximately 4 images in a 2x2 grid. For example, you can use spatial distribution as your key.

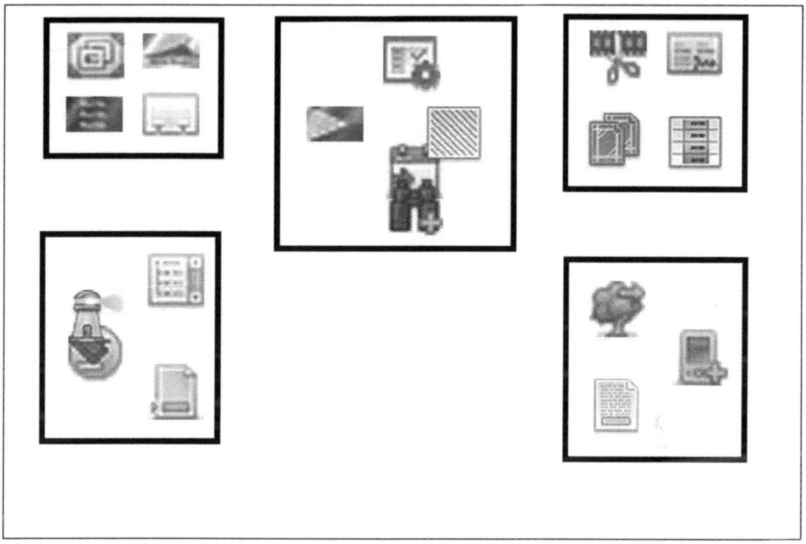

There should be 20 images in the example, so there are probably 5 objects on center top (binocular and calendar are 2 objects) and bottom left (I think there is a coin under the lamp). We can use 2 objects as one marker, it is not a problem.

Now you use a memory palace as a baseline. For the 20 objects exercise you can use a 6-room house. In this example, I use a generic house with different rooms:

| | | |
|---|---|---|
| (5) Bathroom | (4) Living room | (3) Study room |
| (6) Kitchen | (1) Garden | (2) Garage |

Now create a short animation of a route you can take.

You go through empty garden

Into a garage where you see a table with

1. An oak tree sapling (personalize the tree)
2. On signed document (simple spatial linkage)

3. Which photo you take by an iPhone (linkage by action to the device)

Proceed with the photo to the study room where on the desk

1. You make a copy of the photo you just took (hence copy icon)
2. The copy gets notary stamp (certificate transformed from object to action)
3. And is filed into a drawer (make sense of the 4 drawers thingy)
4. You cut the background from the original (adapted use of scissors)

With the original photo, you proceed to the living room and on the sofa there

1. You glue a background slide to the photo (need to make sense of the object with diagonal lines)
2. You search the calendar for national holiday (the binocular on a calendar)
3. You paint the flag of golden green blue land - ia (does not have to be a true country)
4. You laminate the image (need to make some sense of the gear)

With the laminated photo, you go to the bathroom mirror where

1. You put clips to hold the photo (bottom right)
2. Take a frame out of the bathroom drawer (bottom left)
3. Glue the photo you have to the frame (top left)
4. Rinse the photo to remove extra glue (top right)

You proceed to the kitchen sink

1. Add the laminated frame to your amazing DIY lamp (left). Only now, your actions make sense. Notice DIY hides money saving and thus the coin.
2. Check your iPhone for the next task (the document and app bar do not belong to the kitchen, but we did not prepare a different room)
3. Start creating dinner menu (use the app icon)

Personally, I find this exercise difficult due to limited spatial orientation. Our students who use memory palaces all the time complete it in under 1 minute.

## Effective Chunking With 2×2 Grid

Memory champion Wang Feng uses a very simple and efficient chunking method. Wang Feng is arguably the fastest mnemonist alive, so his method works. The simplicity of this method is only superficial, and you need a lot of practicing to master it – more than other methods we teach. Influenced by the structure of his native Chinese he uses very simple markers and then chunks the simple markers in 2×2 grid and remembers the whole grid as one more complex marker.

If you work with definitions and formulas, you do not have enough details to create complex markers from the text. Instead, we recommend creating simple markers. Simple markers look like pictograms, clip-arts, characters, icons: a very simple depiction of complex ideas. If you want examples, use Google image search with search tools -> type -> clipart turned on. Our 20 images exercise uses this sort of images, and many students find it is very challenging to work with this sort of abstraction.

An example:

***DG***

*How shall I create and structure markers for several things like in paragraph below:*

*"Such application contains a description of the relevant goods, the target market and competitors, rough estimates regarding the size of the market, the price of goods, duration and cost of the work to create new products, the cost of production and profit margins..."*

*What I need to remember:*
*Rough estimates of*
*- Market Size*
*- The price of goods*
*- The cost of work*
*- Revenues*
*How do I do that?*

***Dr. Lev Goldentouch***

*Chunking 2×2 works quite well. You visualize the whole chunk at once. Very fast, and no stories required. I learned this method from Chinese memory champion Wang Feng*

*Lists of up to 16 items can be generated as a 2×2 structure of 2×2 structures. That's why our exercise has 20 items: to push beyond this limitation.*

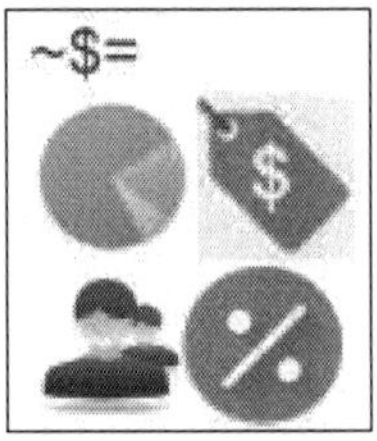


Why does a perfect grid have 4 items? Notice, quite often linking and chunking happens in a different context than marker creation. The context switching slows you down: remember multitasking exercises. The context switch is happening because our working memory is of limited size. The working memory size is 7±2 objects (7 plus or minus 2 objects). Note: 4 X (objects for chunking) + (the resulting marker) + (the link to a previous marker) + (the room to place the resulting marker) = 7 objects! This means that this way we use all the working memory, and have no context switching.

Why are we arranging the objects in 2×2 grid? This is the most spatially compact representation. If we need to visualize the object in one glance, we do not want it to move in 3D, we do not want to scan lines and columns; we want to have a razor-sharp focused visualization.

One of the things we always ask our students is personalizing the markers. How do we personalize the 2×2 grid? For example, we add a different color for each cell of the grid. We also place the grid within compartments of our memory palace. Finally, we link it to a story about the personal route: why we found this specific grid in the specific compartment.

Please notice the processing needs to be blazing fast. Otherwise, we would be better off using larger chunks with context switching for linking (as Anna teaches in her 1:1 lectures). Now suppose the article we read has 5 definitions, then we create one full grid and one partial grid, and we need to place both grids within the memory structure. This is 3 times more operations than creating a 5-object grid would require. To make it worthwhile, we need to get 2×2 grid creation and linking twice as fast as 5-object grid memorization. Such speed requires a lot of practicing. No wonder Wang Feng trains for 8 hours each day...

Even without Wang Feng, super training you can remember 2×2 grids effectively. Start now, and with time, you will memorize as fast as a champion!

## 20 Words Example

The 20 words exercise is very similar to what we see during prereading. We see some words that catch our attention, but we do not yet have enough details for full markers. So we use simpler markers instead.

Go to http://www.KeyToStudy.com/20-random-words-generator/

You will see some 20 random words like

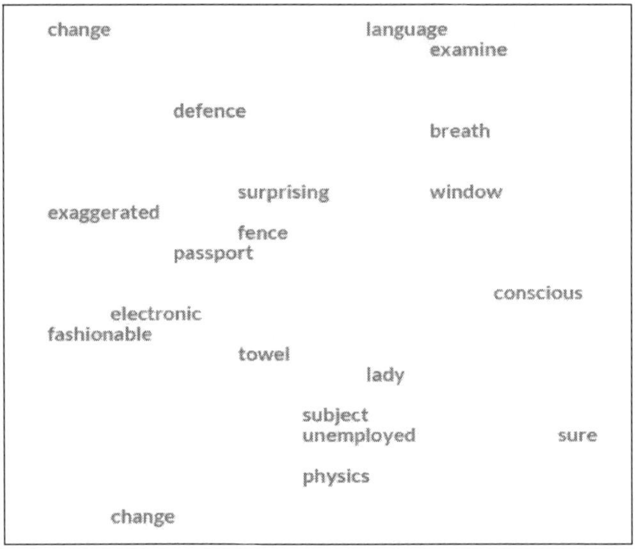


Typically I reorder the words into 2x2 grid according to their location within the text.

Notice, some of my 2x2 grids are rombs, and some are partially empty.

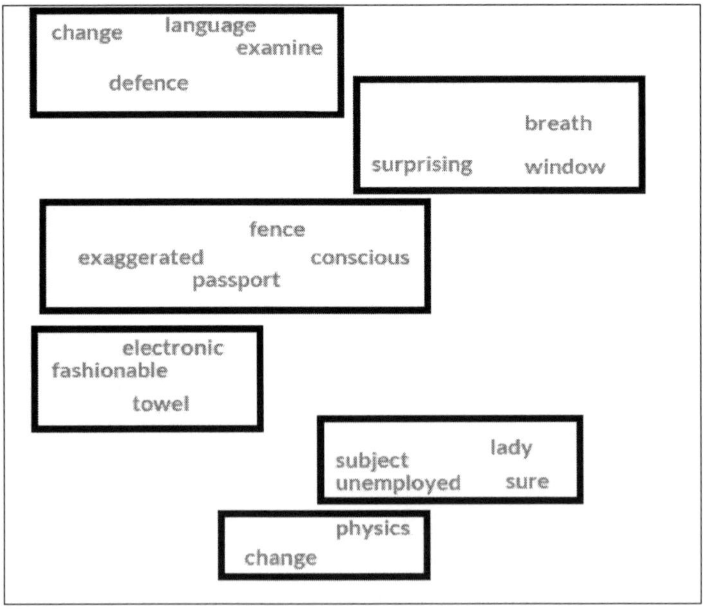

We can use simple pegs
1=pen
2=twins
3=tree
4=door
5=hive
6=lock

Now create visuals using pegs

"**Pen:** *Change, examine, language, defence*" A defence art student holds a pen writing language exam, but the letters of exam keep shifting (Harry Potter scenery triggered by "defence" association)

"**Twins:** *breath, surprising, window*" Twins open a window and gasp in surprise. (May continue Harry Potter theme)

"**Tree:** *fence, exaggerated, conscious, passport*" Harry Potter (we need to mark Harry is not a word) climbs a tree, falls near a fence and loses consciousness; a passport with his exaggerated image falls from his hand. (Unfortunately, some scenes are more complex than others are)

"**Door:** *electronic, fashionable, towel*" Door opens and Hermione dressed only in a fashionable towel electrifies Harry Potter with a taser. (Romance and violence are great drivers for associations)

"**Hive:** *subject, lady, unemployed, sure*" In the meanwhile, a jet sub flies out of a hive and a bum lady with a crown greets it with an OK gesture. (Nothing simple comes to mind, so we can use replacement: subject=jet sub, unemployed=bum, lady=queen, sure=OK gesture)

"**Lock:** *physics, change*" - Harry Potter in his dream unlocks gates that change the laws of physics. (For me change of laws of physics is one marker, like a portal through which ghost comes to earth in *Ghostbusters*, so I do not need to add extra markers)

Most of our students do not have a problem with this specific exercise, but rather with speeding it up. A simple way to speed up the exercise is to use the first visual association we have instead of generating more complex and far-fetched associations increasingly.

Also, notice all of the stories above are an animation sequence/cartoon of approximately 6 seconds. Do not make it longer. Just remember it as a short animation/cartoon.

Anna often suggests using chunks of 5-6 objects, but this often comes with a price of more complex and thus slower associations, so see what works better for you.

### For Further Research:

https://prezi.com/

# Chapter 19: Memory Palaces

Memory palaces are essentially apartments with compartments. They are inherently built to store things and intuitively suitable to chunking information. Placing texts in memory palaces is as simple as putting laundry in your drawers. If we have several objects of the same type, we instinctively put them in the same drawer, which makes memory palaces extremely suited to highly hierarchical and repetitive information.

The memory palace (also called loci) is the oldest method available for memorization, and still it feels like we are very far from using its full potential. If you are interested in using memory palaces for any particular application, I suggest you to try Anthony Metivier's books:

http://www.amazon.com/Anthony-Metivier/e/B0092HJ7PG.

Anthony has demonstrated how memory palaces can be used virtually for anything with accurate examples of how he uses it.

For me personally, memory palaces have been notoriously difficult to use. I have a genetic tendency to misorientation. I do not find things at home, even those things I placed there, even when I used seemingly perfect markers to find them. Therefore, I use memory palaces only if it is the most efficient way to remember something. From this viewpoint, I will try to explain my understanding of memory palaces.

## Safe Deposit Compartments

For me, the best advantage of memory palaces is instant visual chunking. When you have to remember a list of 20 images or 20 words, you can do it in many ways. A memory palace is probably the perfect way to remember the list.

You imagine a safe deposit wall with several compartments. Based on chunking, you take individual markers and put them into the safe deposit. Done!

This is the only method I know that enables a person to solve the 20 words exercise well below 30 seconds. A person would use 4 seconds to evaluate the exercise, 4 seconds to generate 5 compartments with 3 seconds per compartment. (A person trained with multitasking can generate up to 4 markers in parallel.) This is great if you need to assess and catalog a medium collection of items and do not have enough time for other methods.

## Apartments With Compartments

This catchy phrase I learned from Anthony Metivier. For me, it represents the ease with which you can nest markers within each other. You can generate compartments very fast. Then you can generate:

- apartments with several rooms,
- houses with several rooms,
- villages with several houses,
- counties with several villages,
- countries with several counties,
- continents with several countries,
- worlds with several continents,
- constellations with several worlds, etc.

The capacity of this method is staggering. You can encode millions of pieces of information ... more so if you love fantasy/sci-fi/gaming.

## Open The Door

It is easy to embed complex objects within memory palaces. Remember the end of *Men In Black*: the hero opens a safe deposit box and beyond the door a whole universe exists. You can put mind maps, PAO and any other memory structure beyond a door, which is always accessible.

## Read The Signs

The Major System and its variations enable easy encoding of names and numbers. These encoded details can be placed like signs or labels on various doors in your memory palace. Do try to make each door different: in color, style, texture, and then put a colorful sign on it. This is my interpretation of what is called the Dominic system. This method actually may be very efficient for encoding some legal and anatomical data.

## I Like To Move It

Who said memory palaces had to be stationary? You can encode a train route, a fantasy world, a voyage abroad as memory palaces. You have the main moving object with several multifunctional compartments, and then you have at each stop apartments with various goodies. When I learn words in foreign languages, I put them in context: friend's home, museum, restaurant, shops, etc. I can encode elements of local culture within. Adding the time dynamics and multiple moving objects it is possible to memorize various chemical cycles and disease processes.... Really useful.

## Disadvantages

With all the advantages above, there are some disadvantages too:

- **The irony of fate**: There is an old Russian movie of a person who arrives at a house on a street in Russia, and tries to open his apartment when he realizes he is actually in the wrong city. I try not to overuse memory palaces since this effect occasionally happens to me. If you try to be creative in details, you introduce ideas that were not in the text. If you are not sufficiently creative, your apartments start to look alike. Some people become disoriented faster.
- **Home improvement**: As long as you need to memorize something static, memory palaces work fine. What happens when you need to add apartments or add cities to a small compartment? What if you need to remove an apartment, how do you remember that? Modifying your memory palaces may be tough...
- **Colliding universes**: When you try to push associations between memory palaces, it is a sort of nightmare. You need to construct some elaborate and not very natural piping or strings within the apartments. It does not feel good, even though I learned some personal hyperlinking tricks (http://www.KeyToStudy.com/personal-hyperlinking-format/).

It is easy to store information within memory palaces, but hard to use it either creatively or analytically.

If you need to learn fast and the information you learn is not about to change – memory palaces may be perfect for you. We see this sort of information in legal and medical documents, historical information, and language structures.

With the help of memory palaces, you will memorize like memory champions.

## Forward And Backward

If you walk your memory palaces both forward and backward you double the chance of remembering. Try to generate dual linking by creating forward and backward routes in your palaces.

If you use mind maps, walk them top-down and bottom-up from each hyperlink. Once you connect two mind maps, you should be able to get from the root node of one mind map to the root node of another mind map without difficulty. Once you get to the root node, you should be able to recollect the whole mind map.

## Which Palace Is It?

Quite often, we reuse the same markers or memory palaces for various contexts. How do we know we are in the right palace?

One simple way is putting a small representation of the subject as a repeating theme in each room, like a portrait or a window. However, it is even better to combine memory palace with PAO. Then you have a million ways to mark the first room.

## Portals And Hyperlinks/Memory Palace

**FH**

*Sometimes when something just doesn't fit into a particular memory palace and is very dense, hard to memorize, do you find yourself sometimes in this spot, or how do you go about this one?*

*It's like you have 7 stations, then you have to know there is something else you just couldn't put there and memorized the usual way and after that come back and continue from 8 ... after doing this there is a "hole" because I have to know I memorized it normally and then I have to switch...*

**Dr. Lev Goldentouch**

*Always chain things. In my high-level visualization setup, there are objects which are sort-of portals to some other place, like the doors in Alice in Wonderland or Men in Black.*

*Same portals on memory trees or in memory palaces can be memorized as hyperlinks. Just as you can jump between Internet pages using Internet hyperlinks, you can jump between memory pages using memory hyperlinks.*

## Loci Example

Typically, we build mental memory palaces of very specific sizes:

**4** Quadrants that can be handled parallel to each other
**6** Working memory size
**10** Usually, we use 10 for computation
**16** Unless you are a programmer, then you use 16
**52** A deck of cards
**60** This is something you can count using two hands (check Babylonian counting online: https://www.youtube.com/watch?v=cXVdYlxs8_M).
**100** This is something you need for larger numbers

## *Lord Of The Rings*: Memory Palace Example

We can use locations from movies as inputs for our memory palace/loci. For our example, we can use the famous *Lord of the Rings* trilogy to create a memory palace of twenty locations from within the movie trilogy. We will create this in a linear and sequential manner following Frodo's journey from Hobbiton to Mordor.

See e.g. http://lotr.wikia.com/wiki/Portal:Locations for a map.

As such, the loci can be divided into three categories, depending upon which part of the trilogy they were featured in:

*The Fellowship of the Ring*
*The Two Towers*
*The Return of the King*

1. Hobbiton/Shire - Hobbits, round tree, hole dwellers

2. Bree - A village, inn, hobbits servants, food and drink
4. Rivendell - Elven outpost
5. Moria - Underground tunnel complex of dwarfs
6. Tower of Isengard - Iron tower of multicolor wizard
7. Rohan - Grassland with fierce riders
8. Gondor - the greatest kingdom of men
9. Dead Marshes - Marshes haunted by ghosts
10. Fangorn Forest - A forest with ents - tree guardians
11. Mordor - hell-like home of Sauron

**Consider a physical constant:**

speed of light = 299 792 458 m / s

Logic: it takes 8 minutes for the light to pass from the sun to the earth and the sun is 150 mln kilometers away. 150e9m/500sec=3e8 m/sec

**Loci/Peg/PAO combo:**

(Shire) Inn-forest-forest: In Shire servant splits trees

(Bree) king-forest-inn: In the inn king splits beer mugs

(Rivendell) tunnel-tower-marsh: In elven outpost dwarf rises from dead

**Consider a person:**

Emmeline Pankhurst (1858-1928) – English suffragette. http://www.biographyonline.net/politicians/uk/emily-pankhurst.html

This is not a sufficiently famous person for most of us to remember already, yet she is famous enough to deserve being remembered.

Emmeline sounds like a line of emu birds (@ shire)

Pankhurst sounds like pink horse (@ inn)

Born 1858 - 40 years after 1818 (18 the age you can go into the army) - baby drafted and wander the desert with Moses (@Rivendell)

1928 - she lived for 70 years. 70 looks like LO which means laughing out - died laughing out (@moria)

English suffragette - vote for queen (@tower)

# Chapter 20: Triple Fun With PAO

Memory palaces are inherently passive. PAO is one of the most advanced and yet fun to use techniques for memorization. PAO means person-action-object. The PAO system is commonly used in memory championships.

PAO is extremely effective for encoding chunks of 6 digits, which makes number crunching a breeze. You can adapt PAO for your own usage.

The classic PAO method includes memorization of a dictionary with 99 unique entries. Each entry contains a person, an action, and an object, like Bob Dylan playing guitar. Now when you have a 6-digit number you look up 2 digits for the person, then 2 digits for the action and finally 2 digits for the object. Instead of Bob Dylan playing guitar, you get O.J. Simpson painting on a car. The resulting combinations are funny and creative by design, so it is easy to remember them. It is also very easy to place the personality within your memory palace.

As far as I know, the PAO was invented by card-counters, although I could not find a reference to substantiate this statement. Each card face was associated with a personality (Kings, Queens, and Princes) and even with specific royalty of the relevant time. The order of cards was readily associated with some sort of activity, like a party. An example of a typical PAO system for cards can be found at:

https://memoryexcursion.wordpress.com/1-2-how-to-memorize-a-deck-of-cards/.

The PAO system was later modified for numbers and popularized by Joshua Foer. An example of PAO for 0-99 shows how typical numbers can be remembered.

https://quizlet.com/18659473/memory-00-99-paodominic-system-flash-cards/

The speed of a proper PAO method is approximately 0.5 seconds per marker. Memory champions remember a deck of cards in 25 seconds. To achieve this speed, PAO is encoded into very fast-paced visual cut scenes, similar to TV advertisements. Advertisements are built to optimize our visual attention for the benefit of brands. We can use the same methods for our own benefits. The triplet of person, action and object comes to mind not as a story but as a single image. Below are some simple tips from:

https://memoryexcursion.wordpress.com/pao-system/

1. ***Choose actions that are distinguishable***. For instance, do not have Bob Dylan strumming a guitar, have him smashing it into pieces. Do not have Schwarzenegger bicep curling a dumbbell, have him doing a human flag. Do not have Barney Stinson adjusting his tie, have him ripping his suit.

2. ***Do not use any clothing article as objects***. If you do, make sure it is noticeable. For instance, do not ever use a tie because any male in your list can be associated with it. Do not ever use heels because any lady in your list can be associated with those. You may use Keira-Knightley-style-fancy-hats, though.

3. ***Use objects that are not too small or too large***. Do not associate Clint Eastwood (I am using a reference to *Gran Torino*) with his honorary pin; do not associate him with his Gran Torino either. Instead, use a stool. (Apparently, he mocked Obama by talking to an invisible stool at the 2012 Republican Convention; I have yet to watch:

http://www.youtube.com/watch?v=933hKyKNPFQ&feature=related)

4. ***Before you try to memorize any number***, run through your PAO list until the list is ingrained in your brain and is second nature. Once the PAO list is sufficiently ingrained, seeing any one element brings to mind the other two.

If these tips sound familiar, it is because they are shared by all memory methods. The three parts of PAO reinforce each other and create memorable markers that can be easily linked into mental films. Alternatively, you can chunk PAO into triplets where the person comes from the first detail (number), the action from the second number and the object from the third number.

A very different, logical approach to PAO is provided by Use Cases:

(http://www.gatherspace.com/static/use_case_example.html).

To make use cases livelier, I imagine my personalities act accordingly to the application script. Specific and graphic persons and actions should be maintained.

It is best to have positive and funny PAO imagery since you occasionally and unintentionally will share them with your friends. Some of my friends consider me quite a clown since I tell aloud some of my PAO imagery when describing how things work. Alternatively, I see people become drowsy when my personalities come from obscure historic references. Choosing the right personalities for your PAO ensures your message gets through when you relive the PAO links.

Like any other advanced memory scheme, PAO is great for chunking. Each personality can do many things on a given stage within your memory. Chunking objects in a way that is handy for your personality is a great way to ensure they are not forgotten. You may combine PAO with loci and the Major System. In this way, personalities can move between rooms, or be trapped in compartments, tell obscure sentences (Major system, subject-specific mnemonics) and do all sort of amusing things.

There are many ways to collect personalities. You can use any celebrity (actors, politicians, business professional, etc.), personal acquaintances, cultural phenomena, animals, magical creatures and any combination thereof (chimeras). You can collect personalities systematically, including:

- persons as pegs (a person for number),
- persons as perspectives (optimistic, pessimistic, emotional, etc.), and
- persons as subject leads (Bill Gates = IT, Warren Buffet = financing etc).

## My Own Method

It is well known that gaming enables development of new mental templates and facilitates learning. The game environment facilitates perceptual visualization – like loci on steroids. In addition, I love RPG and strategy game genres. Therefore, I based my own loci method in a game setup. A game is not limited to any rules except for the consistency of the game universe: all things within the game universe follow the same genre rules and storyline. There are clear roads and portals leading from one space to another, each with its own set of details. The rules of the game follow some sort of mental template, and there are common sense tactics where to run and what buttons to press.

An enormous bonus of this method is the use of autobiographic memory. I actually experience myself just as if I live in the game world. I interact with characters and environment. Typically, characters are common ideas that appear in various places in the text, but sometimes they are people performing various deeds or formulating their positions. The constant details that arise in a particular context become decorations within the environment. The decorations follow the same genre so I do not forget which room and in what game they belong.

To remember the whole game, I run the game from the beginning to the end. Sometimes I fail and learn from failure. If I forget an object, I add a needed action to the object to continue with my quest. If I successfully complete the game, I celebrate, by playing in my mind some theme song.

There is a certain danger of getting over-involved in the game. Therefore, I painstakingly monitor and make sure I do not introduce to the game anything but the details representing concepts supported by the text. The game world should stay minimalistic, and should experience very few changes between re-reads, so no dissonance is formed. It is also important not to "play" the game too much: the understanding of the subject may change and it should not be too fixed in our minds to allow modification.

The main modifications I introduce to loci methods are living the game, active characters connecting sceneries and consistent motive throughout visualization. I think my method is more suited for young people who spend a considerable amount of time gaming. The visualization is a lot of fun. Try it with real examples.

## Linking Exercise

Suppose you need to remember 100 objects, how do you do that?

One simple way is generating 10 stories. Each story has 10 objects. Then, create a super story with the first item of each story.

Now let us make the process more efficient. We can generate 20 stories of 5 objects and use PAO to encode the beginning of each story. It is much easier to remember PAO plus 5-object stories than 10-object stories since our working memory is 7±2 objects long.

To make the memorization even more stable, we can remember each 5-object story forward and backward and add PAO on both sides. Since 2-digit PAO can encode a million variations, and you can create stable stories of 5 objects, you have a tool to remember 5 million objects. Now you can start counting cards and training for the memory championships!

## For Further Research:

https://memoryexcursion.wordpress.com/pao-system/

http://en.wikipedia.org/wiki/Memory_sport

### Memorize Cards:

https://memoryexcursion.wordpress.com/1-2-how-to-memorize-a-deck-of-cards/

### Numbers:

http://theskillfulbrain.com/?p=205

http://headinside.blogspot.co.il/2011/10/pao-system.html

https://quizlet.com/18659473/memory-00-99-paodominic-system-flash-cards/

### Use Case:

http://www.gatherspace.com/static/use_case_example.html

http://en.wikipedia.org/wiki/Use_case

**Gaming:**

http://venturebeat.com/2014/11/12/playing-call-of-duty-has-long-term-learning-benefits-for-the-brain/

http://www.lifehacker.co.uk/2014/11/25/motivate-living-life-like-movie

https://www.psychologytoday.com/blog/cutting-edge-leadership/201410/5-steps-being-successful-anything

https://www.psychologytoday.com/blog/metacognition-and-the-mind/201410/can-brain-training-be-brain-draining-0

# Chapter 21: Major System To The Rescue!

Now suppose we encounter a name or a place, how do we encode it? We could use a memory palace or PAO, but it would be not very effective. How can we encode seemingly meaningless syllables, without repeating them all the way through the learning curve? Well, we find a meaning for each and every one of them! The result is a linked chain of very simple markers we need to remember in a specific order. When we recall the chain of markers, they magically recreate the object we encoded.

## History Of The Major System

The mnemonic Major System is quite ancient. In its most pure form, each number is a letter and letters form words that can be easily remembered. In Hebrew, each letter is a number, and Kabbalah is using this to achieve miraculous deeds. In Hindu, there is a similar tradition called the Katapayadi system that was used to encode geometrical and astronomical data in poetical verses. In the western tradition, the mnemonic Major System was introduced by Puritan reformers in the 16th century as a more pure way to remember things.

Dominic O'Brien used this methodology with memory palaces to develop his Dominic technique and win eight world memory championships. I do not claim to be a master of this method, but I do use it when faced with overwhelming odds.

## Encoded Dictionaries/Periodic Table

In the heart of the Major System are dictionaries. We encode one dictionary (like numbers) by another easier dictionary (letters). We can use other dictionaries and get a similar effect. When we learn something complex and new, something that cannot be easily remembered, a dictionary can be used.

The first time I needed to use this method was when learning chemistry. I had very simple imagery for several elements, and was very good at combining them. However, I had to remember very complex chemical processes in the semiconductor industry, and I simply did not have enough images. I had to develop a dictionary for the whole periodic table, open and close parenthesis, and the numbers 0-9. Then I could remember any chemical composition. Later, I used a similar method to remember combinations of letters and numbers like passwords and abstract information. As long as you keep 1:1 correspondence between the hard things you need to remember and something you can remember easily, you are safe.

### How Do You Memorize THAT?

From time to time, I am faced with memorization tasks in which the best way to memorize them is using a dictionary. For example, a couple of months ago a student asked me how to organize shirts by color. I used a very simple dictionary: green=grass, yellow=sun, black=ground, etc. He remembered 20 colored shirts in no time. If a task seems very complex, but also very repetitive, the Major System will help.

### Do We Need Spaced Repetitions?

When performing research on spaced repetitions, the scientists always generate information that cannot be easily remembered. To trick the system, magicians occasionally learn the Major System for phonetic sequences and show supernatural skill. There is some preservation of effort: first, you need to invest a lot of effort learning a dictionary, but then you save a lot of effort using it.

### How Do We Explain This To A Child?

Some variations of Major System (like using the first letter in each word) provide a delightful and easily explainable method. You can easily teach a child a funny verse when the verse in fact encodes the order of planets, chemical structure, physical constant or some code. The effort is invested by the creator of the mnemonics. For users of the mnemonics, the process is almost effortless.

## So Common And Yet So Elusive!

Rare things force us to strain our minds, to create unique and specific markers. However, when we see something as generic as a common name it is easy to misplace it. Dictionaries help. Every name, every definition has its etymology and something there should be useful for a marker, and you can use it as a dictionary entry.

## Synesthesia

One of added values of synesthesia is replacing one set of dictionaries by another: music by letters, feelings by colors and so on. In this sense, synesthesia is closely related to the Major System. By learning synesthesia, coding becomes automatic. Every programmer knows working with a code highlighter REALLY helps.

While the Major Mnemonic System is usually learned to remember numbers, it can, in fact, be used to remember ANY dictionary. If something is too abstract, unremarkable or elusive so that you cannot remember it, consider adding it as an entry in your dictionary.

## Memorizing Numbers Example

pi = 3.14159265359

Pi is something we need to remember. There are many ways to remember pi.

### Mnemonics:

You can remember pi by creating a story with words of a certain length. For example, the word "how" is 3 letters. A simplest mnemonic to remember pi is, "How I wish I could calculate pi." A cool mnemonic giving 15 digits (3.14159265358979) is, "How I want a drink, alcoholic of course, after the heavy lectures involving quantum mechanics," originally due to Sir James Jeans (Gardner 1966, p. 92; Castellanos 1988, p. 152; Eves 1990, p. 122; Davis 1993, p. 9; Blatner 1997, p. 112).

You can find many mnemonics online, so you do not have to reinvent them.

## Major System:

For example, consider

| Digit | Consonants |
|---|---|
| 0 | S or Z |
| 1 | D or T |
| 2 | N |
| 3 | M |
| 4 | R |
| 5 | L |
| 6 | J or ZH or SH |
| 7 | K or hard G |
| 8 | F or V |
| 9 | B or P |

You can change the table for your own language-friendly phonetics so the letters do not mix. For example, Arabs typically mix B and P; Spanish mix B and V; and the Japanese mix L and R. Play a bit with a table until you find a comfortable combination.

Then PI (3.14159265359) becomes
M DR DLB NJL ML B

Now transform the consonants into words
My DeaR DoLeV, No JaiL MaLe Be...

As you can see, I am not used to working with the Major System. If I used it every day, I would come up with something like:

**My dear Taliban,**

**Shalom! Will the big bomb in my Virage injure Imam Haytham in Kabul? Say no! They fear to be caught shopping by bomb cults.**

(https://wmjas.wordpress.com/2010/08/11/)

## Dominic System:

Dominic system is closely related to the major system and is mapped as follows:

| Digit | 1 | 2 | 3 | 4 | 5 | 6 | 7 | 8 | 9 | 0 |
|---|---|---|---|---|---|---|---|---|---|---|
| Letter | A | B | C | D | E | S | G | H | N | O |

Maybe you are not 100% happy with these mappings, but give them a chance, they are quite well chosen! Most of them are fairly obvious: 1-5 map to the first five letters of the alphabet; '6' begins with the letter 'S'; '8' sort of looks like the letter 'H' wearing a hat on its head and feet. 'O' looks like 'zero.'

Therefore, to continue our Pi exercise, 3.1415927 becomes CA DA EN BG. We need to translate these initials into people, preferably using a pre-memorized list of person associations. Perhaps we get something like:

CA Chester Arthur
DA Dan Aykroyd
EN Eugene Nowak
BG Bill Gates

**PAO:**

https://quizlet.com/18659473/memory-00-99-paodominic-system-flash-cards/

Using Dominic system flashcards
31 41 59 26 53 59

(31) Captain America (41) ghostbuster-zapping (59) hulk
(26) Ben Stiller (53) taking dump on (59) hulk

This is quite simple. In fact, PAO is probably the best system to remember numbers.

Most numbers are 6 digits long:

**Dates**: day, month, year, e.g., mm/dd/yy

**Engineering**: number, fraction, power, e.g., X.FFFe-PP or X.FFFe+PP

**Financial**: number, fraction, order of magnitude e.g. XXX.FF (K/M/G)

Therefore, if you need to remember a lot of numbers, it is great to know PAO intimately. You do need some extra practice to keep PAO always in your mind, and you do need extra care not to lose the decimal point or sign.

## Logic:

Pi is used to transform square into a circle.

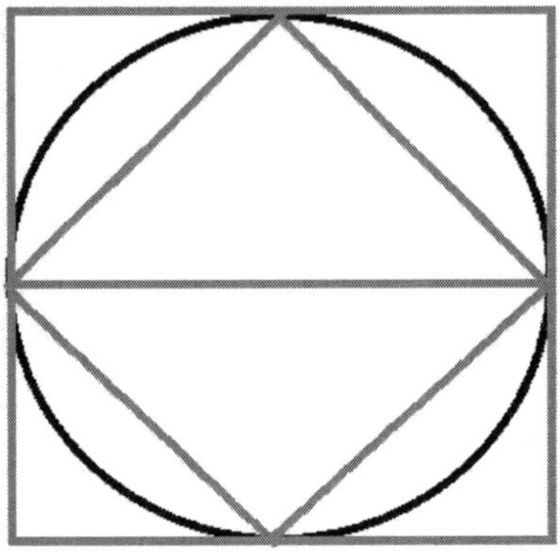

Take a circle diameter as the basic unit, the perimeter of the circle is pi. Pi is somewhere between the bounding quadrat perimeter 4 and bounded quadrat perimeter 2*sqrt(2).

Clearly, there are better geometrical approximations, but at least you will always place the decimal point and sign correctly. Try to use some sort of logic to cross-validate your other memorization techniques.

# Chapter 22: How To Memorize Detailed Text

Now we have all the elements required to memorize a paragraph. Either we can technically encode the paragraph in a memory palace with the PAO and Major System compartments, or we can get creative!

Many of our students need to learn boring and complex material rich in details. How do you remember complex statistics or medical descriptions? You break it into smaller steps, use a lot of humor, and try to keep a consistent tone in details and imagery. Below are examples from discussions in our Udemy course.

~~~~~

## Learning Something New

**NH**

*So I opened up Wikipedia and I started to learn about GSP Belgrade.*

*The things I tried to remember are:*

- *Public Transit Company*
- *Created in Oct 14, 1892*
- *First line was a horse tram between Slavija and Terazije.*
- *Has 145 lines, 12 are trams, 8 are trolley bus and 125 are bus lines.*
- *Hours of operation are 4am to Midnight with limited night buses.*
- *There are about 6,200 employees*
- *They use about 1000 Vehicles*

*I have difficulty actually turning this data into images.*

*I can attach the Oct 14 to my mum's birthday; however, I don't really know what to do with the other stats.*

*Any advice?*
~~~~~

**Dr. Lev Goldentouch**

*Thank you for the question. The way to proceed is an issue of personal style. I will try to present my personal approach. Eventually, the more you know the easier it will be to learn. Let us try to encode based on my prior knowledge:*

*The Belgrade GSP started to work during the Homestead Strike on Carnegie steel mill. It has 125 bus lines (I encode 125 as 5*5*5 and have a special marker for it, like 3 hands touching), 12 trams (lucky number, one more and they would hit the unlucky 13. I use a trellis as luck symbol) and 8 trolleys (8 looks like infinity and trolleys are infinitely cumbersome for a city). They are closed from Midnight to 4am (there is a 2009 movie called "4am is the New Midnight"). There are 1K vehicles (I have a special marker for a kilo). The number of employees in Wikipedia is 6166, (I have a number 666 encoded as Satan, so just remember 1 non-satanic employee).*

*Now if I really do not want to forget, just make up a funny story. Sometimes I actually prefer to remember information as comics:*

*During the Homestead Strike, the workers came to your mother's home and shake hands with her 3 times. The shake was infinitely long and she was lucky when it was over. It felt like midnight in poorly rated movie and the hand was getting very heavy. Then a fourth worker came in and stood second in the row, and all 3 previous workers started growing horns.*

*Try to find your own personal style.*

*Good luck.*

~~~~~

**KF**

*Can I use this exercise / method for each type of text?*

*I chose today the text about Adductor muscles of the hip http://en.wikipedia.org/wiki/Adductor_muscles_of_the_hip. I find it very complicated to find pictures for some words.*

*I want to learn all the muscles of the adductor group:*

- *Adductor brevis*
~~~~~

- *Adductor longus*
- *Adductor magnus*
- *Adductor minimus*
- *Adductor magnus.*
- *Pectineus*
- *Gracilis*
- *Obturator externus*

*Can I use the method of markers or need I something else?*

*Then I tried another article: Pilates. I started with history – http://de.wikipedia.org/wiki/Pilates#Geschichte*

*I took the German article. My English is not so good.*

*The first sentence: Joseph Hubert Pilates (1883–1967) war Turner, Taucher, Bodybuilder und Zirkusartist.*

*In English:*

*Hubert Joseph Pilates (1883-1967) was a gymnast, diver, bodybuilder and circus performer.*

*For me there are a lot markers in one sentence and I start to find pictures for:*

- *Hubert*
- *1883 / 1967*
- *gymnast*
- *diver*
- *bodybuilder*
- *circus performer*

*Am I on the right track?*

**Jonathan A. Levi**

*Thanks for a fantastic question, Klaus.*

*Let's start with the muscles of the hip. This is an extremely difficult one, but you should rely on existing knowledge to create markers. Your knowledge may differ from mine, but let me demonstrate how I might create markers.*

***Adductor brevis***

*My mind jumps to "brevity," and I picture a scene from the movie "The Big Lebowski" where he uses the word "brevity" – this is my marker for that word, always. It's a vivid image in my mind of the character.*

*Brevity means short (brevis in Latin), and so I remember that this is shorter than the next one, adductor longus.*

***Adductor longus***

*The "long" in the name obviously gives me a marker, and I might just remember that it's the longest muscle in the leg, using the marker of the image supplied in Wikipedia.*

***Adductor magnus***

*Magnus means "great" in Latin, but we may not know that. I see that this muscle is very small, and I think that it must be a pretty great muscle to keep up with the other 2 longer muscles it's next to.*

*I use as a marker a picture of the world's strongest man, Magnus Ver Magnusson. He is very strong, and this little muscle must be too, as said above.*

***Adductor minimus***

*See similar techniques as above*

***Pectineus***

*I think of the "pectoral" muscle, which is in a similar position to the shoulder. My marker is my pectoral muscle, which I've seen a million times, and which rotates my shoulder in just like this muscle does for the leg.*

*If you need to make another marker here, that's fine. Think of something silly or outrageous, like feeding a bird out of your lap and having it "peck" you your inner leg accidentally.*

***Gracilis***

*This muscle is thin and graceful. I picture a graceful woman in a long ball dress who also looks thin.*

***Obturator externus***

*Similar methods to above.*

*Now, that was tricky, but it should give you an idea. I'm really going for "vivid" and concrete imagery, and I'm trying to tack on to anything that is already part of my existing knowledge. Movies, English words, Latin words, muscles I already know – any connection I can make, I make. Now, if you covered up the labels on the muscles, I could recite the names to you because I have a silly memory or story connected to each one. I don't remember Adductor Brevis, I remember The Big Lebowski... "So you're not into Brevity... I get that..."*

*Now let's talk about the Pilates question. You're definitely on the right track. This is a very information dense paragraph. I am interested in knowing how involved he was with sports and activity, given what he designed with the Pilates program, and so I would definitely make markers for gymnast, circus performer, bodybuilder, and probably even diver. I don't know that the dates would be that important to me – maybe just the death date. His name is pretty important, too, but I don't have a marker for Hubert, so the first thing that came to mind was the Sesame Street character "Bert" – but in a different hue, like green. It's silly, but it's a functional marker for me.*

## Handling Mental Blocks

Occasionally, we try to focus on the task at hand and our mind goes blank. Now, what should we do next? Do not give up! There are tricks that can help to some extent.

**Relax**. Very often, if you simply relax your mind block will evaporate. Try some simple visualization exercises using simple objects, people or scenery. Familiar food and friends, nice resort landscapes and familiar places are very good for visualization and relaxation. Breathe deeply to fill your blood with oxygen. While not entirely relaxing, remembering scenes from my favorite movies and games also work great. These simple and rewarding visualizations activate the reward centers in the brain, which enable an efficient learning cycle.

**Change position**, maybe walk or jump in place. Some motoric activity activates a set of brain centers also responsible for visualization. This may be sufficient to activate your visualization abilities and your SuperLearning powers.

**Dual coding.** We often encourage our students to alternate several methods of visualization, including memory palaces versus mind mapping, PAO versus pegs, mnemonics versus visual memorization, etc. When one method of memorization malfunctions, it is easy to switch to the secondary method. Always keep a backup in case your main memorization tools malfunction.

**Repeat another day**. Some autonomous processes that happen when we sleep may activate a specific visualization we need. Simply waiting a day may be sufficient for this magic to happen. This is especially true in the case of a déjà vu when a specific memory simply does not surface into consciousness. Many experts recommend keeping a notebook and scheduling reminiscence sessions.

**Search online.** Often we do not remember what we need, but remember an association generated by what we need. Simple wandering online near the keywords that appear relevant may be sufficient to activate our memory.

**To summarize**, always have a backup in case of mental block. Quite often creative relaxation, sleep and physical activity will help.

## For Further Research:

http://www.mind-expanding-techniques.net/visualization-exercises.html

https://en.wikipedia.org/wiki/Motor_imagery

https://en.wikipedia.org/wiki/D%C3%A9j%C3%A0_vu

# Chapter 23: Mind Mapping

Long books and texts are built like a tree. The book contains chapters; the chapters contain sections, and the sections contain paragraphs. Each paragraph usually contains two main markers and occasionally several auxiliary markers. Now, the best way to encode a tree is probably a mind map. Mind maps are also excellent for encoding logical markers, science and engineering information, and markers operating with abstract notions.

Very often, I reference Tony Buzan books for mind mapping. Tony Buzan popularized mind maps and made them available to the public in the early 1970s. Instead of focusing on the classical mind map structure, I prefer to describe the modified structure I use.

For me, a mind map represents an article or a book chapter, but it can be larger or smaller. A group of mind maps may create a larger mind map like trees create a forest.

## What Our (Adapted) Mind Mapping Looks Like

1. Many of you have experienced fancy mind mapping applications with beautiful designs. You do not have to do that in your head. You need to **keep only the following basics**:

- **Anchor:** The root node or anchor is the place from where you access your whole mind map. Whatever imagery you use for the anchor, make it stand out and be unforgettable. The anchor is like a personal title you give to an article. If you invest *t* time (where *t* = 1 unit) in a marker, do invest 5*t* time in the anchor, it is *THAT* important. The anchor should summarize the essence of what you need to remember. The anchor is like the trunk of a tree.
- **Retrieval markers:** The anchor is connected to the retrieval markers, which are like landing pages for various lines of thoughts. These markers are created *AFTER* reading the article and are used as triggers to remember the root node from as many

perspectives as the article supports. Do invest 10*t* time in the retrieval markers, or you may forget the whole mind map in a way that only spaced repetition can cure. Disclaimer: I do not like spaced repetition and use it only when I cannot create stable memorization. Retrieval markers are like the roots of a tree.

- **Main branches:** The main branches are allocated for main ideas springing from the trunk. Typically, you have three to six main branches per mind map, which correspond to sections within an article. The main ideas should come with viable markers. Do invest in main ideas 3*t* time.
- **Smaller branches:** The smaller branches are allocated to supporting ideas, controversies, and facts. These are the bulk of your markers, and you should have approximately two per paragraph, subject to the density of the text. Do invest in markers *t* time, after all you *ARE* speedreading. Please note each branch should have a visual representation (an icon, a 3D object or a room) based on the methodology you are using. Typically, you create markers during the prereading stage.
- **Leaves:** The details, facts, numbers, and specific information generate leaves. Leaves are typically encoded back as details of the branch that supports them (color of the marker, its texture, its shape, and design). However, if these details are complex (names, dates, formulas), they are encoded into separate yet smaller branches. All the leaves are typically encoded immediately after reading a paragraph.
- **Strings:** Most of us should not only retain what we read, but also generate new thoughts. While most of the articles we encounter are built like a tree, the way our thought functions is more of a spider weaving a web between trees to catch elusive bugs of new creative ideas. Thus, we

connect the small branches and the leaves of various trees with a translucent web of strings that I usually call hyperlinks. Hyperlinking is my addition. You will not find hyperlinks in the original mind mapping theory, but you cannot operate mind maps effectively without connecting different trees. In software, we use pointers and references with a similar effect.

2. **When do we use mind mapping**? Mind mapping is not very useful for memory sports. You cannot effectively encode decks of cards or sequences of numbers into a mind map. It is probably not very efficient when you need to work in real-time: during conversations and lectures. However, almost any computer program, textbook, article or presentation can be effectively encoded as a mind map.

3. **Mind mapping over a clock face**. I am so used to working with data structures that mind mapping over a data structure comes naturally for me. The form of mind mapping Anna uses with students is the more classic mind map. She asks you to imagine the face of an analog clock with numbers 1 to 12. Now the trunk or the bigger branch always connects where the clock strikes 12. You still have 11 hours to position additional markers/branches. Since each marker is a visual entity, you visualize the clock with the marker near the relevant number, like an icon. It is recommended to put markers on the odd hours 1-3-5, etc. Then use the even hours as a reserve for the markers we need to add later on, like results of our analysis, details we missed in the first read, etc. The clock face allows you to remember the exact order of markers (drawn clockwise), the relationship between markers and some other details.

4. **Can mind mapping be used with other forms of memorization**? Typically, it makes sense to make a hybrid between mind maps and other forms of memorization. For example, it could be PAO like a spider connecting leaves, or the mind map could be a memory palace, which is a botanical garden where every tree holds a story. Occasionally the articles have numbers or strange names, like legal paragraphs

or body parts, in that case, a variation of the Major System may be used to label the mind maps and serve as retrieval markers.

5. **Moving trees:** Mind maps can be easily moved around. You can easily cut branches from a tree. You can easily graft one mind map to another (remember the even numbers on the clock face?). You can spin association strings between mind maps. You can easily progress along each branch to the leaves of concrete details or the roots of specific applications. You can flatten a tree into a flowchart or a use-case. You can even make multidimensional trees (see hyperlinking and chunking.) Unlike other methods, mind maps are extremely handy to manipulate.

Anna teaches mind mapping as the default way to remember text. I use mind mapping as a default way to memorize and analyze new ideas and complex scenarios. We hope with this small explanation, you will find mind mapping of more use.

## Mind Mapping Example

**Giant Crack in Africa Will Create a New Ocean**

http://www.livescience.com/10592-giant-crack-africa-create-ocean.html

https://www.flickr.com/photos/123907127@N02/14147302450/

**Paragraph 1:**

A 35-mile rift in the desert of Ethiopia will likely become a new ocean eventually, researchers now confirm. The crack, 20 feet wide in spots, opened in 2005 and some geologists believed then that it would spawn a new ocean. But that view was controversial, and the rift had not been well studied. A new study involving an international team of scientists and reported in the journal Geophysical Research Letters finds the processes creating the rift are nearly identical to what goes on at the bottom of oceans, further indication a sea is in the region's future. The same rift activity is slowly parting the Red Sea, too.

**Paragraph 2:**

Using newly gathered seismic data from 2005, researchers reconstructed the event to show the rift tore open along its entire 35-mile length in just days. Dabbahu, a volcano at the northern end of the rift, erupted first, then magma pushed up through the middle of the rift area and began "unzipping" the rift in both directions, the researchers explained in a statement today.

"We know that seafloor ridges are created by a similar intrusion of magma into a rift, but we never knew that a huge length of the ridge could break open at once like this," said Cindy Ebinger, professor of earth and environmental sciences at the University of Rochester and co-author of the study.

**Paragraph 3:**

The result shows that highly active volcanic boundaries along the edges of tectonic ocean plates may suddenly break apart in large sections, instead of in bits, as the leading theory held. And such sudden large-scale events on land pose a much more serious hazard to populations living near the rift than would several smaller events, Ebinger said. "The whole point of this study is to learn whether what is happening in Ethiopia is like what is happening at the bottom of the ocean where it's almost impossible for us to go," says Ebinger. "We knew that if we could establish that, then Ethiopia would essentially be a unique and superb ocean-ridge laboratory for us. Because of the unprecedented cross-border collaboration behind this research, we now know that the answer is yes, it is analogous."

**Paragraph 4:**

The African and Arabian plates meet in the remote Afar desert of Northern Ethiopia and have been spreading apart in a rifting process — at a speed of less than 1 inch per year — for the past 30 million years. This rifting formed the 186-mile Afar depression and the Red Sea. The thinking is that the Red Sea will eventually pour into the new sea in a million years or so. The new ocean would connect to the Red Sea and the Gulf of Aden, an arm of the Arabian Sea between Yemen on the Arabian Peninsula and Somalia in eastern Africa.

**Paragraph 5:**

Atalay Ayele, professor at the Addis Ababa University in Ethiopia, led the investigation, gathering seismic data with help from neighboring Eritrea and Ghebrebrhan Ogubazghi, professor at the Eritrea Institute of Technology, and from Yemen with the help of Jamal Sholan of the National Yemen Seismological Observatory Center.

~~~~~

***Root***: *new ocean in Africa*

***Article prereading:***

*Huge ocean crack in the red sea around Ethiopia and Yemen is spreading apart causing seismic activity*

***Tags/anchors:***

*Israel seismic activity*

*Africa departing from Europe*

***Mind map with 5 branches***

***Paragraph 1 (1 o'clock branch): crack***

*(1) Found new controversial ocean crack in Ethiopia spreading similar to the crack in red sea.*

*(2) May spawn a new ocean*

*(3) P1 Details:*

- *35-mile -rift = 50 km crack*
- *20 feet wide = Giraffe's height wide*
- *Found in 2005 = (2=tween)(00=toilet)(5=hive)*
- *Ethiopia = Queen Sheba*
~~~~~

***Paragraph 2 (3 o'clock branch): Volcano***

*(1) Volcano erupted pushing magma and unzipping the raft*

*(4 o'clock) All at once*

*(1) Ebinger co-author "never knew it unzips all at once"*

*P2 Details:*

*(3 o'clock branch)*

*(2) Dabaho volcano north end = W volcano up-map*

*(4 o'clock branch)*

*(2) Cindy Ebinger = Sandy evergreens*

***Paragraph 3 (4 o'clock branch):***

*(3) Earth plates can break as whole not as bits*

*(5 o'clock branch) Ethiopia lab*

*(1) Dangerous for Ethiopia, not dangerous at the bottom of ocean*

*(2) Ethiopia as a lab, many nations work together*

***Paragraph 4 (7 o'clock branch)***

*(1) Afar desert in Ethiopia: where African (elephant) and Arabian (camel) plates meet*

*(2) P4 details (7 o'clock branch)*

- *Afar desert in Northern Ethiopia = A far sandy dune of Queen Sheba up-map*
- *Spreading 1 inch a year for 30 mil years = 30 mil thumbs push plates apart*
- 186-mile Afar depression and the Red Sea = *250 km a far depressed red sea*
- *Red sea will connect to Gulf of Eden = Red sea and paradise gulf will connect through the rift*
- *Arm of the Arabian Sea between Yemen on the Arabian Peninsula and Somalia in eastern Africa = hand of camel see between yes-men and black pirates in right-map part of Africa*

***Paragraph 5 (9 o'clock branch)***

*More researchers from Ethiopia, Eritrea and Yemen*

## For Further Research

http://www.KeyToStudy.com/personal-hyperlinking-format/

http://www.KeyToStudy.com/high-level-chunking/

# PART 5: PRIMING AND TIMING

# Chapter 24: Multitasking

Quite often, our students focus on HOW they read and not on WHAT they read. This focus may generate overload and reduce both reading speed and reading comprehension.

**Please**

- try to do all the preparatory work during prereading,
- do all the performance analysis after reading, and
- concentrate on reading when you read

One way to do it is active reading. A very different way to address the subject is reducing the stress level.

## Reducing Stress

Reducing stress levels is a sure way to happiness for most of us. Around 20% of us suffer from stress or anxiety disorder, and an additional 50% of us simply complain about stress and anxiety. Probably 90% of the people reading this chapter and 100% of people writing it need to relax. There are many ways to relax including meditation, sleep, sports, social activity, reducing coffee and sugar intake, and practicing gratitude, which gives a very different perspective.

## Measuring Performance Weekly

Another suggestion: do not measure your performance too often. Do it once a week, not five times a day. Over analysis is a sure way to paralysis. Do not stress yourself more than you need, do not measure the things you do not REALLY need to measure. Relax and let go. The amount of mental energy released will probably generate a quantum leap in your life.

~~~~~

***DJ***

*Really like this post. Isn't there an application that can be used to track the amount of time spent in an app? I do a lot of reading on my iPhone but I always feel inadequate and like I'm not meeting the daily reading and practicing goals if I'm not consciously tracking how much time is spent doing each one.*
~~~~~

***Dr. Lev Goldentouch***

*Thank you for your honesty. Many people feel this way.*
*Anna/Jonathan might be able to help you with timing and measuring.*
*Controversially, I think that it is better not to measure your reading more than 20 minutes a day. Checking your progress too often may generate a compulsive habit that may keep you from concentrating on content and reaching your full potential.*
*Try to calm down and be confident in your skills; your experience may improve as a result.*

~~~~~

***TS***
*My issues are my eyes constantly move out of the lines when I am reading, and my brain tends to be very racy and fixate on words or sentences previously read. In addition, my eyes tend to skim over sentences and words, and I have great difficulty consciously controlling my eyeball movements and, as a result, no comprehension.*

***Dr. Lev Goldentouch***

*It seems you overestimate the amount of problems right now.*
*Once your confidence builds up sufficiently high, your focus will switch from how you read to what you read, and this will make the difference. Just relax and keep reading. Try meditation – it helped with my over focus. Sports also help, especially swimming.*
*If you can afford a 1:1 session with Anna, she can easily help both with technique and with extreme self-awareness, but this is not a must.*

~~~~~

Whatever you do, use your stress to motivate you and to focus you. Do not allow it to control you or interfere with your activities.

## Good And Bad Multitasking

Some of our students point to Eyal Ophir's work to demonstrate that multitasking is bad. While we do not argue with dangers of bad multitasking, we provide several concepts and training exercises that reduce the damage caused by multitasking. In Chapter 18, we described chunking as a form of good multitasking. In this chapter, we introduce **preread-read-analyze cycle** as a way to quit bad multitasking.

The working memory is the pinnacle of our attention and focus. We can work with 7±2 objects at the same time, and the more objects we hold in the working memory. the slower it becomes. If you are summing up numbers with two digits, you pretty much use your whole working memory (load numbers, sum ones, sum tens, add together, and do not forget the carry number). If you tried to add two series of two-digit numbers at the same time, your calculation would probably fail because you do not have enough working memory to execute two such sequences. Instead, we are trained to add and subtract three or four such series. To do that, we replace the whole content of the working memory, e.g., load set A – process set A – store set A -load set B – process set B – store set B and repeat. There is some overhead for this context switching, but it still enables efficient computational multitasking.

We can apply the same process to reading complex texts. First, we need to read, then we need to remember what we just read, but immediately afterward we need to switch context. We need to decide how the paragraph we read makes or does not make sense and what logic it adds to our knowledge base. Then we switch context to reading another paragraph and so on. If we try to switch context every word instead of every paragraph, the act of reading would take forever, and if we try to read too much before switching context we could lose a huge chunk of content.

## Train Multitasking

About 2% of people can do multitasking without significant degradation in performance. Our modern lifestyle makes you wish you were within this 2%. To some extent, this can be trained.

**Switching memory context:** By summarizing two or more colored math series very fast, we learn to control and color the context in which we remember the information. It this sense after some training we can effectively multitask up to four tasks

**Ambidextrous activity:** Garfield was the first left-handed president of the United States. James Garfield could write Latin with one hand and Greek with the other at the same time. By practicing ambidextrous activity, we can learn to double our processing speed and multitask two activities, like writing and talking with people.

**Serial multitasking:** If you did not train multitasking, try to switch small tasks one after another. Not all tasks are suited for this process, and you should train to chunk similar tasks to be performed one after another with no waiting in between. To do that visualize how you perform the tasks one after another before you start performing them.

## Multitasking Computations

It is notoriously difficult to multitask. In this exercise, you calculate the sum of the numbers of the same color, e.g., red with red, green with green.

The idea is to keep in your head outputs of previous computations per color and update them with each new result.

http://www.KeyToStudy.com/multitasking-computations/

## For Further Research:

http://www.KeyToStudy.com/active-reading-sq3r-system-preread-read-analyze-cycle/

http://www.adaa.org/about-adaa/press-room/facts-statistics

http://www.adaa.org/workplace-stress-anxiety-disorders-survey

http://en.wikipedia.org/wiki/Analysis_paralysis

http://news.stanford.edu/news/2009/august24/multitask-research-study-082409.html

# Chapter 25: Preread-Read-Analyze

We teach our students to preread, read and reread. This technique comes from the so-called SQ3R system that is commonly used in US schools. The SQ3R cycle contains five operations that are performed sequentially per paragraph or a section containing several paragraphs.

1. **Survey:** We also call this prereading. Usually we skim or scan the content before we read it to prepare our mind for new information. This is thoroughly covered in our course materials.

2. **Question:** Before reading the text, we can ask ourselves why we are trying to read the text or ask, "What is in it for me." Clear motivation improves reading process. Getting to the content from different perspectives improves our benefit. Typically, we merge this step with prereading. Scanning-questioning-skimming is a good way to filter out what articles we want to read and how much effort to allocate for each.

3. **Read:** Clear your mind and just read the content. When reading, you maximize the benefit of previous SQ steps, do not reread and dwell in irrelevant details. Anna strongly suggests learning to prioritize text AFTER graduating 1000 wpm 85% comprehension or you risk being stuck in speed versus comprehension tradeoff.

4. **Recall:** We add details to the markers AFTER reading each paragraph. This is our way to ensure we recall the paragraph. During training, we first make sure to read-recall several times until we get 100% retention, only after several weeks we trust the brain to recall automatically.

5. **Review:** Analyze the content from multiple perspectives. See what you learned and try to connect it to previous knowledge. Personally, I probably spend more time on this step than all previous steps taken together. If you do not review the article properly, it is hard to understand it and occasionally you will need to revisit it over and over.

Be active BEFORE and AFTER you read. Ask questions, build strategies, look for support of your insights, synthesize new ideas, try to implement new techniques; however, when you read, try to clear you mind and focus purely on the text. Anna always says "do not read and analyze at the same time, your working memory is not built for it." Our preread-read-analyze process was built as simplification and clarification of SQ3R process.

Scan/skim when prereading, read with open (and prepared) mind, visualize/analyze after reading. We structure the reading process in a form that optimizes brain-processing abilities. Trying to mix steps may overload your brain (working memory/visual cortex, etc.) and reduce both speed and comprehension.

SQ3R is a great alternative to our preread-read-analyze process, addressing the same needs in scientifically sound and widely acceptable format. One way to ensure you will retain material is addressing the material from many angles. By using a structured reading process, we ensure we address the material from many angles without unnecessary repetitions and without losing precious time.

## Calculate Reading Speed

Every text editor has a word count feature. Use a timer/stopwatch to measure how much time it took you to read a text. Now insert the text into a text editor or http://www.wordcounter.net/ and find the word count. Divide the number of words by the time in seconds it took you to read.

Your reading speed will vary according to complexity or "density" of the material you read. Do not be alarmed by fluctuations.

Example:

Number of words read = 10,000
Number of seconds = 80
10,000 / 80 = 125 wpm

## Calculate Saccade Width

In many exercises, we ask you to input saccade width in pixels. The saccade width in pixels can be calculated from the actual saccade width that would appear for example in a newspaper.

With average line width of 1000 pixels, a typical computation is as follows:

**Basic level** = 3 columns = 5 words for column on 1000 px template = 300px per saccade

**Intermediate level** = 2 columns = 7 words per column on 1000 px template = 450px per saccade

**Advanced level** = 1 column = 12 words per column on 1000 px template = 900px per saccade

Notice that some displays have better resolution and some words are longer than other words (depending on the language). Please go to Saccade formatter (link below) and see if the calculation needs to be modified for your device and language.

**Links:**

**3 columns:**

http://facstaff.elon.edu/gibson/COM322/Handouts/Newsletter_Stuff/Three_Column.html

**2 columns:**

http://facstaff.elon.edu/gibson/COM322/Handouts/Newsletter_Stuff/Two_Column.html

**1 column:**

http://facstaff.elon.edu/gibson/COM322/Handouts/Newsletter_Stuff/One_Column.html

**Saccade Formatter:**

http://www.KeyToStudy.com/multicolumn-saccade-formatter/

## Calculate Retention Score

Anna suggested calculating your retention score using http://swoogle.umbc.edu/SimService/phrase_similarity.html. You can put the original text in the "Phrase1" line and your own summary in "Phrase2" line and check how close you are.

## Calculate Effective Working Memory Size

Ask someone to read you random numbers of X digits. After hearing the number, try to recreate it. To improve apparent working memory try to chunk the digits into several groups, four digits each.

Average working memory is approximately seven digits. By training with a partner, you will have an effective working memory of approximately twelve digits.

## Calculate Multitasking Limitations

Try adding several independent series using http://www.KeyToStudy.com/multitasking-computations/

You can see that one series will be very easy, but two series will be harder.

Using four series multitasking is very challenging. Try having a 2x2 grid with the previous result and current result. With practice, you will be able to multitask four activities.

## For Further Research

http://en.wikipedia.org/wiki/SQ3R

http://www.slu.edu/x32711.xml

http://www.KeyToStudy.com/creativity-101-power-multiple-perspectives/

# Chapter 26: Scanning And Skimming

There is a large amount of literature regarding scanning and skimming for specific purposes as complementary to reading (see For Further Research below). Specifically you can use both skimming and scanning for prereading, but also you can use the characteristic eye motion of skimming and scanning for saccade reading.

**Saccades** are very fast eye jumps when we focus on interesting words in various parts of the page instinctively during prereading and column-by-column during actual reading. During **skimming** the eyes jump very fast between several positions or columns on a paragraph, while the eyes do not move within each column. We try to use our peripheral vision to gather information from each position while we focus on it.

There is a physiological phenomenon called "saccadic masking" that actually blinds us between columns, and we use this "blind time" to generate markers and details. If your eyes are not sufficiently trained to use peripheral vision, you can still focus on various areas of the text trying to pick its meaning: headings, dates, names, rare words that catch our attention. In skimming we try to look at the text and get a general inventory of what is in it, without trying to follow the logic of each argument, so our eyes movement can be (well...) saccadic.

A faster alternative to skimming is **scanning**. The scanning methodology really shines when our visual angle is large enough to encompass the entire row width (easy to achieve with newspapers, Kindle and mobile devices). Then instead of jumping eye motion, one can scan an entire paragraph top-to-bottom in one continuous motion or saccade. During scanning, the saccade masking happens at the end of each paragraph, and markers are also generated at the end of each paragraph.

If the line is slightly wider (up to 2-columns width), it is easy to read the text in zigzag motion, still reading a whole paragraph in one saccade. When scanning article in zigzag motion, try to keep wave-like eye motion and not full stops, do not focus on the extreme points of the line (if your visual angle is 7 words move focus between 4th word from beginning and 4th word from the end). Many people have photographic memory with a time span of several seconds, which allows scanning longer text lines or several text lines in one glance.

Typically, we use the scanning methodology when looking for some specific word or phrase. Our eyes simply do not lock their focus until we find the pattern we are looking for. Only when we find something that looks like the pattern we are looking for, the eyes will automatically focus on that information.

The easiest way to learn the specific eye motion of skimming and scanning is by following scanning and skimming learning tactics. Try using skimming by reading various blog articles: focus on the title, the abstract, the key concepts that appear in each paragraph, the conclusion, graphs/tables/infographic if available. After skimming if you like the article, do read it as you would regularly read it. After finishing reading the article, think about it and try to find a question that is answered within the article. Now scan the article for the answer. When you are comfortable doing this with one article, do full search training:

1. Scan 50 articles and choose 20 that are relevant to your search
2. Skim 20 articles and learn the basic ideas of the subject you are interested in
3. Select 5 articles for reading, read all of them
4. Scan all of the relevant articles for answers to follow-up questions.

Once you can use eye motions characteristic to skimming and scanning as a basis for saccade training in speedreading, you should try to choose which visual flow enables the best tradeoff of speed and retention. If you get vertigo with skimming or scanning, you will probably try minimizing. It makes sense to know both scanning and skimming techniques and rely more on the techniques with which you feel natural. We have some anecdotal evidence that shows that ADHD/hyperactive students prefer skimming, while OCD/over-focused students often preferred smoother scanning experience. Scanning requires a better working memory and takes longer to learn, while skimmers benefit from multitasking training (fast context switch). I am not sure one can comfortably read above 800 wpm without skimming and above 1600 wpm without scanning. In any case, you would need either skimming or scanning for prereading and for web search.

The next time when you need to read something, ask yourself, do you want to scan the text, skim the text, or read and retain the details. Choose your reading tactics accordingly to save time.

## Eidetic Memory

Everybody wants to have a photographic memory. Unlike common myth, the photographic memory is limited both in the amount of details and in the amount of the longevity of the mental image. Eidetic or photographic memory typically lasts for several seconds, not more. A person with eidetic memory can read a section or maybe a couple of pages and recollect the text from visual memory.

This is something you can easily learn. Focus on an image for several seconds. Now put the image down and try to recreate the image from your memory. Focus on each detail, no matter how small. The more you train, the more accurate your mental image becomes until you will be able to keep a whole image in your memory.

Now go to texts. Start with a paragraph, and gradually increase the amount of visual data you can remember. This way you will eventually generate an eidetic memory. When you remember where every piece of text is in the original paragraph, you may use it as markers. You will not need further visualization. This is the method Anna uses when reading.

## Find The Differences

"Spot the differences" game is great when preparing for the complex skimming task. While skimming we come up with our own prejudice regarding the subject, and try to see what new information is introduced by the text. The differences are often small. You should be able to focus on details. If you can spot the differences between two images, you will be able to detect the difference between your prior understanding and new visual structures from the text.

A totally different way to spot the differences is discrimination between several mental structures. You see two seemingly identical memory palaces, and yet they are not the same. Spot the context in which the memory palace appeared by small details you imagine within the palace. With time you will become very good in generating the details that enable specific identification of the memory palace you need.

## Code Highlighter

If you have programming experience, try to switch on and off the code highlighter. For any normal person, using the code highlighter is significantly easier than reading all the code in the same color. You can use color patterns of the code highlighter to recognize design templates and follow the code's logic.

However, very few people add any color to their UML design or PowerPoint presentation simply because it does not look professional.

Nothing should stop you from coloring what you read in your visual markers. Highlight the visualization you generate, as a code highlighter would process your code, and even complex subjects will become simpler.

This method is extremely handy when dealing with equations and grammar. In fact, if you use a lot of equations or musical notation, you may consider training synesthesia.

## Perception Speed

When you scan the text, you try to find something familiar in a flood of unrelated information. This is similar to looking for numbers in series of letters. The faster your perception speed is, the better you can distinguish numbers from letters in a long chain of letters, the better will your scanning ability be. As an added value, you may get some synesthesia training. Use a specific color for each letter and each number, and if you practice long enough, letters and numbers will generate strong color association.

## Sometimes Skimming Is All You Need

**Theodore Roosevelt** was known as a very rapid reader and a tireless reviewer of books. Even by today's standards, his reading speed would seem incredible. One of his reading qualities, besides speed, was knowing when to skim and scan, while still absorbing the thrust of his reading material.

In a letter to his son, Kermit, about the best way to read Dickens, Roosevelt said, "The wise thing to do is simply to skip the bosh and twaddle and vulgarity and untruth, and get the benefit out of the rest." Roosevelt was also fond of reading favorite books more than once. He even left a list of novels that he had read "over and over again."

While in the White House, President Theodore Roosevelt was said to read a book every day before breakfast, and occasionally reading three books in a day.

## For Further Research:

### Skimming and Scanning:

http://www.howtolearn.com/2013/02/skimming-and-scanning-two-important-strategies-for-speeding-up-your-reading/

http://www.slideshare.net/AmandaMAllison/reading-techniques-skimming-vs-scanning

http://www.southcentral.edu/images/departments/ASC/documents/Skimming_vs._scanning.pdf

### Photographic Memory:

https://www.psychologytoday.com/blog/open-gently/201504/theres-no-such-thing-photographic-memory

# Chapter 27: Prereading

Before reading a text, we need to preread it. While prereading, we typically use scanning in order to decide if the text deserves reading and skimming to create an "inventory" of the text, including names and dates that we try to memorize before actually reading the text.

There are several reasons for prereading:

1. When reading the articles, we need to **focus on the content** of the article and not on ideas and emotions it generates. During prereading we deal with all the extra information and associations, so when reading we can be very focused on the content itself

2. **Proper comprehension requires variable reading speed** with long pauses to encode dates and names. Unfortunately, it is very hard to modify reading speed in mid reading. Instead, we create auxiliary markers for names and dates BEFORE we read the text.

3. Several memorization methods require the **creation of a "setting" or "theme"** which is used to encode markers. Prereading facilitates the creation of such a scheme.

4. **Not all content is equal**. We can decide to read slower or to skip the paragraph altogether as irrelevant during the prereading stage.

Below are some examples of prereading from my life. I do not expect you to generate similar habits during the first several months of training, but after a year, you may find your routine is very similar to mine.

## Prereading And Reading News Blogs

A news blog is the best media to train prereading. First, I read the title. If the title is remotely interesting, I read the excerpt at approximately 5000 wpm. If the excerpt is remotely interesting, I open the article as a new browser tab (this method is suited for PC not mobile) and forget about it until my tabs are full of articles. I use 24-inch 1920×1080 monitors, so this takes some time.

Once I am happy with the result, I preread the whole article with variable speed. I start at 5000 wpm and read the whole article. If the article was a waste, I close the tab. Otherwise I reread the interesting paragraphs, usually around 1500 wpm. I allocate around 1 minute per article. Very seldom is the article very long, complex or useful. In this case, I move the tab to the left of my Gmail tab for further integration (occasionally rereading, typically as a blog post idea in Google docs/Asana/Trello or a mail to a friend). Rereading the article for the third time, my retention of the article is very good for a very long time.

## Prereading And Reading Tech Articles

When I am asked to solve something I have no idea about, I do some Google search magic and open several tabs with cool scientific articles. For each article, I preread the whole article at 5000 wpm because there are potentially cool ideas hiding in different places of the articles. From the approximately 20 articles I have preread, I select 3-5 and send them to my colleagues. For each of these articles, I already have mental coloring of the interesting areas. I reread those areas at 2000 wpm, and then again at 200 wpm the definitions and the formulas. After reading all the articles, I stop to think. Finally, I reread the whole 3-5 article batch at 3000 wpm to generate fuller understanding of the subject. Occasionally, I understand the articles are too fragmented, and I need to read some fundamental book.

## Prereading And Reading A Tech Book

Typically, books are more boring than articles since they need to be systematic, so I try to avoid long books. If I do need to read long books:

- I preread the introduction sections at a constant speed of 5000 wpm until I find the subjects I am looking for.

- I mentally color the interesting sections and yet continue to read at 5000 wpm.
- When I finish the book or the section (I do not do more than 100 pages at 5000 wpm without getting a serious Pomodoro break), I revisit the interesting sections at a constant speed of 1500 wpm.
- If I do not understand something, I revisit it after finishing a subsection (between 1/2 and 3 pages) at a low speed of 200 wpm.
- Occasionally I reread the interesting sections completely at 5000 wpm to generate more unified understanding. The "unified understanding" means proper linking between various smaller structures of mental markers.

## Prereading/Reading Computer Code

Then I need to implement the subject in computer code. Computer code below 10,000 lines is small, between 10,000 and 100,000 lines is medium and above 100,000 lines is large. For large codes, it usually takes several days until I generate their structure in my mental markers. For medium code, (if the code is readable and not overly engineered) it takes a day or two. Orientation in small code base should take approximately 20 minutes. Then, I am left with several markers for short code segments of 200-400 lines with a mental marker per segment. Orientation within a short code segment is an issue of seconds. Typically, I need to modify a given code in 3-5 segments to integrate my ideas within the code. I do spend some time testing making sure everything works as expected. If fact, debugging takes a large part of my day.

## Technical Writing

Finally, I need to document what I have done. Usually, I just pour my mental markers into a PowerPoint presentation and add visualizations of testing results before and after the modification of the code. Occasionally, I reformulate the presentation into a patent or a specification document for my colleagues. Then I use speedwriting. I follow the structure of my mental markers but also add the details for each marker.

### Prereading Sentences: Grammar And Meaning

Not every part of a sentence is equally important. You need to understand what you are looking for when you are prereading/skimming the text. Is it an event, a definition or a feeling? Accordingly, you can easily summarize long texts into 1/4 of their original length. The summary words will form the basis of your markers. Occasionally the important words can be selected by simple grammatic analysis.

### Prereading: Newspaper Example

Take an informative news line:

"Four people, including a young girl, have been killed after a car exploded on a roundabout in Sweden's second city of Gothenburg, police say."

First, remove auxiliary phrases. Usually, they can be skimmed. "Four people have been killed after a car exploded on a roundabout in Sweden."

We start with the verbs "killed after exploded." These words explain the basic plot.

Notice I always add adverbs and negations when considering verbs. These small words may change everything.

Now add nouns. "Four killed after car exploded in Sweden."

Do not add adjectives, but keep prepositions.

This summarizes what most of us should remember after reading the full sentence.

Feel free to choose if you want the rest of the text, or if you are good with 1/4 of what you just read. This qualifies for 70% retention.

To achieve 90% retention, you do need to remember the auxiliary phrases.

### Prereading: Textbook Example

Now let us take simple textbook sentences:

"When something creates a problem, the performance or the status quo of the situation drops. Problem-solving deals with finding out what caused the problem and then figuring out ways to fix the problem."

Notice that now verbs can be dropped (create, drop, deal, finding, figuring, to fix) because they do not generate meaning.

Focus on rare nouns: "problem, situation, cause, ways." "Causes and ways to deal with problem situations" will qualify for 70% retention, and again this is 1/4 of the sentences.

## Prereading: Food Review Example

Finally consider a food review:

"We had an amazing evening for two couples. Night Kitchen has the right combination between amazing food, and a fun and warm atmosphere. I would also say the value for money is very good. We tried different dishes and enjoyed all, personally I really liked the nookie."

We need to judge how good the evening was. Therefore, the focus would be on adjectives: "amazing, right, fun, warm, good, different." No need to understand what exactly happened there. "amazing, fun and warm" would summarize the experience.

The Pareto principle suggests that 80% of the meaning of the text is focused in 20% of the words. Find the right words in each sentence and everything else falls in place. Verbs, nouns, and adjectives each may play a different role in the way we remember texts.

## Fun Reading

By the end of the day, I am exhausted. I visit some funny site like www.fishki.net or www.omgfacts.com. I do not preread them since the articles are very short and fun. I read about 2000 wpm and focus on images

I hope this answers some questions regarding my personal reading style. I preread at 5000 wpm, select interesting objects and reread at 2000 wpm, reread some hard places at 200 wpm, and reread the interesting objects again at 5000 wpm. Most importantly, I take a lot of breaks between readings.

## Consciousness And Attention Dissociation (CAD)

Many of our students read one thing while thinking about something else. This discrepancy is known as consciousness and attention dissociation and is counter-effective. For example, if you try to generate markers and worry about the quality of your markers at the same time, your attention is focused on the text, but your consciousness is dealing with your insecurity. As a result, your reading speed and retention will drop.

A different take on the same idea is this diagram.

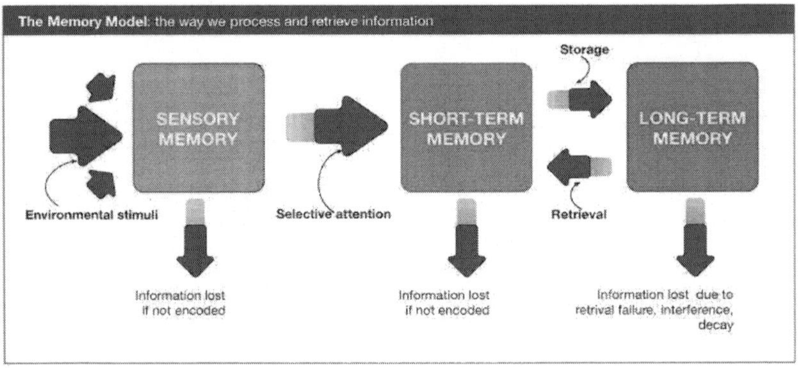


While some consciousness can exist without attention and vice versa, as your consciousness wanders away, your attention becomes increasingly selective. As your attention wanders away, your visual markers will get lost in storage.

To make things worse, consciousness and attention dissociation may be feeding itself. As your consciousness registers less visual inputs, it focuses on its own meta-activities. Many students when missing details within the text stop reading and start doubting "What did I miss in the text? Am I studying properly? Maybe I should try something else?" As the mind wanders away from the text, it is very hard to focus back ON THE TEXT. This sort of "paralysis by analysis" is one of the hardest problems we face while teaching our best students.

Here are some solutions you can try to break the "paralysis by analysis" problem:

1. **Read something interesting.** Relax and have fun. The results do not matter. As we drop the requirement of perfect reading at high speed, the brain has as easier time focusing on the text instead of the reading process. The reading improves, and new reading habits are generated. Unfortunately, when facing an exam or other stressful activity, the bad habits may surface again reducing the efficiency of this method.
2. **Focus on one thing at a time.** Reading is the work of attention, and analysis is the work of consciousness. By alternating reading and analysis, consciousness and attention sync with each other. Do not worry if you need to read the same paragraph several times. Only when you are fully in focus, add the prereading stage to the mix and speed up. With time, the attention and consciousness will sync faster until there is no need for this practice.
3. **Speed up!** Paradoxically, as you speed up, there is no time for consciousness and attention dissociation. While you expect that your retention will drop at higher reading speed, it may increase. In addition, when reading fast, boring texts become more interesting simply due to the amount of conscious effort involved in understanding.

To summarize, as your attention wanders away from the text, relax, focus on one thing at a time, and try to speed up.

## Stroop Effect

The markers we generate during prereading are not fully formed markers. They are more like visual associations, and visual associations are prone to errors.

The Stroop effect deals with colors. When the name of a color (e.g., "blue," "green," or "red") is printed in a color not denoted by the name (e.g., the word "red" printed in blue ink instead of red ink), naming the color of the word takes longer and is more prone to errors than when the color of the ink matches the name of the color.

The Stroop effect was discovered in Germany in 1929. The findings of the experiment should not surprise you. When the color and its printed name coincide, we get the information much faster and more accurate than we get with just the text. If the color and its printed name contradict each other, reading is both slow and error-prone.

## Do Not Prejudge The Text

When we read a text, we have an extensive set of personal judgments and understandings. If the text is similar to what we expect to see, we get semantic facilitation and absorb the text like a sponge. However, if the text contradicts our thinking, we may misunderstand what we read or may require a longer time to read it.

It is very easy to try to force your prior knowledge on the text when speedreading. I remember, just after I married Anna, she used to read a lot of professional literature. When asked she would say, "This is a very interesting book, and it says what I already know in different words." It took Anna 5 years of teaching practice until she could finally see the nuances. Try to avoid this mistake if you value your time.

## Why Prereading Is Not Reading

Some schools teach students to preread at high speeds of approximately 10,000 wpm. The student is to read the whole book and generate some understanding of the subjects read.

Howard Berg's claim to fame began with the 1990 *Guinness Book of World Records*, in which he was first recognized as the world's fastest reader with a heroic speed of 25,000 words in a single minute. The ability comes from a childhood spent in the library, reading incessantly: "It was the only place to play," he says.

Hitting 3,000 wpm in college, Berg realized there was nowhere to go but up. He ultimately taught himself to read-and-flip the pages in a book like most of us shuffle a deck of cards.

Howard Berg claims to read 15 lines at once. By widening the visual angle and reading as much as 12-15 lines at once, it is possible to scan the text very fast. However, the brain probably cannot cope with so much information, so such a speedreader would be able to generate approximately 7 details and one marker from every 15 lines.

If the text is not very dense, not very important and not very complex to understand, it is possible to speedread that fast and leave the reading table with the same amount of understanding as a regular reader.

## The Basis Of Prereading

This is essentially the basis of prereading:

**While prereading**, we try to get as much and as fast as we can. Sometimes we do not need more. However, if we do need more we start reading.

**When we read**, we vary our reading speed according to text difficulty. We follow long and complex logical arguments, and we remember a myriad of small details. If you do not remember the details, you probably are not reading at 1000 wpm, but prereading at that speed, and should read the texts again.

## For Further Research:

### Pomodoro Technique:

https://en.wikipedia.org/wiki/Pomodoro_Technique

### Prereading Sentences

https://en.wikipedia.org/wiki/Lateral_thinking

### CAD

https://www.psychologytoday.com/blog/theory-consciousness/201506/consciousness-attention-and-conscious-attention

# Chapter 28: Harness The Power Of Perspectives

## Asking The Right Questions

When prereading, we need to ask ourselves questions. The purpose is to focus on relevant information rather than select random words. We ask ourselves the following questions:

- How are we going to relate to the article?
- What benefit are we going to generate from it?

This section deals with questions, how to ask questions, and not become stuck when asking them.

## Priming

After we preread an article and before we actually read the article, we want to prime ourselves for reading. Our brain is a filter, and it filters out everything we do not expect to see. By asking ourselves good creative and logical questions, we tune our brain to retain more of the material within the article. We generate the context for details and logical structures to build upon the themes for the markers we create.

## Power Of Priming

There is no second chance to make a first impression.

Before you read the text, you should try to generate the best approach to the text.

- How are you going to use the text?
- Do you trust the author?
- To which extent do you need every detail in the text?

Additionally we need to prepare ourselves to absorb new information.

- What else do we know that can influence our perception of the text?
- What subjects will we link the text to?

- Are we going to build a memory palace or a mind map?
- Which theme/style will we use?

The brain is much better handling the information it is prepared to handle. Use this property to your advantage.

### Proactive Approach

By asking ourselves how we can react to the article, we become more proactive. A proactive approach enhances comprehension and fuels motivation. Ask the following questions:

- What did we learn?
- How can we reuse the article in our material?
- How can we build an argument contradicting the article?
- How can we build a simulation testing the article?

### Connection With The Author

Every article is there for a reason. By understanding the main messages, we connect with the author on a human level and retain the information better. The article comes with a specific new message in the voice of the author. Ask the following questions:

- What was the purpose of this message?
  - To make us do something?
  - To declare a discovery?
  - To make obscure understandings clearer to us?
  - To connect seemingly unconnected events?
  - To overview recent trends?

### Anchoring Information For Further Retrieval

Some markers are used as **anchors** allowing us to retrieve information in the future. Other markers simply connect to anchors generating further details and linking to additional information.

*The anchor markers are there for a reason: they answer some fundamental question, and we plan to remember both the question and the answer.* Think of it as dual coding: if you have both the question and the answer, the possibility of you forgetting both is much lower than the possibility of forgetting each.

## Prediction/Correction

When we read the article (after prereading) we predict what the author will say, but then correct it by what is actually said. This is our inner questions and answers session we convey at the end of each section. Using questions as a method of maintaining our inner dialog (Socratic Method) boosts our understanding and our ability to accept the content.

## Creative Connections

This method is a bit different from the logical thinking we typically use. We allow the strangest, out of the box, unrelated connections to surface by continually asking the same questions and coming up with different solutions each time. Example questions:

- How can one use this idea?
- What other thing could provide a similar result?
- What does this story remind me of?

Eventually, we may come up with things and connections that surprise us. Many inventions surfaced during bath time or came during sleep. We do not need to wait for this: we can make the ideas come forward by asking crazy questions and not rejecting crazy answers.

## Creativity 101: The Power Of Multiple Perspectives

While I had a long and organized training on creativity, Anna is a master of out-of-the-box thinking. She claims she uses one and only one trick, but she perfected using it. Anna calls this trick "multiple perspectives."

Draw a shape or write a word. Now take 2 minutes and write as many associations as you can. The average number is 15. I can do 40 on a good day, limited more by writing speed than by creative potential. How do I come up with 40 uses for a finger or 40 objects that look like a rectangle in 2 minutes alone?

I am utilizing the power of perspectives. I have an array of perspectives I always try:

- What is this item made of?
- How can I use this item?
- What everyday object looks like this item?
- How can this item be used for war, food, construction, art, entertainment, sports, grooming, etc?
- What historic or symbolic meaning is associated with this item?
- Where can I see similar items in nature?

I have many more of these questions, and I ask them very fast. Each question projects the item into a range of virtual landscapes where I try to fit the item. For each landscape, I get several perfect fits for the item or a reason for failure and thus a link to the next landscape to try.

When we take an item and rotate it (a topological operation will do) in 3D space, we have accomplished a similar task using multiple perspectives at a medium-level visualization. With each new angle of the marker, we get new details and colors. Each detail and color is associated with details and colors of the knowledge we are trying to encode.

A third task of perspectives opens up the hyperlinking process. When viewing a new piece of data, we try to project it onto various bodies of knowledge we already have in our heads. If there is a connection, we generate a link between the marker and the existing object.

Try out these exercises yourself, or if you want, schedule a teaching session with us via info@KeyToStudy.com.

## For Further Research:

### Dual Coding:

http://en.wikipedia.org/wiki/Dual-coding_theory

http://citeseerx.ist.psu.edu/viewdoc/download?doi=10.1.1.113.5460&rep=rep1&type=pdf

# Chapter 29: Innovation Focus

Not all texts are equal. Occasional texts require more priorities: either we need to read them slower to understand small details, or to reread them to create the full big picture. Other texts are not important enough, and reading them is a waste of time. By focusing on content I can learn from, I create priorities in my reading.

## Optimize Your Priorities

When I read a text at high speed, I am reading at a speed that does not allow 100% retention. Reading at this rate, I do not retain some of the content I read which occurs even more when I am stressed or in a hurry. *How do I choose what I want to remember and what I want to skip?*

Choosing what to remember and what to skip is a complex subject. Any strategy is probably better than random selection since it enables revisiting the text and filling in the gaps. Yes, every strategy should come with a complementary strategy to fill in the gaps at a lower speed.

## Optimization Strategy

1. **Is this content in the field of my expertise**? If so, I probably need to remember the authors, the terminology used and where I saw it. Otherwise, maybe I should just focus on the main idea and write myself a link somewhere for a future revisit.
2. **Do I need specific numbers or just trends**? It is easy to remember trends and graphs, much harder to remember actual numbers. Is it worth the effort? After all, it is very easy to find numbers when revisiting the article.
3. **Does this article belong to specific chunks of things that interest me or is it opening a completely new domain of knowledge**? Usually, it is sufficient to remember the differences between the current article, and available knowledge in the

domain, enforcing stronger links within the knowledge domain.

4. **If I wanted to take three things from this article, what would they be? How would I use them**? When revisiting, what other three things could I learn? For the high priority things, I use more detailed markers and more detailed linking with many strong links. This process can be done per article, per section, per paragraph with increasing detail level at larger portions of the content.

## Working Memory

Human working memory is 7±2 objects. The working memory is a desk in your brain you use to process information. The faster you can pile up things on your desk and later clean the desk, the faster you think. The more objects can fit on your desk, the more complex are the ideas you can manipulate. It is not surprising working memory is tightly linked with IQ.

When we train speedreading, our reading abilities are limited by working memory. **With a *developed* working memory, we can generate more details and links per marker and manipulate markers faster.**

Chunking is a simple way to increase you working memory. Instead of remembering 5 objects (remember 7±2) you can remember 5 groups of 4 objects in a 2x2 matrix. This way your working memory can hold 20 objects, which is approximately all the information you can acquire in a typical section of text.

Practice separately 20 images and 20 words exercises, since the required skills are closely related but not the same. When you see obscure images, try to think, "Of what does this remind me?" and remember the visual association and thus the original image. When you see words, try to create one marker with 4-5 details for each 4-5 words you see. Both skills are invaluable when you speedread.

## For Further Research:

**Garfield:**

http://www.anythingleft-handed.co.uk/fam_history.html#politicsus

**Wang Feng:**

http://en.wikipedia.org/wiki/Wang_Feng_(mnemonist)

**KeyToStudy Exercises:**

http://www.KeyToStudy.com/20-random-words-generator/

http://www.KeyToStudy.com/random-images-generator/

# PART 6: SPEEDREADING AND COMPREHENSION

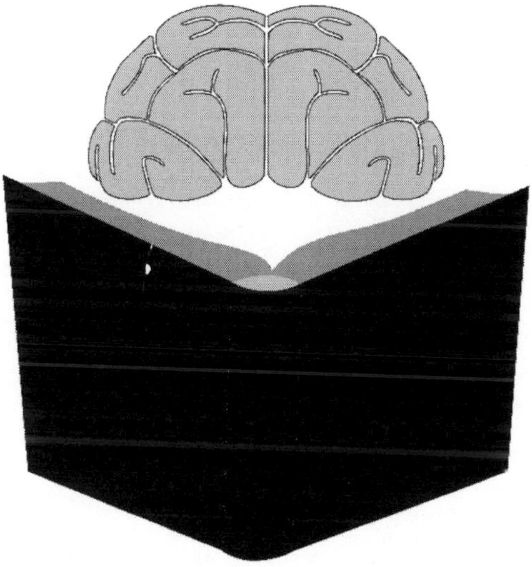

# Chapter 30: Reading Using Metaguiding

When reading it is easy to keep a constant pace. This way we can increase our reading speed over time. Here are some reasons why we understand the text better when we read fast:

1. **When we keep a fast pace, we do not have time to obsess on HOW we read; we are fully focused on WHAT we read.** A very common problem is people obsess with their markers instead of focusing on the text at hand. A fast pace does not leave time for distractions and therefore, you will start generating the right markers.
2. **Reading and rereading the text in small chunks breaks the logical chain of arguments** and focuses us on information that is not clear instead of information that is important. When we read fast, we reread large chunks of text only when we do not understand what we just read sufficiently well.
3. **When reading slowly we can get infinitely bored.** As we go against the clock, the sport itself gets exciting. The adrenaline pumping in our veins does not allow us to lose focus.

Dali used to sleep with a key. When the key would fall, the sound would wake him up from his sleep, and he would start painting. Going against the clock is our way not to lose focus and go into the land of daydreaming. We use metaguiding as our key.

## Metaguiding

To force our eyes to go faster, we use the speedreading methodology known as metaguiding. As children, we often read while putting our finger near each word we read. When we become older, we no longer need this, and we do not use our finger for reading anymore.

Metaguiding revives this practice, only now we put a finger on each line we read and not on each word. Instead of trying to follow our reading with our finger, we try to increase our reading speed until it catches up with the finger. The effort required to catch up does not allow us to reread the text or phrase we previously read.

Unlike other processes, we use (visualization, memorization, skimming, analysis, and time-management strategies), the actual speedreading is a pretty straightforward process. We assume:

- You have already encoded all the names, dates and other dense information within the paragraph in prereading, and the relevant markers are readily available to be used.
- The text is of average density; cannot be skipped; and does not require thorough analysis.
- The text is based on prior knowledge we have, and we can easily understand what we are reading.

These assumptions work probably 90% of the time, maybe more. Under our assumptions:

- We do not need to reread the text.
- All we should do is read the text in front of us as fast and accurately as we can, generating markers as we read.

## Metaguiding Device

A finger is a very simple and readily available metaguiding device. For people who have dyslexia or ADHD, it is better to read with a card, so we do not see what text lies ahead. On the computer, one can use continuous scroll to the same effect.

Some speedreading programs flash words one by one at a constant speed, which is not a good method because:

1) Words get out of context especially in phrases,
2) You cannot control the speed with which you read or take a short micro-pause, and
3) You depend on external software that will not be there in other situations in your life.

You may learn more using a program that flashes several words, like Acceleread.

## Metaguiding Speed

We recommend moving your finger with almost constant speed. Try to keep moving your finger slightly faster than your comfort zone to increase the reading speed. Quite often, the finger is a bit slower in the first paragraph of the page (to generate context) and in the last paragraph of the page (to ensure that the whole page is understood). The headings naturally generate pauses in reading, which enable construction of section markers.

Try to read faster so that you catch up with your finger. If you start losing comprehension, slow your finger down. Otherwise, consider moving your finger still faster.

## Metaguiding In Preread-Read-Analyze Cycle

If you read something, you will use metaguiding only in the reading stage. Make sure you preread the section before you start metaguiding and analyze the section after you stop metaguiding. A section in this sense is approximately 2 to 3 pages of text.

## Advanced Metaguiding

Advanced students read fast. At some point, this is just too much effort for the finger. Instead, we can use the paging process to set up the rhythms. At approximately 3 to 5 seconds per page (faster when using Kindle), turning the pages sets up a metaguiding rhythm of the reading process. In this sense, we can use larger sections of approximately 20 pages.

At each step of the speedreading process, we need to control our reading speed. Metaguiding is a simple way to keep a constant and high reading speed.

## For Further Research

http://www.acceleread.com/

# Chapter 31: Suppress Your Inner Voice

An amazing fact is most people read only as fast as they talk. When reading 250 wpm, we hear each word in our head. The fastest talking person can handle 600 wpm. Unfortunately, at that rapid rate I, or most people, do not understand a word of what is said.

I do read 2000 wpm and understand everything. To do that, I suppress vocalization and run images in my head. Here creating markers comes handy when you suppress vocalization. Creating markers is how we operate concepts in our head without vocalizing them.

**Warning:** If you do not create markers fast enough, do not learn subvocalization suppression. You can still do all the other exercises in this book. Suppress your vocalization only when you feel positive you are ready.

The brain cannot efficiently perform two vocalizations at the same time. This training not only teaches you speedreading but also opens you to efficient multitasking.

The exercise below is the simplest way to reduce subvocalization when reading text line by line. Choose to visualize one marker per line. You are allowed to subvocalize 1 to 2 words per line.

## Beginner Exercise

Slowly (100 wpm) repeat aloud, as you are reading the words, sentences and paragraphs, 2-4-6-8-10. Your job is to multiply by 2s as you read along. After you reach 10, continue reading, but start-over, 2-4-6-8-10, and so forth, to the bottom of the page. Do not focus on the counting; let it become a mindless song, a jingle. Your job is to focus above the words and feel your eyes sweep left – middle – right, sentence-after-sentence.

## Intermediate Exercise

Now "silently" do the "2, 4, 6, 8, 10s" while reading. You can mentally raise the volume on hearing the numbers, and it will drown out the subvocalization of the words. Our left-brain is a serial processor; it can only run one program at a time. When we focus on hearing the numbers, it is like a jingle that gets in your mind and will not leave, and that song takes prominence over subvocalizing the words.

## Expert Exercise

The objective is to not need the numbers, and not hear the words you read. Open up a TV or radio or another noise source and focus on what you are reading. Make the brain focus on the text a hand and not on the conversation on TV. Now slow down your reading and focus on the conversation. Try to understand the conversation while reducing the reading speed to compensate. Continue for 3 minutes and switch your focus back to the text.

## Generating Rhythm

When teaching speedreading, we often ask our students to use rhythm. Rhythm means a "movement marked by the regulated succession of strong and weak elements, or of opposite or different conditions." One of our students summarized the usual effect of a lack of rhythm. "The first 5 minutes are easy then get harder; I slow down and I have to rest." Usually, this means you are working incorrectly, and probably not keeping the rhythm.

Rhythmic breathing is an important health exercise. You can practice your breathing rhythm with visualization, improving your rhythm and your health. In other words, better breathing leads to better thinking. Eventually, you will need to apply these skills to SuperLearning, and some prior experience is handy.

The first encounter of a student with rhythm is subvocalization suppression. We ask our students to count and move a card to control their reading speed. The independently moving card and progressing count forces our brains to process information FAST, overcoming the subvocalization. At this point, counting and the card are no more required and many students do not keep any rhythm. Interestingly, some of our students report significant progress in further stages of our course by using a metronome. While this is a cool method, a simpler method would work. For example, most lines are made of three saccades. Counting 2-4-6 and breathing (inhale-hold-exhale) accordingly would introduce the rhythm. Then you could stop counting (once again) and use just your breath to control your speed.

If you read yet faster, do not hyperventilate. You can synchronize your breath with paragraphs. Take a deep inhale when prereading, keep air while reading, and exhale while creating markers.

Later on, you can read sections of two paragraphs in one breath, using the 8:4:8:4 breathing rhythm of yoga in the exercise above, since analysis/marker generation and prereading together should take about half the time it takes to read a paragraph. Notwithstanding your reading and breathing level, you should stop after each paragraph to create markers and you should breathe properly.

The next level of rhythm applies to larger sections of several pages. When you read several pages, you need to pause and think about what you read. Remember the forgetting curve: you just dodged the 1 to 5 seconds limitation when you stopped at the end of the paragraph, now you are getting to the 5-15 minutes stage. Fortunately, Pomodoro timing dictates you to take approximately 5 minutes rest for approximately every 15 minutes of work.

Rhythm up the Pomodoro breaks with your necessity to analyze the document. Do not read during the break. Do get a drink, toilet, close your eyes, or stare mindlessly at the monitor to give your brain a chance to process. After an hour of work, take an even longer break. Recollect the markers (1-hour repetition) and switch activity. Talk to someone or watch cute cat videos. If you learn too long, your brain will get more information than it can process and become inefficient. After the break try to do something entirely different for an hour, if you can since this form of serial multitasking is extremely efficient.

Whatever you do, simply keeping a rhythm will do wonders for your endurance. You can SuperLearn without keeping a rhythm, but with rhythm, SuperLearning is SO MUCH easier.

## For Further Research

### Rhythm:

http://en.wikipedia.org/wiki/Rhythm

http://holisticonline.com/yoga/hol_yoga_breathing-Rhythmic.htm

http://www.care2.com/greenliving/13-health-benefits-of-deep-breathing.html

http://www.wikihow.com/Improve-Your-Thinking-Skills

# Chapter 32: Eye span

Our eye muscles are limited. If we were to focus on each word we read, we would not be able to read above 600 wpm, and then we would suffer a massive headache and eyestrain. Students who try to push reading speed without learning saccades often complain the words become blurry, and they cannot read at all for 2 weeks before they can resume the regular speedreading. Clearly, this does not happen to me, to Anna, and to students that graduate the course. This is not because we have exceptional stamina, but because we **read smarter**.

Our eyes have a tiny spot in which they are focused. Outside of this spot, our vision degrades and gets increasingly blurry. On the edges of peripheral vision, we can only notice large movements without being able to understand them. Therefore, our instinct is to focus on the word we read, the word after it and so on. However, we do not need our top resolution to understand the text we read. We can read quite well even if our eyes are focused elsewhere. We do need some short adaptation before our brain rewires.

By focusing on one spot and picking up letters and words on different spots, we increase our eye span, or the ability of the brain to interpret signals from visual areas with lower resolution. This skill is notoriously hard for the eyes and brain. Therefore, for every couple of minutes of practice we need to take a couple of minutes of rest (focus our eyes on the horizon and relax).

Very soon, we will be able to see 5 words while focusing on the central word of the phrase. Advanced students see 12 words with one focus. These 5-12 words form a saccade.

Suppose our saccade is 7 words wide and an average text line in our book is 12 words. Then we can focus on fourth and eighth word of the line only and see 2 saccades with 3 words overlap. It is important to avoid overscan at the edges of the book. Therefore, we do not focus on the first word, but we need overlaps, since some words are very long and catch the space of 2-3 regular words.

Suppose we have eye-span of 9 words, and we need an overlap of 2 words. Then we can saccade with relative ease 7*500=3500 wpm. At 12-word saccade and 2 words overlap, we get approximately 5000 wpm. This is probably the upper limit of our current method and the speed you should be using for your scanning technique. For scanning and skimming, you can increase your speed even more by reading several lines at once. In fact, some people (me included) are capable of getting a full Kindle or iPad mini page in one span focusing in the middle of the screen. This is both very fast and very comfortable since I do not have to move my eyes often. However, this does not apply for very long lines, and the reading speed drops significantly as lines get wider.

By reading with the peripheral vision, we can increase reading speed and decrease eyestrain significantly. If your eyes hurt when reading, then you are not doing this correctly!

## Shultz Tables

Our eyes have their clearest vision in the central zone of view. Everything that lies outside this central zone is seen as a frog would see it. This broad field of vision makes the searching process shorter. It is possible to widen our field and quicken our vision by using "Shultz tables."

| | | | | |
|---|---|---|---|---|
| 5 | 13 | 22 | 4 | 15 |
| 3 | 10 | 9 | 21 | 2 |
| 8 | 14 | 24 | 12 | 25 |
| 20 | 7 | 23 | 6 | 11 |
| 1 | 18 | 17 | 16 | 19 |

Rules to work with Shultz tables

- Find numbers silently, in increasing order from 1 to 25 (without omission). The found numbers are specified only by a sight. As a result of such training, the time to read one table should be no more than 25 sec.
- Before beginning to work with the table, the sight is fixed in its center to see the table entirely.
- When scanning for 25 numbers, fix your eyes only in the center of the table. Horizontal and vertical movements of eyes are forbidden. Distance from the table should be similar to the usual text.
- It is very important to let your eyes rest between the tables at least 25 seconds.

The main goal of the exercise is expanding the peripheral vision by keeping the eyes fixed.

If you are tired of regular tables, you can play with a twist. Try http://www.KeyToStudy.com/visual-angle-training/ and take for example, 25 candidates.

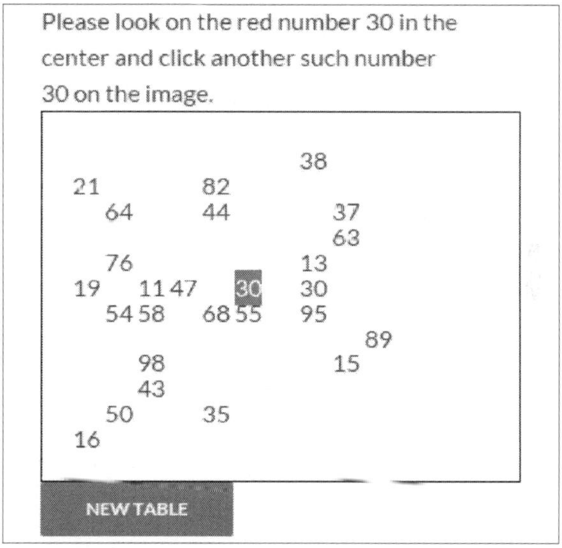


Think fast! Here it is:

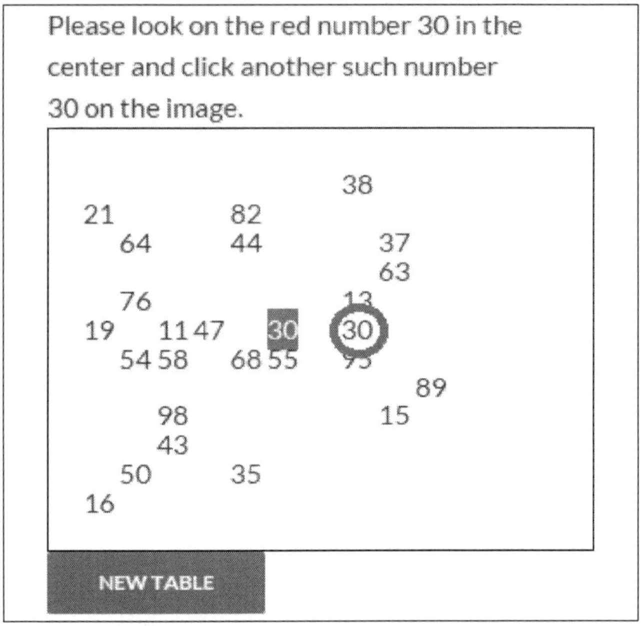


Click on it! Continue to the next set...

The exercise is very similar to actually scanning the text. If you have developed synesthesia (e.g. see numbers in colors), you will solve the exercise faster. Try http://www.KeyToStudy.com/accuracy-synesthesia/

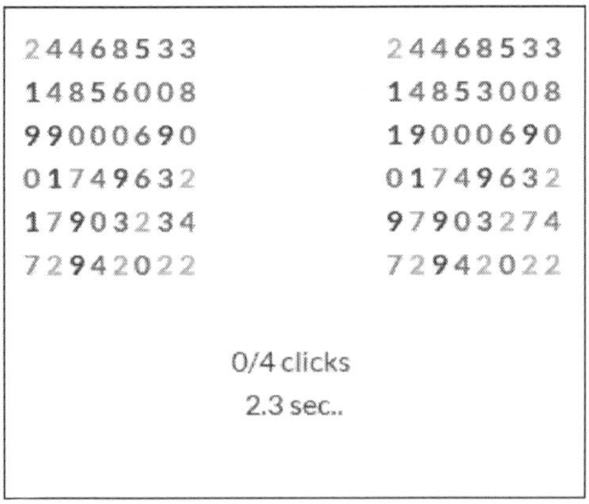

This exercise is more like skimming, since you have 4 differences you need to find and 2 columns to look into.

Try to be as fast as you can...

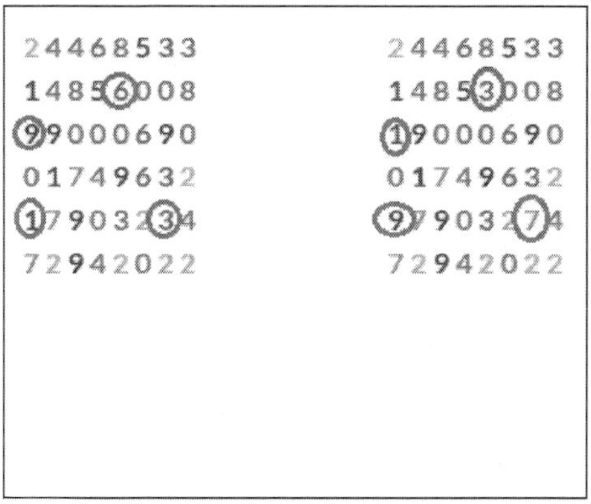


Do click on each difference you spot.

Once you start seeing numbers in colors (it is a slow process, so be patient), do try to switch to letters.

# Chapter 33: Manage Pauses

When we use saccades, we need to control our time properly. The eye will stop a couple of times per line, but you should make longer stops at the beginning and the end of each paragraph.

## Using Negative Time

Managing pauses when we learn is an important skill nobody discusses. Below is a recommended SuperLearner strategy inspired by a discussion on our Udemy course regarding small pauses we have when we learn. My personal opinion is we should use these pauses as one would use negative space. Therefore, I will call these small pauses "negative time."

## Some Little Known Facts

First, let us understand what constants of time we are talking about.

| Phenomenon | Duration | Usage in SuperLearning |
|---|---|---|
| Microsleep | between 0.5 sec and 30 sec | analyze the section we just read |
| Page turn | around 1 sec | rest... |
| Analyze image | ~0.5 sec | prereading |
| Saccade | 0.02 sec | read the text |
| Saccadic masking | 0.01 sec | we "Go blind" and create/modify marker |

These numbers were first measured using a device called a Tachistoscope.

## Do We Go Blind?

There are some computations showing that at least 40 minutes per day we spend in blindness, but our memory fills in the gaps using some cool trickery. These saccadic lapses probably cannot be controlled. Other times we consciously choose to close our eyes to get a better understanding of the text or to reduce strain on our body. These microsleeps should not be confused with short 5-minute breaks we take for "Pomodoro time" to be efficient during the day. In fact, we spend much more time not reading than we spend reading, and this is perfectly okay. When I speed up my reading above 1000 wpm, I notice my comprehension starts to drop, so comprehension x speed stays approximately constant.

## Why Do We Need So Much "Time Off"?

Our body and our brain were built for tracking animals in African bushes and not for speedreading Tolstoy's *War and Peace*. Therefore, we do need some clever hacks for the brain to adapt to the new way of information consumption. The brain is hardwired to track one object for a long time and not to jump between objects every 10 microseconds. The extra strain is above the brain's power to process the information, and the brain starts to miss details. The extra rest allows you to use your brain with maximal efficiency.

## What Is The Recommended Strategy?

We use 10-microsecond saccadic mask for the prepare-read-analyze cycle. At the end of each paragraph, we take a longer 0.5-second break to fix the visual marker, generate its links and prepare for the next paragraph. At the end of each page, we take another 1 second to daydream and rest our eyes. At the end of each section (approximately 15 pages), we take several minutes to analyze what we just read and how we can use it in our life.

Below is the discussion from a student regarding pauses.

## Time Management Of Pauses

*I would like to have a clarification between micro pauses and long pauses. I have no doubt longer pauses are consciously done, but what about short time pauses? Doesn't the eye naturally pause between a paragraph/page and the other (we're talking about fractions of seconds) or is it something I have to be 'conscious' about? I mean is it possible to review markers in fractions of seconds?*

*I understand I may come from a bit of a skeptical perspective – certainly because I haven't tried short pauses yet – but the main point of the question is to have a better understanding of what exactly I should focus on to improve in my training sessions on short pauses.*

*A second point: if a paragraph is interrupted by a page shift, should I first finish the paragraph instead of pausing at all costs at the end of the page, because I normally would finish the paragraph for the sake of understanding.*

### Dr. Lev Goldentouch

*Basically, you go blind for several milliseconds, and you daydream markers during that time. This sounds surreal, but it works. You do not consciously cause saccade jumps – it happens since your visual angle is limited, and you want to minimize overlap between focus points.*

*Regarding the broken paragraph: you pause consciously at the end of the paragraph/section (logical unit), not page (physical unit). However, the physical act of turning page generates a pause that you can effectively use. Personally, I use it to micro-rest (turn brain functions down for a couple of milliseconds). See e.g., microsleep.*

## For Further Research:

### Negative Space:

http://en.wikipedia.org/wiki/Negative_space

### Saccade:

http://www.KeyToStudy.com/use-negative-time-saccade-masking-microsleep/%22http://en.wikipedia.org/wiki/Microsleep

http://en.wikipedia.org/wiki/Saccade

http://en.wikipedia.org/wiki/Saccadic_masking

### Pomodoro:

http://www.KeyToStudy.com/use-negative-time-saccade-masking-microsleep/%22

http://en.wikipedia.org/wiki/Pomodoro_Technique

**Prepare-Read-Analyze**

http://www.KeyToStudy.com/use-negative-time-saccade-masking-microsleep/%22http://www.KeyToStudy.com/prepare-read-analyze-cycle/

**Microsleep:**

http://en.wikipedia.org/wiki/Microsleep

# Chapter 34: Fun with Colors

When reading, you may need to change your reading speed through the text. While we do not recommend this to a new student, an experienced reader may assign in his/her head colors for specific parts of the text and change the reading speed accordingly. If the text is complex, this practice enables more accurate scanning and rereading.

## "Coloring" The Text You Read

Sometimes the text I read is heterogeneous and addresses the issues from many points. To keep track of various perspectives I "color" the text according to the dominant perspective of each paragraph. I try to follow the "colors" in the visualization themes, and I try to be capable of reproducing the article photographically with "color" to improve navigation when I re-examine the article. The most important tip here is keeping the colors consistent with the article, not your thoughts.

The seven colors I use roughly correspond to the six thinking hats. You can use some dialectical approach instead, but I find it very simple to follow the basic color scheme. I added one more color for my purposes.

**Green**: This is probably the rarest and important color in the text, corresponding to entirely new and surprising ideas. The green color stands for creativity. Any text marked as green deserves pause, thought, and thorough linking. To remember, associate green with personal growth.

**White**: This is the color of support material. Any associative link needs to be supported by facts, data, authority and some other information. While it may have a small role by itself, it is important to keep the support material for all knowledge we have, and thus the white stuff is important. To remember, associate with white stuff in your brain.

**Blue**: Each text has its flow, and good authors guide their readers in the flow of their text. The thinking behind the methodology is very useful for navigating the text and for recreating similar processes. To remember, associate with a blue river.

**Red**: Often authors cite controversy. Any controversy generates emotions. In historical books, we see cool anecdotes. Those anecdotes also generate strong emotions. Some blogs put great images or cool titles, which create an emotional response. Emotions are easy to remember and use for visual markers. Emotions fires up our interest and imagination. To remember, associate red with fire.

**Yellow**: Many articles open new opportunities. This new idea can be used for... There are relatively few lines of hope within most of the articles we read, and they shed some light on the possible future use of the idea. To remember, associate yellow with a flashlight.

**Black**: Basically, black is the opposite of yellow. Black deals with threats, uncertainty, scams and other demons lurking in the darkness and is rarely used. Associate with darkness. Use an underline to highlight in documents.

**Gray**: If you read something and have no idea how to use it, do not color the text. Instead, make it fade away into shades of gray. Associate with fog. Change the text color to gray in documents.

Now take a text you are willing to mark, put it in your word editor and start highlighting paragraphs with the appropriate colors.

## Synesthesia

The subject of synesthesia (when various senses "leak" into each other) enables reading complex texts. Any programmer knows how a code highlighter makes reading code easier. Synesthesia is just such a code highlighter only in your head! Synesthesia naturally occurs in one out of 2000 people. Moreover, you could encode music, taste or other complex sensory information into visual markers, and you already know what to do with visual markers!

Now, the most interesting part of the story is the simple fact you can probably teach yourself synesthesia! Anna has been using the Stroop effect for a while to prepare people for subvocalization (reading one color and visualizing another).

Many top-level musicians have synesthesia and see some part of music as colors. What they see instead of chords and timbre is some color dynamics. It is easy to remember color dynamics, and one can train partial synesthesia. There are many projects where students are expected to color-code notes, and even color piano projects.

There is a good chance after a while, the number/color or letter/color association will become stronger and you will remember numbers like Daniel Tammet, who has linguistic, numerical, and visual synesthesia.

Synesthesia is an advanced skill, and you will need a lot of practice to acquire it. Happy hunting acquiring the new skill and we are here to support you.

## For Further Research:

### Six Thinking Hats:

http://www.KeyToStudy.com/colouring-text/%22http://en.wikipedia.org/wiki/Six_Thinking_Hats

### Synesthesia:

https://www.ted.com/talks/daniel_tammet_different_ways_of_knowing?language=en

http://www.theatlantic.com/technology/archive/2012/07/can-you-teach-yourself-synesthesia/259519/

http://en.wikipedia.org/wiki/Stroop_effect

http://en.wikipedia.org/wiki/List_of_people_with_synesthesia

http://en.wikipedia.org/wiki/Colored_music_notation

http://mudcu.be/piano/

http://en.wikipedia.org/wiki/Daniel_Tammet

# Chapter 35: How To Train Reading

Training reading is a bit of a tricky balancing act. If you fail the balancing act, you may generate bad habits that are hard to change.

## Speed

The first thing to train in speedreading is obviously speed. Reading speed typically does not increase gradually, but in quantum leaps and occasional regressions. Do not be alarmed either way. Push your progress patiently. Do not strive for changes too large, but do not stagnate.

## Retention

It is important to have high retention. Retention below 80% is not good for most applications. Occasionally you need to be able to get near 100% retention at low speed (memorization) and very high speed at low retention (skimming/scanning). Most of the time you would prefer to slow down your reading speed until your retention is in the sweet spot.

## Strain

It is important not to strain your eyes and brain at any point. Students who push too hard experience burnout. They lose many weeks, and it is hard to regain training momentum.

## Focus

It is important to train all skills and not just one skill you decide is most important. If your skills are not balanced, you will need to work significantly harder.

## Texts

Some texts are just not suited for speedreading. Do not speedread texts that are hard to understand, too short, full of numbers you need, stressful, uninformative, etc. Tech and business blogs are usually highly suitable for speedreading.

## Typical Progress

Before subvocalization suppression: read 250 wpm and try to improve retention until you get 90%.

1. Suppress vocalization until you reach approximately 450 wpm. Retention will drop.
2. Do not try to read faster! Patiently work on retention until you get back to 90%. This will take several weeks.
3. Increase your visual angle. Learn saccades. With a visual angle of 9 words increase your reading speed. Get to 800 wpm.
4. Again, increase retention and stop at 80% retention.
5. Check the full integration of preread-read-analyze cycle until it becomes natural. When you master skimming and scanning, you will get 1200 wpm at 80% retention
6. At that point, you need to contact Anna for a qualification test and see if you are eligible for advanced training.

If you train speedreading in a right and balanced way, your comprehension quality and reading speed increase simultaneously, and you do not get tired.

## Accelerated Pros And Cons

We suggest our students use Acceleread or similar program (like our http://www.KeyToStudy.com/sliding-words/) to practice speedreading. With a program showing words at high speed until our brain catches up, we train fast perception. The programs also display several words preserving some context and enables checking retention afterward.

While this is great training, it is lousy reading. When you need to read and remember, you need to control your reading speed. Moreover, you need to preread and reread if required to understand the text. You need to pause to memorize dates and names after each paragraph.

While you can practice metaguiding and word flashing separately, we have a combination of metaguiding and high-speed words flashing on http://www.KeyToStudy.com/card-exercise-equivalent/.

## FDR Method In Kindle

**Franklin D. Roosevelt** would certainly be included among the leaders in speedreading. Like most people, he began reading two or three words at a time, then stretched that to three or four words, then six to eight words. Eventually, he was able to read (and absorb) an entire paragraph at a single glance. He often practiced reading two or three lines at a single glance ("fixation"). Even more interesting, he would glance quickly at a single page, then turn the page and ponder over what the author was trying to say.

When we train our visual angle, we start from 3x3 tables, and normally progress to 5x5, 7x7 and eventually 9x9. Some speedreaders are capable of absorbing an entire page with one glance. This is relatively very simple on Kindle since the pages are small.

If you consume most of your information from Kindle, you could consider the FDR method: absorb the whole page at once and then reprocess it from memory.

## Free Your Mind When Reading

Reading is hard enough. Free your mind of everything else. If you need to ask questions, correct your markers, or shift paradigms, do it before or after reading. When you are reading focus only on what is in the text. Try not to bring your thoughts into the text. You would have brought your thoughts in during prereading. Try not to think what happens next. You will handle "what next" after reading. Reading itself is a Zen-like experience. Reading should be handled with proper respect and simple elegance.

## Reading Aloud

When speedreading becomes your second nature, you need to read aloud once more. You can preread each sentence and pause between sentences, but you do need to read each sentence slowly afterward. It will be slow since you vocalize every word. However, you can use the time you gain to scan the audience for body language, make eye contact and even improvise occasionally. Do train before attempting this.

## Reading Without Prereading

If you do not want to ruin a surprise, you can read without prereading. In this setup, you are almost forced to reread fast to fill in the details, and your reading speed goes down slightly. This is not a large price to pay if you hate spoilers!

## Subliminal Reading

Occasional students read very fast, remember everything and do not generate markers. This is simply a higher level of the reading skill. The markers are usually produced on a subliminal level, and the reader is not aware of this process. Do not try to get this skill by brute force, but do not be surprised if you do get there. This is very normal.

## When You Should Read Slowly

When you mastered speedreading, slow reading is not an easy task. We describe the reasons for reading slowly, the difficulties that arise from reading slowly, and how to deal with them.

Recently I read an article on reading slowly. Reading slowly is a hard task for a SuperLearner. Suddenly you have all this time and nothing to do; you need to slow down your saccades (take longer periods between saccades), and even vocalize the text.

## Slow Reading Scenarios

1. **Poetry:** When reading poetry or other exquisite literature, it is fun to enjoy the sound of the text and the shape it takes in the book. My technique involves speedreading a sentence or a line and then trying to generate audio markers as we do when learning a foreign language. The audio markers break words into pieces and allow joy from every piece of the word. Alternatively, I subvocalize the phrase in my brain to feel how it would roll down my tongue. This goes well with high-level visualization of the scene described and multisensory markers for the emotional input.

For me SuperLearning improves the feeling of good literature; however, there is so much to do that I hardly have any time for it.

2. **Foreign languages:** Speedreading assumes that you can understand the text and generate the markers faster than you talk. I can do this in three languages. In all other languages, I need to slow myself down and try making markers per word. Typically, the side effect is 100% retention of the text, even when using Google Translate. I am fine with that.
3. **Complex text:** Some complex texts, especially math, may be hard to speedread. Often when reading formulas, you need to generate a marker link per letter since each letter has its own marker. These markers are unique for a specific article since every scientist may choose his own notation. Fortunately, most mathematical tricks are repetitive, and you can generate a marker per trick, but then you should make sure you do not miss anything. When I face a complex formula, I just subvocalize every number and letter and use the right brain hemisphere to understand the mathematical logic behind the formulas.

## For Further Research:

### Reading Slowly:

http://www.psychologytoday.com/blog/tip-the-tongue/201407/reading-fast-and-slow

# Chapter 36: Sample Texts And Marker Generation

## T-Card Example

When I was learning to memorize texts, Anna asked me to use a T-card:

TEXT |------------------| Drawing My markers |

For example, I will use the following text and show my markers: http://en.wikipedia.org/wiki/Big_Bang:

> In the mid-20th century, three British astrophysicists, Stephen Hawking, George F. R. Ellis, and Roger Penrose turned their attention to the Theory of Relativity and its implications regarding our notions of time. In 1968 and 1970, they published papers in which they extended Einstein's Theory of General Relativity to include measurements of time and space. According to their calculations, time and space had a finite beginning that corresponded to the origin of matter and energy.

## First, See My Markers:

Three British astrophysicists, Ellis, Hawking, Penrose

(19)68-(19)70
Einstein Black Hole theory extended

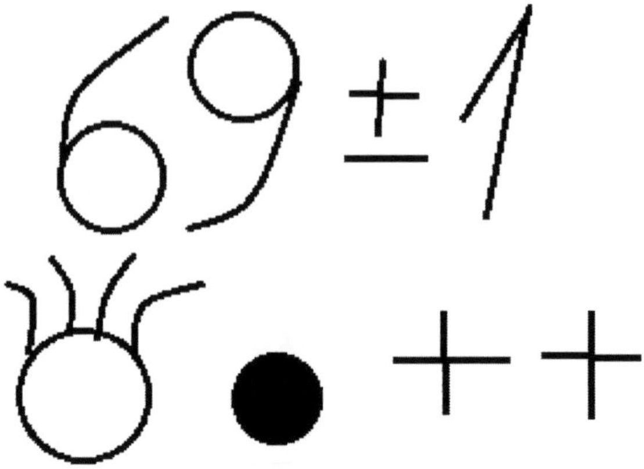


They expanded from single origin of matter: time and space

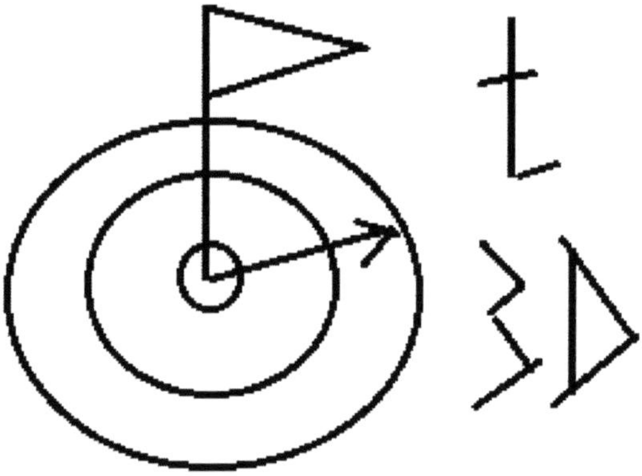

## Text with Markers

| | |
|---|---|
| In the mid-20th century, three British astrophysicists, Stephen Hawking, George F. R. Ellis, and Roger Penrose turned their attention to the Theory of Relativity and its implications regarding our notions of time. |  |
| ~~~~~ | ~~~~~ |
| In 1968 and 1970, they published papers in which they extended Einstein's Theory of General Relativity to include measurements of time and space. | 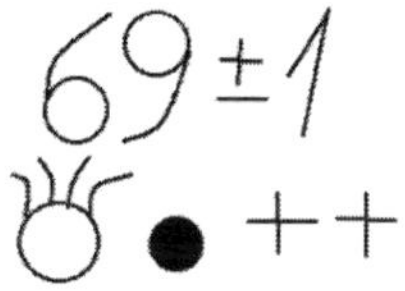  |
| ~~~~~ | ~~~~~ |
| According to their calculations, time and space had a finite beginning that corresponded to the origin of matter and energy. | 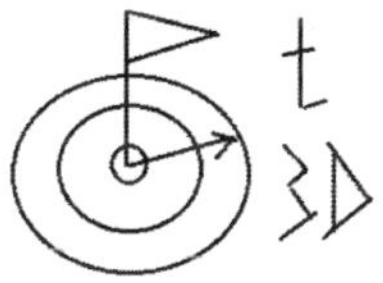  |
| Summary | • Three British astrophysicists, Ellis, Hawking, Penrose<br>• (19)68-(19)70 Extended Einstein General relativity theory with a new notion of time:<br>• time and space expanded from single origin of matter! |

Do not be an artist. Draw the best you can.

Try using 2x2 chunking of markers before learning structures that are more complex.

## Dr. Lev / Example Texts And Markers

I was asked by Suraj to create markers for the texts below. I did not choose the texts and I do not really know why these particular texts were chosen.

For each paragraph of the text, I create a shorter paragraph of markers. Choosing markers is tricky. The markers should cover the most informative part of the text, and yet be memorable.

This is very much like reading the text with a highlighter in your hands. No two people will use the same highlights.

## Example 1

One midnight after a certain engagement "somewhere in France" in which many men fell, I learned of an experience which burned its way into my soul, and I believe will stay there till the Judgment Day. I have read in history of individuals such as the one I am telling of, but never in my life have I had actual knowledge of any but this one, and I hope that I shall hereafter forever be delivered from such. This particular night the firing for some reason had suddenly ceased. A man named Valke was an emergency watcher at a listening post, when the most blood-curdling thing I have ever known occurred.

- *in France –*
- *experience –*
- *till Judgement day => Eifel tower Armageddon*
- *Night-cease-fire-watcher-Valke => Agent Walker (Valke ~ agent Walker) on watchtower at night*

A listening post is a branch off from the main trench toward the enemy or in his general direction, which is dug secretly as you go, the dirt being carried back in bags so as not to disclose its location. These posts must be changed often, as the enemy is apt to discover them, and then look out!

- *Secret -listening - post -*

- *dirt in bags - often change = A bag of dirt in hands of agent who is listening to something*

Valke was standing in the darkness and seclusion of the post when a shriek rent the air, the sound of which he said he would hear through eternity. It came from a man who was prostrate on the ground. He had noticed the body lying there before, a few yards away, and had assumed that the man was dead. He was a Frenchman, and on account of the darkness could be seen with difficulty. But he was not dead, only unconscious, and something had suddenly revived him.

- *Unconscious Frenchmen on ground revived with a shriek = zombie mime comes to live with a shriek*

"O God," he cried, "my marriage ring!" and then he moaned and groaned like a lost soul in agony. Immediately another form raised up to full stature and looked quickly about. Valke had to strain his eyes to see him and he trembled with nervousness. He did not know what to do for an instant. The man's head jerked this way and that. He must have expected someone to hear the cries and groans of the other man, and evidently was looking around for watchers or listeners. The Frenchman kept on groaning, and the man, seeming to fear that if any watchers were near, they would immediately let loose upon him, started to run. Valke kept very still in his dark post.

- *My marriage ring cried French = zombie seeks marriage ring (plain ring)*
- *Valke saw a man stand up afraid of watchers = Walker saw a shadow stand up afraid of towers*

Suddenly the fugitive stopped. He turned and ran back to the prostrate Frenchman. Valke saw the gleam of a knife drawn from a sheath. It was in the hand of the apache. In an instant the horrid thing was done—a swift movement of the arm, a flash, and the blade plunged into the body of the helpless soldier! Then silence: silence more terrible than the groans of agony that it stilled. Valke's fists clinched by instinct, the nails cutting into the very flesh of his palms; and then his right hand went to the holster on his hip. It was all too plain: the hideous vulture of the battlefield knew that "dead men tell no tales," and that the wounded sometimes recover and tell things that lead to fearful reprisals on their enemies. More than that: wounded men cry out and groan; but the dead are quiet. The knife had done its work: escape might be surer for the assassin. That's the logic of ghouls.

- *Man came to Frenchmen with a knife and then silence = Shadow slays zombie with a blade*
- *Valke nails in his palm - dead men no tales - fear of reprisal / dead are quite = Walker put hand on holster: shadows kill zombies to protect horror labs*

Valke drew his service pistol, but hesitated to fire. To do so might betray his listening post and draw the enemy's shrapnel; it might be fatal to the section. In the second that Valke cast up the chances, he heard whisperings from another listening post. The ghoul had risen and was slinking for cover when the crack of a rifle tore a gap in the stillness.

- *If Valke fires need new listening post, hesitation, rifle shot = Walker hesitant: shadows come for sound, sees rifle shot*

*This text is so clear and visual that it requires no marker transcoding; however, I decided to put one just to make clear what it would look like. Occasionally it is easier to understand the dynamics of events if put in some other better-known universe with similar laws.... Whatever I wrote in text I visualized as a first-person shooter MMORG scenario...*

## Example 2

If my health had not required a change of climate, I should not perhaps so soon have accomplished the wish I had often expressed of leaving England for a short time. An immediate removal was judged expedient; and as the ports of Spain and Portugal were either closed to British subjects, or at least not in a state to be visited by an invalid, I determined upon Brazil; to which my friends agreed.—I fixed upon Pernambuco, because a gentleman, who had for many years been acquainted with my family, was about to embark for that place, and from the favourable reports of the people and climate which I had received from several persons. On the 2d November 1809, I set sail from Liverpool in the ship Lucy.

- *Health problem, sail from Liverpool England to Pernambuco Brasil, ship named Lucy, 2-11-1809=*
    1. *Coughing blood*
    2. *From Shipping yard of the Queen*
    3. *To wood capital of Amazonas*
    4. *Ship Lucy (American show star)*
    5. *2-roman 2 - 2 centuries ago, year #9*

We had a very prosperous passage of thirty-five days, without any occurrence worthy of particular notice.

- *Boring 35 days passage = ?*
- *Occasionally no need to remember*

I was agreeably awakened very early on the morning of the 7th December, with the news that we were in sight of land, and likely to get into harbor this day. We soon discovered two vessels, with all sail set, making for us; these proved to be two English merchant ships, bound likewise to Pernambuco; they had never before been at this port, and therefore wished to receive some information respecting it; they judged that, from the manner in which our vessel made for the land, her commander must be acquainted with it, which was the case, this being the second voyage of the Lucy to Pernambuco.

- *7-Dec = On the day of Pearl Harbor*

- *2 vessels join to the same port following experience commander of Lucy = Captain on the bridge, followed by 2 ships, port at sight*

The land is low, and consequently not to be seen at any considerable distance; but as we approached it, we distinguished the hill upon which stands the city of Olinda, a little to the northward; and some leagues to the southward, the Cape of St. Agostinho; a nearer view discovered to us the town of St. Antonio do Recife, almost a-head with the shipping in front of it; the dreary land between it and Olinda, which is one league distant, and cocoa groves northward, as far as the eye can reach; southward of the town are also seen great numbers of coco trees, woods, and scattered cottages. The situation of Olinda is the highest in the neighborhood; and though not very high, is still not despicable. Its appearance from the sea is most delightful; its white-washed churches and convents upon the tops and sides of the hill; its gardens and trees, interspersed amongst the houses, afford a promise of great extent, and hold out expectations of great beauty.

- *Olinda city on hill white beauty=On hill white fortress of linden tree*
- *No need to retain extra info*

The sands, which extend one league to the southward of it, are relieved by two fortresses erected upon them, and by the ships in the lower harbor. Then follows the town of Recife, with the appearance of being built in the water, so low is the sand-bank upon which it has been raised; the shipping immediately in front partly conceal it; and the bold reef of rocks on the outside of these, with the surf dashing violently against and over it, give to them the appearance of being ashore; and as no outlet is seen, they seem to be hemmed in. The small tower or fort at the northern end of the reef, however, soon claims attention, and points out the entrance. We approached the land rather to the southward of the town, and coasted, under very easy sail, at a short distance from the reef, waiting for a pilot. It was not yet noon, the sea was smooth, the sun was bright, and everything looked pleasant. The buildings are all white-washed; the sun shone upon them, and gave to them a glittering silvery appearance.

- *Wait on white coast for a pilot through hidden reef = Hidden white reef*
- *Olinda city on hill white beauty=On hill white fortress of linden tree*
- *Occasionally details migrate from some objects to some other objects. Usually I just leave them there: it is hard to remove them and low danger from keeping wrong detail.*

Nothing this day created so much astonishment on board our ship, amongst those who had not been before upon this coast, as the Jangadas, sailing about in all directions. These are simply rafts of six logs, of a peculiar species of light timber, lashed or pinned together; a large latine sail; a paddle used as a rudder; a sliding keel let down between the two centre logs; a seat for the steersman, and a long forked pole, upon which is hung the vessel containing water, the provisions, &c. These rude floats have a most singular appearance at sea, no hull being apparent even when near them. They are usually managed by two men, and go closer to the wind than any description of vessel.

- *Jangada 6 log 2 men crude vessel for provision = Young Ada is raft of 6 logs with 2 men and a crate.*
- *Special detail: no wind fear = magic sail*

You are the one to choose your reading strategy. I would probably skip the text here and maybe reread it after I get the taste of the adventure to come. Ask yourself:

- What details you need and what details you can skip?

- Do you need at all to read something like the text above, or just skim it?
- Why did the author put all these infinite details into the text?
- Should you read the text slow and painstakingly visualize each and every detail?

## Example 3

Modernity was a reaction against the inadequacies of traditional worldviews. The modernists contended that all the traditional ways of understanding the world and society have become obsolete and there was an urgent need to come up with new moral, philosophical, cultural or political principles to understand and deal with the changing world. The (re)emerging idea of reason had provided them the hope for building a new world on universally objective foundations.

- *Traditional worldview inadequacies = eunuchs*
- *Modernists =enlightenment*
- *=Benjamin Franklin beats eunuchs to improve world*

The postmodernists in turn have argued that these modern attempts to reinvent humanity are insufficient and futile. They have contended that reinventing new and absolute principles amount to newer forms of authoritarianism and have concluded that all such hopes are false. In this context the postmodernists have urged the abandoning of all metanarratives that are foundational principles. This they thought would expose the infinite field of differences within humanity. The idea of constitutive otherness is derived from this insight. Through their critical approaches, the postmodernists have attempted at exposing the mistakes of modernity and have declared that modernity has come to an end.

- *Postmodernists = Nabokov, author of Lolita. I have specific marker for him*
- *Hope to reinvent humanity futile = Nabokov thinks Franklin glasses are stupid*

- *People are different, no single foundation, modernity was mistake that ended = Franklin stood on quicksand and drowned*
- *I do not use the word metanarrative, which is "narrative about narratives of historical meaning, experience or knowledge, which offers a society legitimation through the anticipated completion of a (as yet unrealized) master idea." = a story about stories of Utopia. Since this whole article is about it, by the end of the article you will have your own marker specifically for metanarratives*

The two most important features of postmodernity are their opposition to the idea of progress and their rejection of metanarratives. By opposing the idea of progress they have questioned the modernists' conviction that reason and science would lead to progress. Based on this optimism all the socalled modern institutions aim at this rational ideal. The idea of universal rationality itself is a meta-narrative and modernity has many such metanarratives which consume different local narratives. For instance, with its notion of universal rationality, modernity has its idea of human welfare, which it blindly applies to all possible situations and all human communities. In this process it neglects the ideas of welfare nourished by different societies and communities in relation with their local surroundings. It thus pretends to send out a universal message and often forcefully suppresses or consumes the local narratives.

- *Postmodernists reject progress, universe is irrational = Nabokov throws trains into blue circle with letter "i"*
- *(Blue circle with letter i means irrational universe, progress= train)*
- *(Welfare) What is good for one person is not the same as another = A person standing on feet hand in hand with a person standing on head*

- *I actually have a dedicated icon/marker for this idea as a whole, since it repeats itself*

By advocating the idea of a concept of universal knowledge, the modern West committed a major mistake. It contended that such a notion of value-neutral, objective knowledge could be discovered by the human mind and the modern West did possess it. Correspondingly, it had assumed the possibility of a disinterested knower who possessed such knowledge. It also believed that the entire humanity was benefited by this knowledge. The postmodernists assert that this supposition is a myth. They thus proclaim that modernity has ended.

- *Universal knowledge is a mistake of modern West, there is no such knower, and the knowledge will not help humanity and now it ended. = Condescending know-it-all Franklin made mistakes, knew little and put the world in danger, and now is dead*

In one sense, ruptures were already present in the Enlightenment concept of rational modern society. Kant's rational project had exposed the fragmentation of the modern society and self into three different and autonomous domains of reason; pure, practical and aesthetic rationalities. Kant had attempted to reunite this with aesthetics, but the problem of fragmentation persisted. This has been recognized as a problem of the Enlightenment project in general; the central unity underlying all aspects of human experiences Versus. fragmentation of the self and of society. Hegelian idealism and many other philosophies of modernity tried to find a solution to this problem, but had failed to achieve complete success. In Nietzsche's writings we find an ultimate proclamation of this fragmented society that was devoid of any universal sacred values and meanings. Nietzsche's Zarathustra preaches the death of God and the coming of the Superhuman.

- *Here it gets hard.*

- *When I read texts I often use "dictionaries" I previously built and then create one complex scene. The whole scene is one marker in some sense.*
- *Dictionary I made when learning philosophy:*
  - *Enlightenment = shining book*
  - *Kant = pure brain*
  - *Nietzsche = superhuman god killer*
  - *Hegel = synthesis*
- *Scene (6 objects < 7 objects limit):*
- *Ruptured shining book - pure brain broken in three parts - trying tie the brain parts together - shining book ruptures more - book synthesis attempt failed - superhuman god killer proclaims the book is dead*

## Example 4

The city of Colon is divided into two quarters—the native, or Panamanian, and the American. The former is picturesque, but has nothing to do with the Canal and is some distance from it. The Canal cannot be seen from the city. The American quarter, in which the Canal employees live, stands on the sea shore, and is made up of bungalows, shops, hotels, hospitals—all that goes to make up a city—save saloons. All are built of wood, painted white, and completely screened with wire gauze, rusted black by the dampness, a protection from mosquitoes and other beasts, bugs and vermin. Raised on concrete supports mostly with long, gently sloping roofs, and buried in a forest of palms, the town, the first the visitor will see, seems absolutely Japanese, is very pictorial and full of character. The design, I believe, of the houses was made by the American engineers or architects.

- *Panama canal city of Colon = two Americas canal in the middle with a column*
- *= Wood American Colon, Wild West city on concrete columns protected from mosquitos by black paint*

Very few of the higher Canal officers live at Colon, which is the Atlantic seaport of the Isthmus, the eastern mouth of the Canal, though Colon is west of Panama—such is the geography of the country. The mouth of the Canal will be fortified; breakwaters and lighthouses are being built.

For authorities on fortification it may be interesting to state that the forts will be so situated that the locks will be completely out of range of an enemy's guns. Personally I am not a believer in wars or navies. If my theories were practised there would be no need for fortifications.

- *Canal fortifications safe from guns*
- *Author pacifist*

Near Mount Hope, which—for the French—should be called the Slough of Despond, or the Lake of Despair, is a huge swamp about a mile or so from Colon, on the left bank of the French Canal, seen on the right of the lithograph. This swamp is now filled with all sorts of abandoned French machinery. Dredges, locomotives, and even what seem to be lock gates, show amid the palms in the distance. Huge American cranes for raising this French material—which the American engineers have made use of—and discharging cargo from the ships in the French Canal—which is here finished and in use—loom over the swamp, the banks of which are lined with piers and workshops full of life—a curious contrast to the dead swamp in which not a mosquito lives, nor a smell breathes.

- *American mountain of hope is a french lake of despair*
- *Swam filled with french machinery American cranes attached above the swamp*
- *Swamp banks with dead mosquitos and workshops*

Between Mount Hope and Gatun is much more of the swamp and much more abandoned machinery, but the Canal is not to be seen from the railroad, or any evidence of it, till the train stops at the station of Old Gatun, with its workmen's dwellings crowning the hillside. I regret I made no drawing of these, so picturesquely perched. At the station of Gatun—the first time I stopped—I saw the work- men—in decorative fashion—coming to the surface for dinner. The lithograph was made from a temporary bridge spanning the locks and looking toward Colon. The great machines on each side of the locks are for mixing and carrying to their place, in huge buckets, the cement and concrete, of which the locks are built. The French Canal is in the extreme distance, now used by our engineers.

- *Gatun (=get on) on hill above swamp, workmen dwelling with train station and huge cement buckets*

There is a flight of three double locks at Gatun by which ships will be raised eighty-five feet to the level of Gatun Lake. From the gates of the upper lock—the nearest to the Pacific—they will sail across the now-forming lake some miles (about twenty, I believe) to the Culebra Cut; through this, nine miles long, they will pass, and then descend by three other flights of locks, at Pedro Miguel and Miraflores, to the Pacific, which is twenty feet higher, I believe, than the Atlantic.

- *=Ship elevator (3x2-lock) 85 feet at get-on hill*

*more details skipped*

This is a typical text. It makes no sense to retain 100% on the first read: that would take forever. You keep some, lose somc (if you read extremely fast), and if you lost too much, you reread later.

# PART 7: ANALYSIS AND CRITICAL THINKING

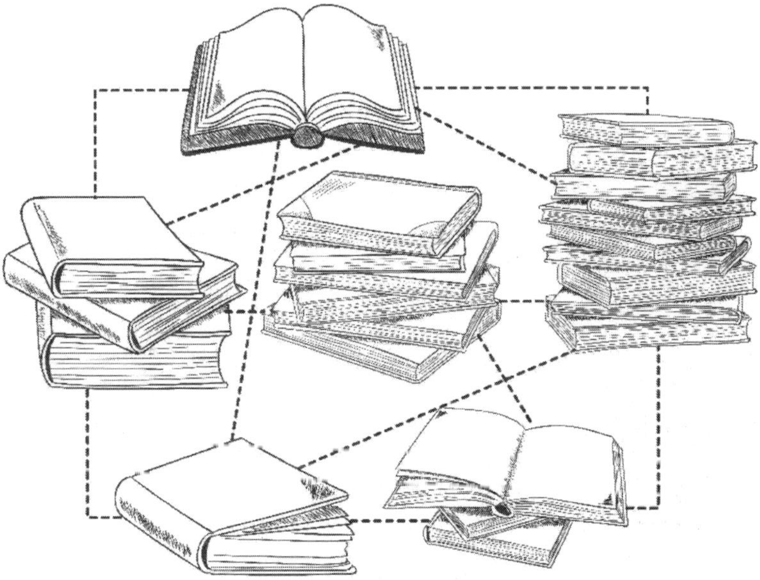

# Chapter 37: Simplifying Texts

Suppose we finished reading the text and realize we missed something very important. In the beginning, this happens very often, and we simply reread the text (paragraph or section, not individual words or lines) until we remember all the facts. With practice, we make fewer mistakes, and we can fill in the gaps by simply rescanning the text with our eyes, looking specifically for the details that we missed (names, dates, etc.). Occasionally we encounter texts that are just too complex to handle. What do we do? We simplify the texts!

Occasionally texts or paragraphs are just too dense or too complex to be understood as written, and then we need to analyze them for our convenience. See the Further Research below for an example of metrics for text complexity.

## Rewording

Some texts contain long and complex words, including words we do not fully understand. In this scenario, we can use online services like Rewordify Tool to simplify the content. This is especially useful for those of us for whom English is a second language.

I decided to test the tool on some obscure text written by David Robinson:

(http://works.bepress.com/david_robinson/16/)

***Original Text:***

*Under circumstances of intense competition and the need for expediency, conflicting priorities arise and the entrepreneur may be faced with certain dilemmas. It may even be that entrepreneurial managers may sometimes inadvertently overlook the ethical elements of business decisions, or worse still, choose to ignore them. Recognizing a business ethical dilemma requires a certain basic awareness of ethics. Dealing confidently with a dilemma requires far more, namely the assurance that one is able to concisely define the dilemma and then resolve it appropriately and amicably. In seeking to do so, entrepreneurs must usually rely on their own judgment to determine an appropriate outcome for all concerned.*

***Using Wordify text the original text became something simpler:***

*Under facts or conditions that surround intense competition and the need for advantage, disagreeing (things that are the most important) arise and the small business starter may be faced with certain two-headed problems. It may even be that creative (with business) managers may sometimes accidentally and carelessly (ignore/not notice) the (honest and right) elements of business decisions, or worse still, choose to ignore them. Recognizing a business (honest and right) two-headed problem needs/demands a certain basic knowledge of (related to the rules and beliefs of doing the right thing). Dealing (in a way where you're sure you're right) with a two-headed problem needs/demands far more, namely the promise that one can (well-said in a short way) define the two-headed problem and then resolve it appropriately and in a friendly way. In trying to do so, small business starters must usually depend on their own judgment to decide/figure out the right/the proper result for all concerned.*

Now I confess I prefer the original text, but I understand why the second text is significantly simpler. It is like using a dictionary for every complex word in the text.

## Generating Shorter Sentences

Long sentences are a sign of poor writing, yet many authors use very long sentences. We need to break them down. How? We use Text Compactor or TLDR Chrome plugin (links below). Alternatively, try to put stops/periods in for the author and reread shorter sentences.

In code, or in math, a similar result is achieved by adding parentheses or giving a special symbol for a repeating formula.

## Analysis Of Text Structure

I ask myself, "What I would write here if I were the author?" Then I compare the result with the text on the page, try to find differences and repeat until I am happy with the results. In some universities, there are courses on expository text structure. The text can be broken into smaller parts by reviewing the role that the author intended for the text.

## Skipping And Rereading

Occasionally it is best just to skip the text, and read the following text, the graphs or the tables within the document. These may provide enough information to understand the text when rereading.

In rare cases, the explanatory data is within the references of the original article, which may result in a chain reaction until we get to the fundamental articles. The fundamental articles are usually well-written, and can be understood as-is.

## For Further Research:

**Text Complexity:**

http://www.ascd.org/ASCD/pdf/journals/ed_lead/el201306_Fisher-Frey-Rubric.pdf

**Rewordify Tool**

https://rewordify.com/

**Text Compactor:**

http://textcompactor.com/

https://chrome.google.com/webstore/detail/tldr/giepilabiomhlcmlefmbfkgeoccfhhhc

**Expository Text Structure:**

http://www.readingrockets.org/article/how-teach-expository-text-structure-facilitate-reading-comprehension

# Chapter 38: Support Your Details

After reading a paragraph or a section, we pause to analyze what we just read. The first thing we need to understand is what part of what we read was actually there and what part we added by mistake.

## The Four Stages Of Competence

1. **Unconscious incompetence:** The individual does not understand or know how to do something and does not necessarily recognize the deficit. They may deny the usefulness of the skill. The individual must recognize their incompetence, and the value of the new skill, before moving on to the next stage. The length of time an individual spends in this stage depends on the strength of the stimulus to learn.

2. **Conscious incompetence:** Though the individual does not understand or know how to do something, he or she does recognize the deficit, as well as the value of a new skill in addressing the deficit. The making of mistakes can be integral to the learning process at this stage.

3. **Conscious competence:** The individual understands or knows how to do something. However, demonstrating the skill or knowledge requires concentration. It may be broken down into steps, and there is heavy conscious involvement in executing the new skill.

4. **Unconscious competence:** The individual has had so much practice with a skill it has become "second nature" and they perform the skill easily. As a result, the skill can be performed while executing another task. The individual may be able to teach it to others, depending upon how and when it was learned.

## Knowledge And Its Support

Taking things that you know for granted is a common mistake. Taking things for granted is a mistake that I make even now, after many years of training. Instead, you should ask questions and verify the facts.

- What facts support our knowledge?
- What resources do we use?
- Who are the authority figures behind the current paradigm?
- What was the previous paradigm?

Probably nothing is truly known. We have some very good understanding of what is most likely to happen and why it happens. Then we learn that it is a part of a much larger and partially unpredictable pattern or erroneous paradigm. We are outraged and insecure. We point out how and where we learned what we know and prove our control of the knowledge. Right?

Well, almost. It takes a lot of effort to learn the "support" of every link: where and when we learned it.

- When we learn cognitive psychology or similar experimental science, we are taught to remember the experiments that build up the body of knowledge.
- In mathematics and similar theoretical sciences, we need to remember the first people or article that came out with proof.
- However, if we read a book, it is very hard to find the actual support for every paragraph within the book. The best we can do is remember the relevant chapters of the book and remember what we read there.
- The information we learn in blogs, TV or other mass media the situation is even worse. We cannot afford to trust them and we cannot afford to check everything they write, so there is a limit to how much we can trust them, and reference them.
- Finally, there are our friends that have no doubt they know everything and much better than the obscure bloggers, yet they refuse to tell their sources and

> request total trust. All I can say here is choose your friends and your enemies wisely, and try to cross-reference their comments.

I am not telling you anything new, yet you would probably be surprised if I asked you to remember for each link between visual markers the support (the source of this knowledge) of this particular link. Arguably, this doubles the amount of information we need to learn. Moreover, since the "support" is based on names of obscure people, we will need to spend extra time to learn about these people.

Believe me; I hate this part of our training even more than you do. However, the evidence that supports this approach is piling up. I have been working with several highly effective professionals who drive their power from knowing "who is who" in their area of expertise and spending a significant amount of time to learn better the main characters. Moreover, when I ask these people how they know what they know, I am immediately referenced to the proper articles, which are remembered very well. This memory is very specific, yet these same professionals cannot find their keys and forget their wives' birthdays. The people who find it important for their career to learn the support for their knowledge consistently reach a very high degree of professional success.

I started to doubt retroactively everything I know. For each piece of knowledge, I ask myself, "Okay, where have you learned it?" To my amazement most of the time the sources are highly unreliable: I cannot find the proper articles and books. I can remember holding the book in my hand, and what I was wearing when reading it, yet I cannot find the book on the Internet. This is another point: what you cannot find in Google is usually hidden and unavailable for further references.

Socrates allegedly said, "I know that I know nothing." Unless we make the extra effort to remember the support of our knowledge, we may easily find ourselves in a very similar situation. For all practical uses, justified true belief is knowledge, so make sure to have proper justifications.

## Clear Thinking

How analytical and rational is my thinking? Only one way to find out: get tested!

I discovered a clear thinking site entirely by mistake, and I was shocked by the quality of personality traits testing. Within very few and very accurate questions, the computer can pinpoint strengths and weaknesses of your thinking. The site loads slowly, but once everything loads the test is lots of fun. Once you discover your personal strengths and weaknesses, try to train the skills advised as well as run further tests from the main page. Make sure to invest time, since these tests are challenging.

## Constructive Thinking

If you possessed all the knowledge in the world, that knowledge will not help you if you sabotage your success. A Psychology Today article, *Build Your EQ With These 7 Constructive Thinking Tools* (link below), suggests a simple set of questions to check your ability to cope with challenges.

~~~~~

When something unfortunate happens to me, it reminds me of all the other things wrong in my life, which adds to my unhappiness.

**Destructive thinking:** You will damage your chances of success. You allow some negative event to influence you in a way that prevents further adequate coping with challenges. A possible way to deal with this is accepting that some things simply happen and move on. This is very simple if you do not have destructive thinking, but very hard if you do.

~~~~~

**Personal superstition:** I have found that talking about future successes can keep them from happening. This is a personal superstition, which is not necessarily the same as common superstitions (such as black cats bring bad luck). It is usually easy to avoid such pitfalls, but if you are not careful, your dark prophecies may be self-fulfilling. If you find enough counter-examples from your life, the superstitions will no longer have a hold on you.

~~~~~

If I were to succeed this once, I would feel very good and always succeed in the future.

**Naïve optimism:** The tendency to overgeneralize in a positive way from one good event to all related events in general. While we tend to love positive thinking, it is important to understand the risks when you take them. Even the most successful people fail occasionally, and if you cannot accept the possibility of failure, you may be devastated when you eventually fail.

~~~~~

When I am faced with a difficult task, I think encouraging thoughts that help me to do my best.

**Behavioral coping** or what we also call "problem-focused." This item taps your ability to get yourself through the tough times by concentrating on what needs to be done, building your feelings of self-confidence to give you a boost. With this mindset, you may jump too fast into action, and you may take the first available approach, rather than searching for additional information.

~~~~~

I believe if I think bad thoughts about someone that person will suffer.

**Esoteric thinking** or the belief that you can magically influence outcomes. Esoteric may prevent you from seeing things clearly and coping with situations properly, it may cause you to invest in dubious schemes and take unjustified risks.

~~~~~

I think there are many wrong ways, but only one right way, to do almost anything.

**Categorical thinking** in which you view everything in black and white terms. Typically, moderate positions work better than the extreme ones. If this quality defines you, you may have trouble adapting to compromises and acting as a responsible adult.

~~~~~

I think about how I will deal with threatening events ahead of time, but I don't worry needlessly.

**Emotional coping** or the ability to calm yourself down by helping yourself to feel better. If you're strong in this area, you've figured out ways to avoid worrying and instead to focus on the positive. By seeing situations as challenging rather than fear provoking, you'll be able to conquer them more effectively.

~~~~~

People with categorical thinking and esoteric thinking tend to adapt better in high uncertainty situations and project calmness when the situation is murky, but may fail in moderate situations and generate an unnecessary crisis. People with higher behavioral and emotional coping skills can better handle unavoidable failures and generate success. If you are high on self-destructions, superstitions or naive optimism, you may consider changing your approach or seek a personal coach/therapist.

Success and failure, crisis and boredom follow each other. A person who adapts quickly to any situation will benefit in any environment. These coping skills may be learned.

## For Further Research:

**Socrates:**

http://en.wikipedia.org/wiki/I_know_that_I_know_nothing

**Justified True Belief:**

http://en.wikipedia.org/wiki/Gettier_problem

**Clear Thinking**

http://www.clearerthinking.org/

http://programs.clearerthinking.org/how_rational_are_you_really_take_the_test.html

## Constructive Thinking

https://www.psychologytoday.com/blog/fulfillment-any-age/201506/build-your-eq-these-7-constructive-thinking-tools

# Chapter 39: Flow Up Or Slow Down

When optimizing reading speed versus the chance of rereading, we need to consider not only our retention but also our ability to focus on what we read. Occasionally we would prefer to slow down, but in other cases, we would prefer to raise the difficulty level and reread as required. We will do that to get into "flow."

To enjoy work and learning, to enjoy life itself, I rely heavily on something called "flow." The feeling is very pleasant, invigorating and positive. Here is the definition of "flow" from Wikipedia:

> *Flow is the mental state of operation in which a person performing an activity is fully immersed in a feeling of energized focus, full involvement, and enjoyment in the process of the activity. In essence, flow is characterized by complete absorption in what one does. Proposed by Mihály Csíkszentmihályi, this positive psychology concept has been widely referenced across a variety of fields. According to Csikszentmihalyi, flow is completely focused motivation. It is a single-minded immersion and represents perhaps the ultimate experience in harnessing the emotions in the service of performing and learning. In flow, the emotions are not just contained and channeled, but positive, energized, and aligned with the task at hand. The hallmark of flow is a feeling of spontaneous joy, even rapture, while performing a task although flow is also described as a deep focus on nothing but the activity – not even oneself or one's emotions.*

It is commonly accepted that one of the ways to reach "flow" is by having a perfect match between the personal skill and the task. Most people simply cannot generate this "perfect match" most of the time, so it remains a domain of artists, sportsmen, and monks.

Since I became a "SuperLearner," I noticed that I seldom get bored and often get deeply and emotionally involved in my work. Why does this happen? Well, previously in 90% of my work I was overqualified for what I was doing. When the job gets boring, we get relaxed and the brain partially "shuts down" into an autopilot mode. Simply speeding up the simple parts generates enough load on the brain to disable this shutdown mechanism. If anything, the brain becomes overly active and free to enter the "flow" state.

**Notice for SuperLearners:**

***Do use short breaks to rest every time you have a chance or you may get a serious headache.***

The next step is activating measurable goals (read the articles, write the post/code/presentation, generate an idea) and use creativity (visualization, associations, etc.) to achieve the goal. Fortunately, this is exactly something the SuperLearner does!

Being a SuperLearner is only a part of the package. We have a full set of tricks to speed up everyday tasks, computer usage, mobile usage, and generate a meaningful communication. We speed up all activities to the point that they stop being boring and generate the "flow"!

Being a SuperLearner not only allows you to generate funny water-cooler discussions or the ability to find the perfect job, but it also enables deep satisfaction from work and everyday life.

## For Further Research:

### Flow:

http://en.wikipedia.org/wiki/Flow_(psychology)

http://en.wikipedia.org/wiki/Mental_state

http://en.wikipedia.org/wiki/Mihaly_Csikszentmihalyi

http://en.wikipedia.org/wiki/Positive_psychology

http://en.wikipedia.org/wiki/Motivation

http://en.wikipedia.org/wiki/Critical_thinking

http://en.wikipedia.org/wiki/Attention

http://en.wikipedia.org/wiki/Emotion

http://en.wikipedia.org/wiki/Learning
http://en.wikipedia.org/wiki/Happiness

# Chapter 40: Generate Understanding

An interesting tool to explain the difference between retention and comprehension is Bloom's taxonomy of cognitive levels. While there is controversy related to the validity of the taxonomy, and which variation of the taxonomy is correct, I will use it below as a visualization tool.

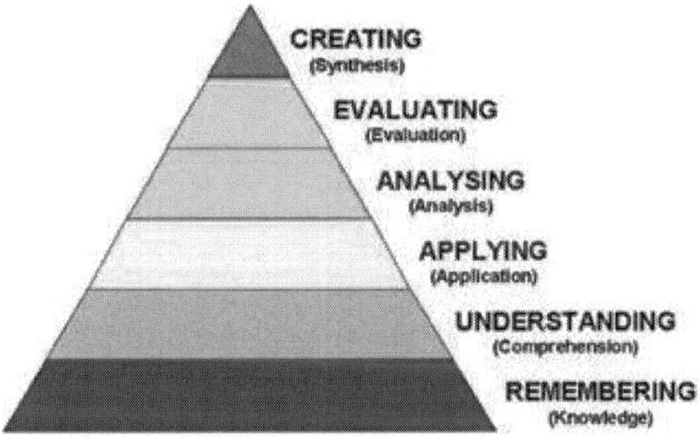


For a more detailed explanation of each step, see Further Research below.

As you can see, there are several cognitive processes associated with learning that are different from each other.

If a person can memorize something, this means that the person can recreate and identify the piece of the knowledge memorized. However, additional levels of cognitive processing are required to manipulate the knowledge:

- Interpret it in another context,
- Apply it when facing new challenges,
- Compare it with other concepts,
- Modify it into new contexts,
- Judge its effects.

To do all of these operations we need to be able to divide the idea into its components and understand how the components connect with each other. Additionally, we need to connect the whole idea and the relevant components to other ideas we have acquired.

For example, you are about to learn a formula. A simple way to do it is use the Major Method memorization technique. Memorize all the letters and math symbols in the formula. Then each time we need to recreate the formula, it is readily there.

Does it mean we will be able to use the formula to solve a physics exam or to build a functioning mechanism? No, probably not, and if someone changes the notation, we will be at a loss because we can only recreate the memorized formula.

We probably need some other way to remember formulas. To do that we can divide the formula into elements and understand how each element influences the result. Alternatively, we can try to understand how to derive the formula. Then, we will be able to modify the formula when the underlying assumptions no longer hold.

Another example is definitions. Students often learn definitions word by word. Then somebody changes the underlying assumptions or provides a different definition. Is this different definition right or is it wrong? It is better if the student can derive the definition in the first place or understand the effect of each phrase within the definition. Then, it is easier to find similarities and contradictions in the alternative definition.

You can read an article, remember it word for word and not learn anything useful. You can read an article, learn something useful that you will utilize every day, but then forget where you read it and the name of the article.

Proper learning experience assumes that comprehension and retention are present together all the time; otherwise, how are we going to build additional layers of knowledge on top of that?

After saying what I just said, you would expect me to present a mind-blowing toolset that will solve all the problems. It is very easy to improve both (see Further Research below). However, there is not very much I can currently offer to speed up higher cognitive functions. They will take time. At some point, reading may become slow again. Not because you are doing easy reading or trying to remember. You will be busy trying to solve higher-level questions: how to derive argumentation, analyze assumptions and results, modify and apply the solution to existing challenges.

## SuperLearner Value Pyramid

I am a bit obsessed about various forms of information and knowledge. Therefore, I have included this short value pyramid:

| TYPE | MEANING | SUPERLEARNER TERM |
|---|---|---|
| Wisdom | Ability to use understanding properly to change the world around us | SuperLearner mission |
| Understanding | Knowledge and its impact on people and universe | Colored or multi-sensory content visualization |
| Knowledge | Different forms of information plus connections and associations between them | Interconnected chunks of markers |
| Information | Structured data containing meaningful insight | Visual markers |
| Data | Basic input from sensory or processing units | Details |

## Encoding Understanding In Visual Markers

Now the main difference between knowledge and understanding is the impact of knowledge on people and the universe. What does this mean in our SuperLearner context?

**First**, in prereading, an interest in the text is generated, and we set the tone for the content.

- In the high-level visualization methods, we set up the theme and mood of the visual markers.
- In hyperlinking, we set up the color of the stylized marks.
- In high-level chunking, we prepare the basic knowledge trees and color them.

**Second**, when we read each paragraph, we can modify the color of the markers used to encode the specific paragraph or line. We may also infuse a set of markers with emotional or multisensory input (smell, touch, taste). Please do not overdo with emotions – you do not want to get vivid dreaming or other psychedelic side effects.

**Finally**, when generating and linking markers you can choose a type of dynamics: is it serious or funny, big or small, dramatic or subtle, happy or sad. At the end of each paragraph, you may pause to think. When you encode the markers of the text, you may want to add some markers of your understanding: how and where you can use this knowledge, whom can it help or alarm.

When mastering the SuperLearning skills it is very easy to become extremely technical. Your imagination can stand up for almost any challenge. The emphatic understanding usually comes later on, when you try to manipulate your knowledge base. However, if you do not want to become a mission-oriented robot, why wait?

## Mental Models

Mental models are very useful for problem solving. Put simply, mental models are the set of tools that you use to think. Each mental model offers a different framework that you can use to look at life (or at an individual problem). Consider a toolbox: for every task there is a tool best suited for the job, the more tools you have, the higher chance of having the right tool for the job.

Mental models are very simple ideas of how things work. Those very simple ideas can be easily transferred from one domain of knowledge to another. Typically, mental models do not have units (golden cut, Pareto principle, law of large numbers, uncertainty principle, and survival of the fittest).

The original ideas may appear in math, economics, statistics, physics, biology or any other subject. However, once we learn to understand them, we can transport them from one subject to another. Much more than a specific statement, a **mental model is a perspective, a way to see things**.

When we read A LOT, we ask many questions. We change perspectives to find from the text as much as we can. We use memorization to remember facts. However, if we are not careful when we read, we will lose the most elusive prey of all – new mental models. Serendipity is about preparing your mind for unexpected situations. When we encounter a mental model, we see the following traits:

1. Something that is presented in one context, but we can easily use in another context.
2. An idea appears as both genius simple and somewhat counterintuitive.
3. While the explanation is very simple, the proof is often very hard.
4. The more we think, "How else can we use it," the more different uses we find.
5. If you think, "This sounds absurd, and yet I believe it," this can be a new mental model.

More often than not mental models we find are faulty. The aesthetic beauty of mental models is such that people often tend to publish it without checking the facts. We can use these myths as ways to find our fallacies when we apply the same thinking patterns repeatedly.

Creative problem solving often includes using mental models of one domain of knowledge with problems of other domains of knowledge. It may be very useful to read books and articles not only in your area of expertise but also in many others. Nobody can guess when such mental models will become useful, but it is always better to be prepared.

## For Further Research:

### Bloom's Taxonomy

http://en.wikipedia.org/wiki/Bloom%27s_taxonomy

http://tep.uoregon.edu/resources/assessment/multiplechoicequestions/blooms.html

**Comprehension and Retention:**

https://joshkaufman.net/3-simple-techniques-to-optimize-your-reading-comprehension-and-retention/

http://www.slu.edu/x32711.xml

**Knowledge vs. Understanding:**

http://lifehacker.com/the-difference-between-knowledge-and-understanding-is-e-1624463050

**Knowledge vs. Information:**

http://www.KeyToStudy.com/knowledge-vs-information/

**Mental Models**

http://lifehacker.com/mental-models-solve-problems-by-approaching-them-from-1682835620

http://jamesclear.com/feynman-mental-models

# Chapter 41: Linking Back To Your Knowledge

## Retention Versus Analysis

When we measure retention, we measure the amount of details we remember after reading an article. This great article "*4 Strategies For Remembering Everything You Learn*" (link below) explains some strategies to learn from an article. Usually learning from what we read is the subject of an advanced course, but I think it makes sense to put some of the related materials at the disposal of even beginning students.

At least some of us some of the time do not read to remember, but instead read to learn new things. Knowledge is fundamentally different from information.

***Knowledge is not about the markers you have, but about the links you make between markers.***

Over time, and in the end, the links between the markers are more important than the markers themselves. Try to put several links per marker using various details of the marker as key points for the links.

Very few articles are like stand-alone puzzles. Articles are self-contained and self-interlocked. Most of the articles we read do connect to our prior knowledge. In Kabbala, there is a saying that "only God creates something from nothing." All of us create something based on something else, and these connections should be reflected in what we link.

It is very easy to miss something important. I do it as often as any other person does. I am, however, more aware of this trait, so I am less confident in the information. I check the information by comparing it with other resources, trying to find the innovation introduced by the specific article I read, the point of view of the authors, etc. Even then, I often miss details, and if the article is important for me, I make others read it and compare impressions. I have many friends with partially intersecting interests.

If I can use the article in real life, as a part of conversations, or a call for action, or something to think about when I take my Pomodoro break, I do that. It is important to reflect about everything we learn. Reflection generates new links and allows us to view the subject in a different perspective. I contemplate on new and original perspectives to view the subject, and occasionally I discover things. If I discover something that makes me interested, I write it down. The simple process of writing something down improves retention. Do be selective about what you write down since it is a relatively slow process (below 80 wpm). This study in the Business Insider (*This 15-Minute Activity Will Make You More Successful At Work*, link below) shows that writing daily reflections on the day for 15 minutes has a huge effect on personal productivity. I plan to introduce such a ritual into my life. I just need to find the proper occasion.

## Knowledge Is About Building Connections

- Do not take anything for granted.
- Reflect constantly on every new piece of information.
- Reflect on how the new information connects with what you already know.

## Wallis' Model Of The Creative Process

Researcher Graham Wallis, many years ago, set down a description of what happens as people approach problems with the objective of coming up with creative solutions. He described his four-stage process as follows:

1. In the **preparation** stage, we define the problem, need, or desire, and gather any information the solution or response needs to account for, and set up criteria for verifying the solution's acceptability.
2. In the **incubation** stage, we step back from the problem and let our minds contemplate and work it through. Like preparation, incubation can last minutes, weeks, or even years.
3. In the **illumination** stage, ideas arise from the mind to provide the basis of a creative response. These ideas can be pieces of the whole or the whole itself, i.e., seeing the entire concept or entity all at once. Unlike the other stages, illumination is often very brief,

involving a tremendous rush of insights within a few minutes or hours.

4. In **verification**, the final stage, one carries out activities to demonstrate whether what emerged in illumination satisfies the need and the criteria defined in the preparation stage.

## How Many Repetitions For Long-Term Retention

If you understand very well what you are reading, you may spare yourself from repeatedly reading and memorizing. However, if you cannot generate very good markers, or if you learn something as hard as a foreign language, you will be forced to repeat what you learn.

Long ago, I was told seven repetitions make us remember almost anything. However, now, I am ready to add some science to it. I follow the logic of Wikipedia's article on Spaced Repetition.

Our neurons are hard-wired to forget something with roughly exponential speed. We can fight this phenomenon via various techniques.

Most of our techniques work simply because neurons work as groups, and any new knowledge is supported by other neurons within the group. We trick the brain to include new pieces of knowledge with older and established knowledge and ensure we will not forget anything important. Eventually, we are left only with things that simply cannot be connected to the established neural groups: numbers, new words, names, and/or completely new areas of knowledge. Then we need to activate spaced repetition approach.

We can try to check what we forget and learn it again and again until we succeed. The Leitner system is labor intensive and involves checking the recall again and again. If we fail, we will check it more often; however if we succeed, we will need to check it much less often until we do not need to check anymore. In this approach, the frequency of repetition is governed by the amount of new data we need to learn. Computers make the job easy (using Anki or equivalent). All we need to do is create the cards with the pieces of knowledge we need to retain.

Alternatively, we may assume all the pieces of knowledge are equally complex, like words of a new language. Then we can calculate and time the next recall. In his work, Pimsleur used 5 seconds, 25 seconds, 2 minutes, 10 minutes, 1 hour, 5 hours, 1 day, 5 days, 25 days, 4 months, and 2 years.

This is slightly more than the rule of seven, but the effect of each following repetition is reduced. Please notice the words need to be presented in random order for the method to work.

At this point, I will refer to the Ebbinghaus study of the learning and forgetting curves:

> *"In 1885 Ebbinghaus published his groundbreaking Über das Gedächtnis ("On Memory," later translated to English as Memory. A Contribution to Experimental Psychology) in which he described experiments he conducted on himself to describe the processes of learning and forgetting. Ebbinghaus made several findings that are still relevant and supported to this day. First, arguably his most famous finding, the forgetting curve. The forgetting curve describes the exponential loss of information that one has learned. The sharpest decline occurs in the first twenty minutes and the decay is significant through the first hour. The curve levels off after about one day. The learning curve described by Ebbinghaus refers to how fast one learns information. The sharpest increase occurs after the first try and then gradually evens out, meaning that less and less new information is retained after each repetition. Like the forgetting curve, the learning curve is exponential. Ebbinghaus had also documented the serial position effect, which describes how the position of an item affects recall. The two main concepts in the serial position effect are recency and primacy. The recency effect describes the increased recall of the most recent information because it is still in the short-term memory. The primacy effect better memory of the first items in a list due to increased rehearsal and commitment to*

*long-term memory. Ebbinghaus also described the difference between involuntary and voluntary memory, the former occurring "with apparent spontaneity and without any act of the will" and the latter being brought "into consciousness by an exertion of the will."*

It is interesting to note, Ebbinghaus used to learn meaningless syllables, and he remembered the syllables that had meaning by mere chance much more than others. Moreover, even if he forgot something, he learned it easier the next time he had to re-learn it. Finally, he applied great effort to eliminate any dual coding or memorization techniques from his study to preserve statistical purity. You are not studying memory curves, so you should do just the opposite: add dual coding, add meaning and memorization techniques.

I will summarize the subject as follows:

1. If you learn simple facts in a familiar area, you may retain information without spaced repetition.
2. If you encode the information in many forms (associations, audio, image, the way the word looks), you may need few repetitions.
3. For a new language or other unstructured data, you may need seven repetitions or more with each repetition contributing less than previous.
4. If you do need spaced repetitions, it is best to use computer programs with flash cards.

## Linear And Lateral Learning

Some subjects, like basic math, should be learned in a linear form. You cannot understand complex concepts before you know simple concepts. You need to understand addition before you understand multiplication, and you need to know negative numbers before you learn complex numbers.

Other subjects, like history, can be learned laterally. You can study each area and time period almost independently of other areas and periods. Then, when you have generated enough knowledge, you can start building the intricate network of a "big history," or how some principles cross the borders of time and space.

Most subjects are in the middle. For example, in law and medicine, you learn the basic idea and then you dive into specific cases and their correspondences.

Whatever we study, quite often we understand that we do not understand what we are reading. Then we reread and still do not understand. Finally, we search the Internet and still find nothing. What we do next depends on the subject we are trying to learn. For example:

1. Try to understand better the basic theories and principles used to construct the text
2. Get more examples of similar articles to learn from them
3. Discard the article. Do we need it?
4. Generate thought experiments and simulations, try to see the text in action

By understanding better the nature of your subject, you balance correctly between lack of progress and generating dangerous gaps in understanding that may haunt you later on.

In this book, each milestone (visualization, memorization, speedreading) should be conquered before you move on, but not every exercise should be actually aced. So if you fail some exercise, try to look for a different way to reach the same goal.

## Long-Term Structures

The memory structures you use for long-term retention should be slightly different from short-term structures you create when reading, e.g., more lively but with fewer markers and details, using a somewhat different setting.

You should move markers from short-term storage to long-term storage at the end of each chapter/article. Alternatively, once you finish the whole book (group of articles), reread it and generate long-term structures for whatever you need to retain. This way you will have double coding of two structures describing the same content and a larger chance of remembering what you read.

## No Prior Knowledge

***AZ***

*I seem to have some issues with markers.*

*The problems are as follows:*

** sometimes there is no real background, which makes retention hard.*

** linking is weak at times.*

***Dr. Lev Goldentouch***

*How do you learn something that has no connection with your prior knowledge? This is a sign of bad strategy. You need to learn a basic subject before learning an advanced subject; otherwise, you may be wasting your valuable time, and every basic subject is fundamentally using your common sense. As long as you are older than 13 years old, you have a whole life of experiences to connect your new knowledge to...*

## Optical Illusions

Try to look at some optical illusions at least once a week. There is a lot we can learn from optical illusions about how visual memory works.

Take the following image:

http://www.moillusions.com/elephant-legs-optical-illusion/

Quite often, we start from one idea, and we end up with another idea. The brain plays tricks on us and uses our own association to connect the unconnected. By following the logic of the links from the beginning to the end, we should make sure that we are not jumping between different concepts. For example, use small keys like color tint or small scenery details and theme to ensure we do not jump between themes.

Take the age-old young versus old illusion

http://mathworld.wolfram.com/YoungGirl-OldWomanIllusion.html

From time to time, we remember the same mental landscape with one minor difference: we remember just the opposite of what we read. One of the ways to ensure this does not happen: having dual encoding of logical markers versus creative markers at top levels of reasoning (per chapter).

As a third example, consider

http://en.wikipedia.org/wiki/Grid_illusion

If we put too much structure in our memorization templates, we may start seeing objects that are not there anymore. Monistic or dualistic thinking is just an illusion. Typically, there is a very wide range of possibility. By forcing extra structure, we cause phantom ideas to appear.

## Paradigm Shift

What we think is correct, what we learned for a while, what we believe comes from truthful authorities - all this powerful knowledge is a paradigm. Typically, we act just fine using our paradigms. Occasionally we find out what we know is plain wrong. From time to time, paradigms shift, and we need to learn something entirely new.

Unlearning something is much harder than learning something new. Therefore, the first step is to discard the previous paradigm from the point where a shift happened. "This assumption is not true." Now, the paradigm shift needs to propagate all the way through your logical structures. Try to keep your memory palaces and mind maps well connected to allow the new paradigm to connect properly.

As the new realizations propagate through your visual associations, try to think of how the change may be used for your benefit. It is much better to accept change than to fight it.

Changing your paradigms is a long process. Do not rush it. If you are patient, eventually you will be rewarded for your learning either by new understandings or by more material success.

## Pomodoro Reminder

After reading for 15 minutes, try to rest for 5 minutes. Focus on far objects, breathe deeply, relax shoulders, see funny images, socialize or nap if you feel like it. Balancing focus and recreation, you will stay sharper for longer and be very effective.

It is equally important to balance serious approaches and fun. If you do too much fun, you lose focus and dose off. If you become too serious, the content will be too dull and exhausting. For example, you can use fun breaks and serious content or fun content and serious thoughts when resting.

Try not to mix themes when creating markers or your memory structure may become broken. Break or no break you do need to be consistent with markers.

## Preparing For The Next Chapter

Pause before you start the next chapter and clear your mind. Some people "stretch" their brain before reading. It is a good practice, but if you do not do some mental warm up nothing bad will happen. The worst-case scenario is you will reread the first section.

Personally, before starting a new chapter, I am planning "what if" or "this reminds me of" games to generate specific interest and "load" specific groups of associations from my memory.

## Socratic Method

Socrates used to debate better than most. His method was both simple and powerful. He would assert some idea, and then he would build a chain of corollaries by illuminating the idea from different angles until one of such corollaries would contradict the original idea.

The Socratic Method can be used to clarify meaning, feeling, and consequences, as well as to gradually unfold insight, or explore alternative actions. Take several positions about the text as you would take hats and try to see where the train of thought breaks and what causes it to break.

A passive position towards knowledge leads us eventually to latent knowledge, knowledge we cannot use. Taking an active stand, asking questions about what we learned, we gain a much better understanding of the subjects we learn, and we can use the resulting knowledge to achieve our goals.

## Thought Experiment

Einstein was a master of mental experimentation. Without leaving his living room, he could journey through the vastness of space and the minuteness of an atom by the power of his mind.

We ask ourselves in the most accurate and structured form possible "What would happen if..." and try to generate a new understanding. You can learn from many famous well-documented thought experiments, some predating Socrates. We use thought experiments when we see a contradiction to enable us to see both sides of the argument more clearly, simultaneously refute a prevailing theory, and establish a new theory through a process of mutual exclusion.

Sometimes we are left with mixed feelings (consider Schrodinger's cat who is dead or alive with some certainty) but often we see the assumptions and limitations of our understanding with all possible clarity.

Anna often asks, "Suppose you would meet the author of the article, what would you ask?" Asking yourself this question makes you wonder, and thus makes the mental structures generated by the text much more active and accurate.

## Ten Rules Of Good Studying

The following rules are excerpted from *A Mind for Numbers: How to Excel in Math and Science (Even if You Flunked Algebra)*, Barbara Oakley, Penguin, July, 2014
http://www.barbaraoakley.com/pdf/10rulesofstudying.pdf

**1. Use recall.** After you read a page, look away and recall the main ideas. Highlight very little, and never highlight anything you haven't put in your mind first by recalling. Try recalling main ideas when you are walking to class or in a different room from where you originally learned it. An ability to recall—to generate the ideas from inside yourself—is one of the key indicators of good learning.

**2. Test yourself.** On everything. All the time. Flash cards are your friend.

**3. Chunk your problems.** Chunking is understanding and practicing with a problem solution so that it can all come to mind in a flash. After you solve a problem, rehearse it. Make sure you can solve it cold—every step. Pretend it's a song and learn to play it over and over again in your mind, so the information combines into one smooth chunk you can pull up whenever you want.

**4. Space your repetition.** Spread out your learning in any subject a little every day, just like an athlete. Your brain is like a muscle—it can handle only a limited amount of exercise on one subject at a time.

**5. Alternate different problem-solving techniques during your practice.** Never practice too long at any one session using only one problem-solving technique—after a while, you are just mimicking what you did on the previous problem. Mix it up and work on different types of problems. This teaches you both *how* and *when* to use a technique. (Books generally are not set up this way, so you'll need to do this on your own.) After every assignment and test, go over your errors, make sure you understand why you made them, and then rework your solutions. To study most effectively, handwrite (don't type) a problem on one side of a flashcard and the solution on the other. (Handwriting builds stronger neural structures in memory than typing.) You might also photograph the card if you want to load it into a study app on your smartphone. Quiz yourself randomly on different types of problems. Another way to do this is to randomly flip through your book, pick out a problem, and see whether you can solve it cold.

**6. Take breaks.** It is common to be unable to solve problems or figure out concepts in math or science the first time you encounter them. This is why a little study every day is much better than a lot of studying all at once. When you get frustrated with a math or science problem, take a break so that another part of your mind can take over and work in the background.

**7. Use explanatory questioning and simple analogies.** Whenever you are struggling with a concept, think to yourself, *How can I explain this so that a ten-year-old could understand it?* Using an analogy really helps, like saying that the flow of electricity is like the flow of water. Don't just think your explanation—say it out loud or put it in writing. The additional effort of speaking and writing allows you to more deeply encode (that is, convert into neural memory structures) what you are learning.

**8. Focus.** Turn off all interrupting beeps and alarms on your phone and computer, and then turn on a timer for twenty-five minutes. Focus intently for those twenty-five minutes and try to work as diligently as you can. After the timer goes off, give yourself a small, fun reward. A few of these sessions in a day can really move your studies forward. Try to set up times and places where studying—not glancing at your computer or phone—is just something you naturally do.

**9. Eat your frogs first.** Do the hardest thing earliest in the day, when you are fresh.

**10. Make a mental contrast.** Imagine where you've come from and contrast that with the dream of where your studies will take you. Post a picture or words in your workspace to remind you of your dream. Look at that when you find your motivation lagging. This work will pay off both for you and those you love!

## Ten Rules Of Bad Studying

The following rules are from excerpted from *A Mind for Numbers: How to Excel in Math and Science (Even if You Flunked Algebra)*, Barbara Oakley, Penguin, July, 2014 http://www.barbaraoakley.com/pdf/10rulesofstudying.pdf

Avoid these techniques—they can waste your time even while they fool you into thinking you're learning!

**1. Passive rereading**—sitting passively and running your eyes back over a page. Unless you can *prove* that the material is moving into your brain by recalling the main ideas without looking at the page, rereading is a waste of time.

**2. Letting highlights overwhelm you.** Highlighting your text can fool your mind into thinking you are putting something in your brain, when all you're really doing is moving your hand. A little highlighting here and there is okay—sometimes it can be helpful in flagging important points. But if you are using highlighting as a memory tool, make sure that what you mark is also going into your brain.

**3. Merely glancing at a problem's solution and thinking you know how to do it.** This is one of the worst errors students make while studying. You need to be able to *solve* a problem step-by-step, without looking at the solution.

**4. Waiting until the last minute to study.** Would you cram at the last minute if you were practicing for a track meet? Your brain is like a muscle—it can handle only a limited amount of exercise on one subject at a time.

**5. Repeatedly solving problems of the same type that you already know how to solve.** If you just sit around solving similar problems during your practice, you're not actually preparing for a test—it's like preparing for a big basketball game by just practicing your dribbling.

**6. Letting study sessions with friends turn into chat sessions.** Checking your problem solving with friends, and quizzing one another on what you know, can make learning more enjoyable, expose flaws in your thinking, and deepen your learning. But if your joint study sessions turn to fun before the work is done, you're wasting your time and should find another study group.

**7. Neglecting to read the textbook before you start working problems.** Would you dive into a pool before you knew how to swim? The textbook is your swimming instructor—it guides you toward the answers. You will flounder and waste your time if you don't bother to read it. Before you begin to read, however, take a quick glance over the chapter or section to get a sense of what it's about.

**8. Not checking with your instructors or classmates to clear up points of confusion.** Professors are used to lost students coming in for guidance—it's our job to help you. The students we worry about are the ones who don't come in. Don't be one of those students.

**9. Thinking you can learn deeply when you are being constantly distracted.** Every tiny pull toward an instant message or conversation means you have less brain power to devote to learning. Every tug of interrupted attention pulls out tiny neural roots before they can grow.

**10. Not getting enough sleep.** Your brain pieces together problem-solving techniques when you sleep, and it also practices and repeats whatever you put in mind before you go to sleep. Prolonged fatigue allows toxins to build up in the brain that disrupt the neural connections you need to think quickly and well. If you don't get good sleep before a test, NOTHING ELSE YOU HAVE DONE WILL MATTER.

## For Further Research:

### Strategies for Remembering:

http://www.businessinsider.com/strategies-for-remembering-everything-you-learn-2014-8

### 15-Minute Activity:

http://www.businessinsider.com/this-15-minute-activity-will-make-you-more-successful-at-work-2014-5

### Repetitions:

http://www.tutorialspoint.com/management_concepts/the_rule_of_seven.htm

http://en.wikipedia.org/wiki/Spaced_repetition

http://en.wikipedia.org/wiki/Leitner_system

### Forgetting Curve:

http://en.wikipedia.org/wiki/Forgetting_curve

### Neurons:

http://www.pnas.org/content/108/13/5419.full

### Anki:

http://ankisrs.net/

### Pimsleur:

https://en.wikipedia.org/wiki/Pimsleur_Language_Programs

### Ebbinghaus:

http://en.wikipedia.org/wiki/Hermann_Ebbinghaus

### Schrodinger's Cat:

https://en.wikipedia.org/wiki/Schr%C3%B6dinger%27s_cat

# PART 8: BONUS: LIFESTYLE AND PERSEVERANCE

# Chapter 42: Practicing When Traveling

Some of our students ask if we have any recommendations or tips for practicing while traveling. While you could proceed with regular training, we urge you to benefit from the learning experience in a different way.

Traveling is a great opportunity to learn. When traveling we are outside of our comfort zone, we explore new locations and cultures and generate enough experiences to remember the travels when we are back at home. However, being out of our comfort zones we must me creative and selective to maximize our positive experiences. When traveling there are three stages: preparation, the travel itself, and processing of the experiences when we are back. To some extent, this is similar to prereading, reading and marker generation.

When preparing to travel we may as well learn history and geography of our destination. We can learn historical facts, main locations, local folklore, a few phrases of the local language (if different). The primary motivation is optimization of the itinerary, but simply learning from exposure to the new location is equally important. To some extent, the main goal is opening up an appetite for the specific novelties that are available at our destination.

When we arrive, we try to follow our itinerary, but we also may want to improvise and change the itinerary if there is a good opportunity. Everything we see can be analyzed from various perspectives:

- How old is it?
- What was its purpose then and now?
- What is its history?
- What does it make us feel?
- How can we use this experience in our lives back home?

In addition, we could look for some signs of a new adventure: mysterious and unexpected details that may revolutionize our understanding of the place and generate a totally new itinerary. Usually, it is great to discuss "life" with locals, see what makes them tick and how they spend their lives. It is also great to meet with other travelers from a different background, to teach and to learn things we would never expect to find. When traveling, openness is important. Good travel always comes with a twist. At the end of each day, I try to remember key points of the day so I will have a good story when I get back home.

When we get home, we look at the photograph and try to recreate the experience. At home is the first time we have time to connect all dots of the experience. Often I go to the history books and try to position all the things that I saw within history's time and place, to make sense of the markers, and to link my own experience into a great story. Each travel is a learning experience since we can learn about others and about ourselves. Good travel makes a great story, and great travel changes us forever.

## An Amazing List Of Simple Exercises

The following is a short list of simple exercises you can practice anytime and anywhere. Anna gives this list only to her most prudent students.

Each exercise should take around 10 minutes, and you can practice it daily if you want. Alternatively, you can choose a weekly subject and focus on it for a whole week.

- Mindful memorization: listen to your surroundings and try to remember names and numbers from the first time you hear them.
- Read and remember five cool facts from Wikipedia: people, dates, new words, physics/math constants.
- Read a page and imagine how you will make it into a movie. Try to be creative and make the movie as fun as possible.
- Learn five words from any foreign language
- Watch a TED talk or TV series and make a transcript for them from your memory. Repeat until you are happy with the result.
- Try to visualize someone you used to know well but have not met for a long time. Try to fill in as many details of their life as you can from your memory.

- Try to generate at least five associations for every piece of information you want to memorize. See if you can recreate successfully all five associations after some time. This will teach you about your personal style.
- Look once at a landscape before you, close your eyes and try to recreate as many details as you can from your memory. Open your eyes and compare. Repeat until you feel good with the result.
- Memorize numbers of passing cars. Hint: when you get better you may need special markers for all 2-digit numbers, for example 00 is toilet, 33 Jesus, 45 WW2 victory, 69 (do it yourself), etc.
- Memorize grocery lists and to do's, try not to look at your calendar.
- Keep a journal of your reading: how much, what, when, and what you still remember after a week.
- Select an object, any object and write down 20 ways it can be used for or be a part of another object.

## Changing Your Everyday Life

SuperLearning is a life-changing skill. Once you manage to learn skills FASTER, the next logical step is applying the same abilities in your everyday life.

Therefore immediately after managing SuperLearning our students find themselves doing all sorts of fun things:

1. **Speeding up:** There are things that can be easily sped up: you can fast-forward video or audio, speed-read and speed-write, speed-date and speed-walk. Some students are even talking faster.
2. **Multitasking:** There are things that cannot be sped up, and you can do several of them at once. Yes, you will kind of suck in all of the tasks you multitask, but with SuperLearning abilities regular people will not notice a difference. Therefore, I find myself enjoying some comedy shows in front of TV with an iPad in my hand and discussing with my kids some things from classical history all at the same time. If the action does not get intense, this is fun.

3. **Generating learning experiences:** Driving is hard for me. When I drive, I do not have enough capacity to speed up or multitask. I do report stuff on Waze and listen to the radio, but I also try to memorize some details of the road (this is trivial for some but very hard for me). For example, one of the tips Anna gives to young SuperLearners: try to memorize the numbers of cars around you to boost your memory skills.
4. **Improving quality:** Sometimes we would like to be perfectionists and do things right, but there is just not enough time to do it. With SuperLearning skills, suddenly there is just enough time. In fact, you can set the bar higher than you ever suspected you could. You can do every single day something that used to frighten you and learn from the experience. You do have time to double-check your moves if you want. You have time to watch TED and learn a proper way to tie your shoes or a necktie (I watched three times three different methods for each and still do not get it).
5. **Improving variety:** I will become 40 years old soon. Every 10 years I make a bucket list, so I started to organize a bucket list for the age of 40. Unfortunately, I could not find enough cool new life-changing things for the list that I could afford (I am very limited by lack of free time). Finally, I settled on a 40×40 paradigm: find 40 different ways to do something you like and monitor the progress. I have not started the 40×40-ing yet, and I am not sure to what extent I want to share the experiences. However, I am sure that the ability to do something in 40 different ways is cool in and of itself.

We are constantly evolving. SuperLearning may well be too limiting a word to define your personal path. Please feel free to give feedback regarding your own experiences and the way they are changing to info@KeyToStudy.com.

## Create Experiences / Firsthand Experience

The best creative exercises provide you with mental activity and material out of which you can form ideas. Experience can be firsthand or secondhand, such as reading, listening or watching. However, firsthand experience is far superior. A Chinese proverb states:

I hear: I forget
I see: I remember
I do: I understand

A special type of firsthand experience is...

## Travel

There is no better way to broaden and refresh your outlook than travel. It gets you out of an environmental rut and exposes you to new people, customs, ideas and ways of living. One key to creative living is to view life from a fresh perspective, and travel can give you this new outlook – if you will allow it. Every culture provides a unique way of looking at common situations and solving common problems. Take photographs and keep a diary as you travel.

Charles Cave writes:

I'm an armchair traveler and particularly enjoy television programs about travel. Michael Palin's *From Pole to Pole* was the story of a wonderful trip starting at the North Pole. I was very inspired seeing such places as Finland, Russia, Estonia, Egypt, Africa and Antarctica.

Last week I watched a program about an Englishman who walked from the west coast of France to Istanbul...in eighteen months!

Sorrel Wilby's book *Across the Top* describes a trek across the Himalayas. I have two books about the ascent of Mt Everest. There is something very motivating about reading books on mountaineering.

A good place for armchair traveling and planning your next holiday is the Lonely Planet website (as well as reading the books!).

## Self-Reliance

The more you depend on your ability to think, the more proficient you will become at thinking up new ideas. Experts and consultants should be viewed as collaborators, not dictators. If you rely on someone else to solve your problems and tell you what to do, your creative abilities will shrivel rather than flourish for lack of exercise.

## Personal Contacts

One way to learn how to think creatively is to associate yourself with creative people. Look for people who are fun to talk to and have a keen sense of interest in life. An individual who can stimulate your thought process is what you are looking for.

## Children

One special group of easily accessible and highly creative people is children.

It has been said that insanity is hereditary; you can get it from your children. Another thing you can get from children is a great deal of exercise. A child's world is filled with fantasy, and yours can be too if you make the effort to interact with them.

Try the association game. You both look at something together and ask the child "What does that look like to you?" or "What does that make you think of?"

Playing imagination games with children and creatively interacting with them is one good way to get you back in touch with your imagination.

You may want to explore the Children section of the Creativity Web.

## Games And Puzzles

Certain games and puzzles can furnish you with plenty of opportunities to flex your creative muscles. The game of chess and checkers are both good games as they force you to map out strategies and make moves that depend on what your opponent does. Similar games of strategy are Shoji (Japanese Chess) and Go.

Physical sports such as football, basketball, baseball, tennis, racquetball or handball can also provide creative exercise involving strategy.

Charades is another game that provides great creative exercise in thinking up novel ways to communicate something. The board game Pictionary is a similar style game.

Word puzzles and games are another avenue for creative exercise, and Thomas Edison was a great believer in this.

Today, newspapers carry crossword puzzles and jumbled word puzzles. A great word game, such as Scrabble or Boggle, forces you to think in terms of adding, subtracting and modifying various combinations of letters, all of which helps sharpen and tone your creative ability.

## Hobbies

There are hundreds of hobbies and some of them can be real workouts for your imagination. Painting, drawing or sculpture cannot avoid putting your creative machinery to work. Technical hobbies can also provide creative exercise, e.g., amateur radio, electronics, home computers.

Computers are a hobby with great potential. Think up new uses for computers in the home and write new programs to carry them out. There are several books on the market with titles like *101 Uses for a Home Computer*. I own one such book!

## Reading

Alex Osborn, author of *Applied Imagination* wrote: "Reading supplies bread for imagination to feed on, and bones for it to chew on." However, not all reading is a good creative exercise. The key to using reading as a creative exercise is to read selectively and actively.

Biographies also can be used for creative exercise. Any life worth documenting usually involves some real imagineering on the part of the subject. Perhaps you could profit from their experiences and use their creative ideas as a springboard to launch your imagination. A good book is *Made in Japan*, by Akio Morita – the story of Sony.

Another way to use reading as a creative exercise is to take a topic of interest and read several different viewpoints.

Magazines can also be used for creative exercise. Walt Disney believed in reading Reader's Digest and said:

"Your imagination may be creaky or timid or dwarfed or frozen at points. The Readers Digest can serve as a gymnasium for its training."

One of the best things about the magazine is that it provides a kaleidoscope of topics in every issue. Such diversity can provide great creative fuel.

Here is a list of just some of the contents of a 1996 edition of Readers Digest:

- Short humorous stories
- "It pays to enrich your word power" – vocabulary development
- Pertinent quotations
- Quizzes
- Laughter, the best medicine
- Stories on places, people, real-life drama, & science

Mike Vance talks about the value of reading Mad Magazine, describing it as the idiom of our time showing us the direction we are heading. Alfred E. Neuman has big ears for listening and comes out with some fantastic quotations. The stories and cartoons are provocative and satirical. Buy and read a few issues of Mad and have a go at writing some stories and cartoons in the Mad style. It will greatly enhance your powers of perception!

Another interesting area for stimulating your imagination is to buy a different magazine each month (or borrow from the library). Read something quite different to what you normally read, for example, sports, house and garden, travel, literary, gossip, fashion, comics, motoring, teenage, arts, etc.

## Writing

Writing ability is considered a basic factor in creative aptitude. The act of writing forces you to utilize all phases of the creative process and come up with a tangible product.

For further information, I recommend the following books:

- *Writing Down the Bones* by Natalie Goldberg
- *Becoming a Writer* by Dorothea Brande

## Physical And Mental Health

Relaxation and good health are important to mental and physical health and are essential prerequisites to creative thinking. I like to go jogging. While jogging I have had a great abundance of ideas. I have visualized computer programs, story ideas and solutions to different problems. I attribute the value of jogging and other forms of exercise such as walking, cycling, and swimming to the following:

- Exercise is a form of play, free from restraints.
- Increased oxygen in the blood is delivered to the brain
- Release of endorphins into the blood (the runner's high)
- Meditative rhythm of the running/walking/swimming strokes

There are drugs that purport to increase the brain's ability and performance, but I have seen no evidence to prove this. Psychedelic drugs, I am told, produce vivid imagery that the user is never able to capture. Hunter S. Thompson, in his recent book *The Songs of Doomed*, writes in the preface about his drug habit and what it does to his writing but I do not believe drugs can increase creativity. Instead, the body and mind should be operating at peak efficiency through correct diet, exercise, rest and fresh air.

## Personal Rituals

Any ritual can help if done with the right frame of mind. Some creative rituals are downright strange. One writer had a particular record of Spanish flamenco music he listened to before he started to write. Mort Walker (the cartoonist) soaks one foot in hot water and the other in cold water. John Steinbeck wrote letters to his publisher in a notebook as a warm-up to writing *East of Eden* (These letters make very interesting reading for the creative writer.) Douglas Adams (of *Hitch-Hikers Guide to the Galaxy* fame) is very fond of taking baths to get fresh ideas.

The ritual itself is usually not directly related to creative thinking but is a means of focussing the mind on producing ideas and is a very personal thing. What works for one person will probably not work for another. Remember that a ritual is an external method, whereas creativity is personal and individual.

## Music

An audio environment can be conducive to new ideas and cutting down the mental block. Music can be used to create an environment unique to each individual. Experiment with different musical styles to see what works best. Charles Thompson, in his book *What a Great Idea!*, recommends music that follows these guidelines:-

- Avoid music with lyrics. Classical, light jazz, electronic and instrumental music of various forms can work well.
- Avoid music that demands your attention
- Avoid music with large, sudden changes in amplitude.
- Use music with sustained tones and subtle variations.

**Recommendations:**

- Brahms: Concerto in A Minor, Op 102
- Chopin: Piano Concerto No.1 in E Minor Op. 11
- Beethoven: Sonata No. 14 in C-Sharp Minor Op. 27
- Vivaldi: L'Estro Armonico, Op.2; Concerto No. 5 in A Major

Try different works to see what works best. Taking a break and listening to music can uplift your spirits and perhaps forge some new neural pathways to help you in your creativity. Music has the power to make you feel good, providing a good environment for creative thinking.

# Chapter 43: Remember Conversations

Some of our students want to use SuperLearning methods for conversations and meetings. Since many of us spend a lot of time in meetings and conversations, it is important to use that time with maximal efficiency. Below are some tips that allow you to create meeting summaries in your mind.

**Question:**

*I have not completed the full course yet but so far it seems quite engaging and I realize it will take time to master. I am a Business Analyst in the IT industry and most of the time I have to go through long discussions over phone or F2F. Is there a guideline to create markers while listening? I tried but not much success yet. This course so far seems to be focused on reading, creating markers and remembering. So am curious what about dynamic discussions when there is no scope of having a documentation ready.*

**Dr. Lev Goldentouch**

*Not sure if there are generic rules. So I will answer from my personal experience. When I have long phone conversations, I draw small pictures and write down some keywords on a sheet of paper. The active part of actually drawing something on a paper increases retention (studies show x2). The keywords and small images allow me to recreate the track of discussion when needed. If I need to create mental markers, I usually say something like "let me sum up what I understand so far" and use the summing-up monologue to create the markers.*

**Jonathan A. Levi**

*As far as remembering verbal conversation or lectures, you should begin applying the "markers" skill set you are being taught to verbal conversation, and you will see a lot of major memory benefits.*

*For example, last night, I met someone at a networking event – let's call her Rachel. When Rachel told me her name,*

*I noticed a similarity between her and another person named Rachel I know. I used that marker (the color of her hair, for example), to remind me of her name – I know two Rachels with brown hair.*

*Rachel also told me she went to the University of Southern California. From there, I pictured an experience I had visiting a very close friend when he attended USC, when I was taken on a tour. I created a marker of my friend and me at USC under Tommy the Trojan, a prominent statue on the campus.*

*By creating markers throughout our conversation, I was able to remember important details about Rachel and her background – and will likely remember them long-term.*

*If I attend a lecture, I am able to do similar marker creation to aid in memory.*

*Hope this helps.*

**Dr. Lev Goldentouch**

*Active learning*

*One of the things we did not emphasize enough when writing the course was ACTIVE learning. When you have to learn a MASSIVE amount of data it is not sufficient to trust your memory skills alone, you should actually WRITE DOWN what you learned. It has been proven that handwriting would be most efficient (double encoding with kinesthetic memory), but any other note taking will do.*

**Jonathan A. Levi**

*Indeed. Writing seems to be just one way to "activate" learning. I personally prefer to discuss. A great example of this is taking breaks from reading to share what you have learned with someone else, explaining and debating with them.*

*Of course, we have to use what we learn or our brain will be very effective in regarding it as "no longer relevant."*

## Doodling Will Boost Your Productivity

Doodling at school and work will boost your productivity. Occasionally we write about doodling (or freestyle annotation) and its benefits.

Students drawing on their papers were mistreated by generations of teachers. They were asked to focus, to stop fooling around and to listen to the teachers. However, the human spirit is stronger than education fashions, and student persistently doodled in school into college and later into successful careers. Around 2009 new evidence began to emerge, effectively showing that doodling significantly improves both retention and productive output. Since then doodling became a standard practice for surviving long lectures and conferences.

Why do we doodle? There is no consensus yet, so I will be happy to explain my theory.

When our logical processing in the left-brain hemisphere becomes too busy to listen to the creative output of the right hemisphere, we get frustrated. The creative part of our brain needs to be heard. Without doodling, it would generate daydreaming, strange associations, inappropriate jokes and other interruptions. However, with doodling, the creative processing and logical processing can coexist in harmony, resulting in higher retention.

What do we doodle? There are some initial interpretations to various shapes. The style of the doodles is personal and similar to our automatic marker style. For example, I draw letters and geometrical patterns. One of my colleagues is drawing words in different languages. Some people draw heroes and comic figures, everyday objects, etc. If we have handouts /printed material, the initial accurate highlights are enhanced by ornaments. As the doodle coverage increases, we become calm, focused and more productive.

How do we doodle? Usually, we doodle in our notebooks. People that spend their time on the streets and not in classrooms often draw graffiti. Graffiti is as old as civilization and has been recently recognized as a legitimate form of art. Annotation is another tool for doodling. Many of our students use Diigo for Chrome or Skitch for Evernote to draw their markers. We encourage this activity and ask our students to share the images with us. A trained SuperLearner can doodle without tools using visual associations. By now, I think that I am doodling in my head all the time. For me, a curious side effect of this visualization process is my sense of humor, which became stronger as I practiced creative markers.

Doodling calms us down, increases our focus and creativity, improves retention and makes us more productive. I hope one day a doodling paradigm will prevail, and teachers will be criticizing students for not doodling.

## For Further Research:

### Note Taking:

http://lifehacker.com/take-30-seconds-after-learning-something-to-write-impor-1558329109

### Doodling:

http://www.wsj.com/articles/the-power-of-the-doodle-improve-your-focus-and-memory-1406675744

http://drawsketch.about.com/cs/tipsandideas/p/doodle_marks.htm

https://www.psychologytoday.com/blog/arts-and-health/201401/doodling-your-way-more-mindful-life

http://en.wikipedia.org/wiki/Graffiti

### Doodles of Famous People:

http://flavorwire.com/147177/idle-doodles-by-famous-authors

http://pencils.com/famous-notebook-users/

# Chapter 44: Build Your Own Success

## Persistence, Curiosity, Empathy

What are the values that you plan to pass to your children? How will these values affect their lives? This article *"Pew Report: Parents with College Degree Focus on Persistence"* implies that values of persistence, curiosity and empathy generate better students and more successful professionals. Let us try to understand why.

## Persistence

Persistence is the key to success. If you set up a goal and you persist on your way to the goal, you will get there, or you have very bad goal-setting skills. We may argue about how little joy it generates, or how slow the way to the goal will be, but reaching your goal is THE DEFINITION of being successful. Similarly important and indicative of success is the skill of delaying gratification, which probably cannot be taught. You have it, or you do not. Yet, persistence can be taught, and persistence can compensate for some need for instant gratification.

## Curiosity

Curiosity is the easy way to enjoy learning and intellectual work, which are critical for success. Curiosity generates creativity and motivation to search for new ways and new answers. It is a cure for most learning disorders: if you cannot learn in the classroom, you use the Internet. It is the best first step to knowledge, and knowledge is power. There is always a workaround for learning something new no matter what a student faces. Someone somewhere has faced a similar problem and just might have an answer or the beginning spark of an answer.

## Empathy

Empathy is a tricky one. You do need to communicate with people around you in order to succeed, but you do not need empathy. A narcissistic sociopath may be as good a CEO as his enthusiastic and empathetic predecessor may have been. Empathy has much more to do with mental resilience, than with huge success. Even the most successful people fail, and if you fail, the network of your friends and family members allow you to regain your success and learn from your mistakes. Therefore, empathetic people can take more risks and fail more often, and still succeed afterward.

Now I understand why I teach my kids to be persistent, curious, and empathetic. I wish my parents had also known this theory: my adolescence would have been so much easier.

## How To Be A Better Student

Recently I started using Reddit, answering all those students who look for an extra advantage in their classes. Soon I understood that speedreading and memory techniques alone would not work. I ended up giving this advice (https://www.reddit.com/r/AskReddit/comments/2emx7n/what_are_some_good_study_habits_i_should_get_into/):

1. **Be healthy**. Eat healthy food, sleep 6-8 hours per day, drink approximately 3 cups of coffee, meditate/participate in sports.
2. **Be creative**. Ask yourself questions, play around with the material, think how other people address the subject. Do not forget to have fun.
3. **Communicate**. Talk to your teachers, fellow students, students in classes above and below you. You will get lots of valuable tips and if you are lucky some good friends. I got a Ph.D. position this way.
4. **Be efficient**. I read very fast, remember almost everything and I can teach anyone.

Generally, I think that this is a good advice, but it is missing one key ingredient: **thinking**.

I remember reading this article:

(https://www.psychologytoday.com/blog/memory-medic/201309/thinking-is-the-best-way-remember).

I thought, "That is how I learned before becoming a SuperLearner, and it was quite effective!" All the tricks I teach (speedreading, memorization, creativity, and prioritization) simply speed up the process of learning.

A true learning experience is **THINKING** about the subjects you learn, solving examples hands-on, simulating equations in math lab and dealing with home assignments. When I was a student, it was okay to forget and use notebooks, to make short summaries and use them, to use ready solutions from previous exams just as long as they allowed me to solve the newly presented challenge. It is okay under the stress to start subvocalization and lose a mental marker as long as your hands-on skills kick in.

Therefore, my best advice would be:

**Think and do the hands-on exercises.**

## From C To A In 5 Days

Every student wants to have good grades. Every parent wants his child to be an A+ student without losing creativity and joyfulness. We plan to give some insights on how this can be done.

The real key to studying is not just speedreading or memory tools, but a much wider range of skills. The first time I realized that was when Anna announced she could turn any C- student into an A+ student in 5 days. I was reasonably skeptical, but over the course of several months, I have seen enough evidence to start to believe it. Naturally, I asked her how she did it. The answer was a bit unexpected. While she did teach them some basic techniques that enabled memorization, the key approach was different. "I teach them to approach the school subjects like you approach a theme," she said. "Wait, what?" In the following discussion, Anna underlined the principles. I will try to summarize some of them below.

## Developing Curiosity

The first issue is developing curiosity. Most subjects for most students are so boring that they do not care anymore. However, the same subjects come to life under deeply engaging teachers. To develop curiosity, we explain in extremely "cool" terms why the subject matters. Apparently, over the years Anna heard so many "little-known facts" from me that by now she can make any subject interesting.

## Building Confidence

To develop confidence, the student is asked to complete several tasks that he finds easy. Then the student is given a key method to solve a task he used to find hard. Under the teacher's supervision, the student obviously solves the task. At this point, the teacher explains that the student can solve any task if he finds the right "key" or strategy. Then, the student stops learning, and starts hacking the system. It is fun and extremely effective since we already have most of the "hacks" available in various online sources.

## Generating A Plan

Another key component to success is a clear plan for reaching this success. Without such a plan, it is very hard to organize everything and stay focused. The teacher sits with the student and develops a strategy of how to organize the time, in which order to learn material, how the material builds up into a reasonable body of knowledge and what understanding of the knowledge will satisfy the student's curiosity without challenging his confidence.

## Follow-Up

While five meetings typically generate the framework for success, long-term follow up ensures the success. No time-consuming teaching is done at that point, only a short tip here and there ensures that the student can adapt his newly found skills in a changing environment. In addition, it is always fun to know that you turned someone's learning experience into a success story.

This is one of Anna's little secrets. She is a genius teacher. I do not even pretend I can copy her methods. However, I am trying to analyze how she succeeds so that you will also be able to do the same.

## For Further Research:

https://www.psychologytoday.com/blog/school-thought/201409/pew-reportparents-college-degree-focus-persistence

**Reddit**

https://www.reddit.com/

# Chapter 45: Suraj's One-On-One With Anna

These are only some of the gems I learned from my one-on-one with Anna. In each section, the training has added value to my understanding and has given me footholds to climb higher. I hope some of the examples I mention here will help the reader/student understand the KeyToStudy System and skills better, but more importantly, what I wish to emphasize here is there is no alternative to learning than having it taught by someone who is an expert. There is no alternative to personal coaching when it comes to SuperLearning. It is like going to the gym for the first time. Would you be better off having an instructor to guide you? You bet!

## Markers

Markers provide the essence of the text at hand. The best markers are visual, metaphorical, emotional and relevant. During my one-on-one with Anna, she asked me what I wanted to remember with markers, and I pointed at a Wikipedia article. Then she asked me to select some markers within the text, and I highlighted them here: http://app.pith.li/pith/national-highway-india.
Anna then asked me what one word I could use that would serve as a metaphor for the entire article.

Anna suggested that I use the word "bypass" as a metaphor for the entire article. This was something new and frankly mind-blowing to me because she related that word to "bypass surgery" which would then remind me of the heart and how it is a transportation system for blood in the entire human body. This triggered many connections in my brain and to date I have not forgotten the details of the article after reading it only once.

In this way, Anna was able to show that the essence of a medium-sized article can be contained in as less as a single word. However, in subsequent articles I tried to do the same thing but did not have the same success. This partly has to do with certain subjects rendering themselves more easily to visualization and partly with my lack of experience in creating good markers.

Creating good markers is not as easy as it sounds. We can get better at it with consistent practice and learn to create markers that stick in the long-term memory.

## Flow, Association, And Visualization

Freely flowing, visual and emotional visualization is key in producing good markers. This skill takes practice. We tend to get rigid into a particular way of thinking, and this hampers both the speed at which we can create markers and the quality of those markers as well. As has been said on KeyToStudy.com before, it is similar to looking at a cloud and saying "*this cloud looks like a dog*."

The key here is speed. To increase the speed of creating markers you can use speedreading software at high speeds (way higher than you are comfortable with) and force yourself to get into the practice of reading words as detailed pictures. The other point here is *ease*. Entering into a flow state means you are doing what comes naturally to you. It is not forced.

There is no set way of thinking or strict rules for visualizing; the rule of thumb is "just because." Use whatever works best for you. Use whatever comes easily as long as it is visually compelling. If you are still confused, perhaps you could use further guidance.

## Prereading

At first, I was confusing prereading with speedreading. This is not the case. As Anna explained, if Lev gets groceries from the market, he will have no idea how to place everything in its right place because he lacks the structure needed to put the things in their proper place. Only Anna can put the groceries in the right order and manner because she has the context of "what goes where."

Prereading, therefore, is the process of creating this context, these pegs into which you will then insert the markers. Prereading is therefore, an essential step and must never be skipped no matter how fast you can read.

Prereading orients you towards speed as well, while skimming or looking over the text at first you will know how fast you need to move across it if you have preread the main headlines, sections, divisions, graphics and illustrations within it. It will help you eliminate the wheat from the chaff and aid you in further attaining clarity towards your purpose for reading the text and increase your speed as a result. The general rule of thumb is do not start reading until you know what goes where.

## Mind Maps

Mind maps are popular and therefore easily misunderstood. The hub of the mind map is usually given to the central topic or theme of the text, but this need not be the case. The hub or central node of the map can well be something totally unrelated which serves as a metaphor for the map and helps serve the entire text in a relative contextual flavor. As an example, consider what a mind map for this article would be like http://app.pith.li/pith/jvika.

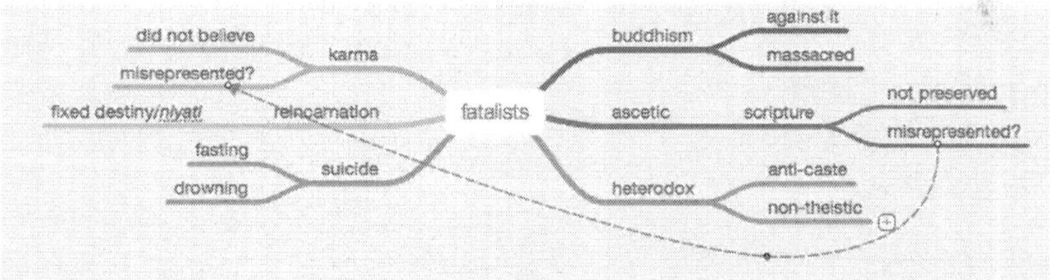


Certainly, you can have the title of the article as the central node and then branch off from there by chunking the article literally but I use the word "Fatalists" as a nodal point and then weave my map around the relativity of that central theme.

The number of main branches in a mind map is also a question of contention amongst learners; people chunk a certain way and then they force their mind maps to resemble it. I am guilty of this. Before meeting Anna, all my mind maps essentially had four main branches each, because that is how I chunked. Anna suggested that I progressively load my mind maps with additional main branches. She suggested five, but given my penchant for symmetrical looking mind maps, she changed it to six.

Moving from four main branches to six was a big jump for me, but it has helped me break my own prison of limited branches and now it is just as easy for me to remember six main items instead of the previous four.

## Saccadic Movement

This is a tricky topic for me to write about since I have not yet really begun to feel the benefits even when I try. Using saccadic movement assumes you have preread the text at hand, and it assumes you are comfortable with at least 300 wpm and have had sufficient practice in reading with a card.

There are a few different types of eye movement such as zigzag movement and S-type. They work great if you have had some exercise in eye span increase and short-term memory training.

Eye movement, for the most part, should be confined to the periphery of a line drawn in the middle of the text and should rarely veer towards the extreme margins. Then the text should be read in a zigzag pattern while ignoring the first and last lines of each paragraph and the first two and last two words in each line.

## Chunking

Chunking can be useful in the elementary stages while learning new words. I will try to show this with an example. I will use the word ***'repudiate,'*** which is a verb that means, "*to cast off, to disown, to refuse to acknowledge, etc.*"

We can chunk the word into two parts 'repu' and 'diate'. We see that 'repu' can serve as a short form for '*reputation*' or '*repute*' and 'diate' sounds like '*date*'. The visual cue when we put them together will have something to do with *reputation* and *date*. Now it is easy to weave a story around these two parts in a matter of seconds. I can imagine my reputation being ruined on a date when I show up, but my date refuses to recognize/acknowledge me.

## Interview Your Memory

Ask more questions. This is the key to all long-term memory. Remember that familiarity with a text is not synonymous with remembering it. We remain oftentimes under the illusion that just because we have read something once or twice and are familiar with the subject matter, we will remember it. This is almost never the case. We must repeatedly "interview" our memory as to what we have learned to make sure it sticks.

Of course, the way to do this is to ask **a lot** of questions. The basic trick here is to remember this poem:

*I've known six honest working men,*
*They've taught me all I knew*
*Their names are **What** and **Why** and **When***
*and **How** and **Where** and **Who**.*

By asking our questions that begin with Who, What, Where, When and Why, we can remember almost anything we decide to. The caveat here is, according to Anna, "Why" questions are the most important because they give us a causal syntax.

Gathering different points of view is another way to create questions that are more relevant. This is not always easy and comes with a lot of practice. As an example, I offer the following story:

While doing the 20-picture exercise with Anna, we came to a point where the visualization I had created consisted of a black horse swimming in a lake with a life-preserver tube. Anna asked me to come up with questions to see this visualization from another point of view. The best question I could come up with was "why" (as in, why is the horse swimming with a life preserver?). This did not impress Anna, and she suggested I try harder. As an example, she asked, "What would replace the horse?"

## Why You Should Take 1:1 With Anna

We invest significant efforts to make all the resources you need to learn readily available. However, there is only so much a reasonable person can learn all alone or even in a workbook. 1:1 Skype lessons with Anna (notice, it is paid and expensive) is the most effective way to learn. Usually, I say one hour with Anna is worth at least 15 hours of independent practice. Here is why:

1. **People make mistakes:** It is very hard to notice your own mistake. Often one bad mistake requires a week or two to wipe and re-acquire the right habits.

2. **A trainer can monitor progress:** We can drive ourselves too hard, focus on wrong things, and give up a moment before we succeed. Training with an experienced professional, we increase the chances to succeed.

3. **Everybody is different:** There are several strategies for all of the skills we develop. In each case, we fit a strategy for a person. It is practically impossible to describe all of these cases on KeyToStudy.com. Anna can fit the specific method for you extremely fast.

4. **The tip of the iceberg:** A huge part of communication is hidden. You can read all of our books, and the books will help you understand the subject. If you listen to Jonathan's lectures, you will generate a feel for the subject. If you learn with Anna, you will master the subject.

5. **Follow-up:** Some of Anna's graduates are offered advanced materials and free mentoring.

Anna has a very busy schedule because her students are happy and her methods successful. However, it is definitely worthwhile to wait for a time slot and attend 5-10 sessions with Anna. Hundreds of Anna's students will testify to the benefit of working with Anna personally!

# Chapter 46: SuperLearning–The Key To The Perfect Job

Recently I read "*Productivity and the Education Delusion*" and "*There is No Job Security*" (links below) and remembered the time when I first started discovering SuperLearning.

After finishing my Ph.D. and a successful exit from the company where I started my first job, I was a bit lost. I wondered, "What to do next?" I was sure my education and working experience would provide me a job in whatever I wanted whenever I wanted and I "let go." I decided to experience as many things as I could and see where it took me. I tried several things and made many mistakes.

Fast-forward several years that could fill a lifetime. I had a wife, kids, lots of stories, lost all my savings, and still no clue what to do next. I was not too excited about getting an executive position (too much stress, I was not cut out for this) or becoming a scientist (too little stress; it was exceptionally boring). Accidentally, I found out that my first real job actually was the only job I really liked.

I decided to give up the few dreams I still had not tried out and went for job interviews. Nobody hired me. I thought I was overqualified, so I underplayed my CV and tried again. Still no luck. To my amazement, the area of my research, the area of my first real job was not there anymore. It had experienced a paradigm shift. Within something like 3-4 years, several works were published, and several technologies released that made my previous experience slightly irrelevant. I had to relearn the entire skill set.

Fortunately, for me approximately at the same time my wife taught me the basics of SuperLearning skills. Probably because the teacher was my wife I was not a star pupil, and with 600 wpm at 80% understanding, I still needed to learn the new skill set.

I started reading. I decided to read 100 articles per day – scientific articles, technological articles, life hacking/psychology.

First, it took me an entire day to complete the reading task. However, very soon, brain adaptation kicked in, and I started to notice the repeating motives and focus on new things. By clustering the new facts in my mind, I could skip 80% of the body for most of the articles, and could read the whole collection in 2 hours, but my retention rate dropped. At this point, my education caused me to analyze the data flow and my brain's ability. I decided to try several tricks I knew from handling communication channels. To my amazement that worked! I could read at 1000 wpm and 80% understanding, moreover I did not have to stop to analyze the material. The analysis came as a by-product. Within 3 months, I learned the entire skill-set I was after and 4-5 skill-sets nearby.

This did not prepare me for the next job that I found: my friend was so much impressed by my ability to learn that he offered me a job where I had to learn yet another 4-5 skills-sets (programming flash, android-JNI, iOS objectiveC and game design). I took the job.

Then I took another job where I needed to master more skills. At some point, I understood that with my SuperLearning I could master any technical skill I wanted in very little time. Now I was getting only the jobs where I got real satisfaction from being in the "zone:" mastering a totally new skill and getting superior results every several months.

Therefore, this is what I do now. I am a consultant. I take only the jobs that no sane person can handle due to complexity. I do these jobs well. I am busy but happy.

With the ever-changing job market and ever-rising technological complexity, there is no safe job. Education, work experience, and good employers may easily become irrelevant in a paradigm shift. Paradigm shifts happen all the time. The only key to job security and a fulfilling career I know is the ability to learn a new skill set in little time and with a high success rate.

## This is the premise of the SuperLearning....

## For Further Research:

### Articles:

http://techcrunch.com/2014/06/06/productivity-and-the-education-delusion/

# EPILOGUE BY SURAJ SHARMA

# The Keytostudy System As A Lifestyle Choice

## What Is The KeyToStudy System To Me?

Simply put, the KeyToStudy System is a daring new lifestyle that pushes the boundaries of human intellect and does so until the practitioner feels evolved – in the true sense of the word. That is a bold statement to make; we know, but it is backed by results. Results, seen not only by the creators but also by the students and practitioners of this lifestyle, which are continually sharpened and shared as each person strives to make the world a better place.

## The KeyToStudy System Has A Long History

The KeyToStudy System is the result of decade-long research and experimentation by the husband and wife team of Anna and Lev Goldentouch. Anna has been teaching speedreading and memorization since 1999. Since 1999, Anna has continuously optimized her methodology. In 1999, it took Anna 120 hours to teach the methodology. Now, it only takes 10 hours of one-on-one training with Anna and very often much less!

Anna and Lev met in 2005 and since then have been working together. Their individual fields of expertise have been combined into truly innovative learning methodologies, which are not found elsewhere. Lev's experience in information theory and artificial intelligence enabled compressing the course and developing new methodologies.

Lev's passion for learning and creative vision has enabled KeyToStudy students to come together to form a community of likeminded students. The goal of the community is to encourage further study and to share ideas to increase each individual's creative ability. By encouraging creativity, the problems faced individually and by larger communities have a greater potential to be solved.

## How Did It Help Me?

When I began putting into practice the methodologies taught, I realized short-term and long-term benefits. There is a very high likelihood you will also experience these benefits.

Short-term benefits include:

1. **Double your reading speed in the first three months of practice.** Eventually, you will reach the "SuperLearning" speeds of 1200-1500 words per minute.
2. **Double your retention and memorization of whatever you read at faster speeds**. Eventually, the student will be able to retain 80-90% of all material after a single reading.
3. **Improve your focus and concentration** while studying/reading.
4. **Perform faster analysis of retained information**. As you become more experienced in using the skills and techniques, you will notice your brain automatically conjuring creative new analysis of the subjects you read. You will find your mind performing additive and subtractive synthesis on stored information and knowledge.

The long-term benefits are known to occur:

1. Increased creativity
2. Imagination management
3. Lower anxiety about studies
4. Lower stress
5. Better problem-solving ability

## Learning Is A Great Investment

As Lev Goldentouch is fond of saying, "There is no price-tag for lifestyle." The student simply must devote time and energy to perfect some of the basic ideas for effective learning. The hours invested in "learning how to learn" save countless hours for years to come, boost satisfaction, and help to get into a blissful state of creative "flow."

Although a great stepping-stone, the Udemy course touches only the tip of the iceberg. Lev and Anna are continually busy coming up with books, tutorials, videos and exercises to improve the KeyToStudy System.

Building an active and flourishing community is very important for Lev and Anna. They feel that your success is also their success. They enthusiastically continue to devote themselves to their students by answering questions, developing techniques and teaching skills to enable the widest variety of students to achieve the students' personal goals of improvement.

# APPENDICES

# Appendix A – Training Texts

## Instructions: Training Texts And Exercises

Each of the training texts in this appendix test your retention when speedreading. Usually I suggest my students train using their own material. You should be improving when reading the material that you read regularly with or without the training.

I suggest you test yourself ONCE A WEEK with one of the provided texts. This is to make sure you are not cheating yourself. Do not obsess regarding small variations in reading speed and retention. Everybody can have a good or a bad day. Do notice long-term trends. We have selected the texts in such a way that the complexity level rises from text to text. As you proceed with training, you should get very good at handling increasingly more challenging texts.

### Instruction For The Exercises

Before reading a text, make sure you have a stopwatch.

1. Read your ordinary text the ordinary way, but timing yourself with the stopwatch, until the stopwatch does not affect your reading.
2. Take a regular Pomodoro break. You do not want to be tired when you read.
3. Open the text you are using to test yourself. Start the timer before prereading the text.
4. Preread the text as fast as you can.
5. Read the text. At the end of each paragraph, if you feel your retention slipping, reread the paragraph
6. Stop the timer. Calculate your wpm as 60*(#words in text)/(#of seconds you read)
7. Answer the questions one by one. Take your time.
8. Compare your answers with the correct answers and generate your retention score.

If your retentions score drops to 70% or below, for the next week do not speed up, but focus on improving your retention. Do not be obsessed with improving your reading speed. If your retention is high, improving reading speed will be easy.

Otherwise, try to improve your reading speed. Do not be obsessed with getting a perfect score, 70% retention is good enough.

# TEXT #1

(Reference: The Project Gutenberg EBook of *Bulfinch's Mythology: The Age of Fable*, by Thomas Bulfinch https://www.gutenberg.org/cache/epub/3327/pg3327.html)

The Romans, like the Etruscans who came before them, were neither poetical nor imaginative in temperament. Their activity ran in practical directions. They therefore invented few, if any stories, of the gods whom they worshipped with fixed rites. Mr. Macaulay speaks of these gods as "the sober abstractions of the Roman pantheon." We owe most of the stories of the ancient mythology to the wit and fancy of the Greeks, more playful and imaginative, who seized from Egypt and from the East such legends as pleased them, and adapted them in their own way. It often happens that such stories, resembling each other in their foundation, are found in the Greek and Roman authors in several different forms.

To understand these stories, we will here first acquaint ourselves with the ideas of the structure of the universe, which the poets and others held, and which will form the scenery, so to speak, of the narratives.

The Greek poets believed the earth to be flat and circular, their own country occupying the middle of it, the central point being either Mount Olympus, the abode of the gods, or Delphi, so famous for its oracle.

The circular disk of the earth was crossed from west to east, and divided into two equal parts by the SEA, as they called the Mediterranean, and its continuation the Euxine.

Around the earth flowed the RIVER OCEAN, its course being from south to north on the western side of the earth, and in a contrary direction on the eastern side. It flowed in a steady, equable current, unvexed by storm or tempest. The sea, and all the rivers on earth, received their waters from it.

The northern portion of the earth was supposed to be inhabited by a happy race named the Hyperboreans (this word means "who live beyond the north" from the word "hyper," beyond, and boreas, the north wind), dwelling in everlasting bliss and spring beyond the lofty mountains whose caverns were supposed to send forth the piercing blasts of the north wind, which chilled the people of Hellas (Greece). Their country was inaccessible by land or sea. They lived exempt from disease or old age, from toils and warfare. Moore has given us the "Song of a Hyperborean," beginning

"I come from a land in the sun-bright deep,
Where golden gardens glow,
Where the winds of the north, becalmed in sleep,
Their conch-shells never blow."

On the south side of the earth, close to the stream of Ocean, dwelt a people happy and virtuous as the Hyperboreans. They were named the AEthiopians. The gods favored them so highly that they were wont to leave at times their Olympian abodes, and go to share their sacrifices and banquets.

On the western margin of the earth, by the stream of Ocean, lay a happy place named the Elysian Plain, whither mortals favored by the gods were transported without tasting of death, to enjoy an immortality of bliss. This happy region was also called the "fortunate fields," and the "Isles of the Blessed."

We thus see that the Greeks of the early ages knew little of any real people except those to the east and south of their own country, or near the coast of the Mediterranean. Their imagination meantime peopled the western portion of this sea with giants, monsters, and enchantresses; while they placed around the disk of the earth, which they probably regarded as of no great width, nations enjoying the peculiar favor of the gods, and blessed with happiness and longevity.

## Text #1 Questions

1) Which of the following is true according to the text?

a) The Romans were more imaginative than the Etruscans

b) The Romans were just as imaginative as the Etruscans

c) The Romans were not as imaginative as the Etruscans

d) Neither the Romans, nor the Etruscans were imaginative

2) Legends and stories of which culture were inspired from Egyptian and eastern cultures
a) Roman
b) Greek
c) Etruscan
d) Nordic

3) To understand these stories and myths, we first need to understand which part of the poet's perspective?
a) The scenery
b) The narrative
c) The structure of the universe
d) The vocabulary

4) Greek poets believed the earth to be
a) Flat & Circular
b) Round & Geoid
c) Flat & Elliptical
d) Spherical & Oblong

5) According to the Greeks, the continuation of the Mediterranean Sea was called
a) Olympus
b) Delphi
c) Oracle
d) Euxine

6) Which is true about the Greek myth of Hyperboreans?
a) They were a happy race free from disease or old age
b) Their country was only accessible by Sea
c) They fought frequent wars with the people of Hellas
d) They lived in caverns

7) Which mythical race lived to the south of the earth according to the Greeks?
a) Etruscans
b) Hyperboreans

c) Æthiopians
d) Olympian

8) The Greeks believed the Elysian Plain was an idyllic place where
a) All mortal souls went after death
b) Few chosen souls went in lieu of death
c) Immortal souls were transported to
d) All mortals souls visited before death

9) On which margin of the earth lay the "Isles of the Blessed?"
a) Eastern
b) Southern
c) Western
d) Northern

**Answers:**

1) Which of the following is true according to the text:
**d) Neither the Romans, nor the Etruscans were imaginative**

2) Legends and stories of which culture were inspired from Egyptian and eastern cultures
**b) Greek**

3) To understand these stories and myths, we first need to understand which part of the Poet's perspective:
**c) The structure of the universe**

4) Greek poets believed the earth to be
**a) Flat & Circular**

5) According to the Greeks, the continuation of the Mediterranean Sea was called
**d) Euxine**

6) Which is true about the Greek myth of Hyperboreans?
**a) They were a happy race free from disease or old age**

7) Which mythical race lived to the south of the earth according to the Greeks?
**c) Æthiopians**

8) The Greeks believed the Elysian Plain was an idyllic place where
**b) Few chosen souls went in lieu of death**

9) On which margin of the earth lay the "Isles of the Blessed?"
**c) Western**

# TEXT #2

(Reference: Project Gutenberg's *Hints on Mountain-Lion Trapping*, by Stanley P. Young https://www.gutenberg.org/files/48711/48711-h/48711-h.htmHE AMERICAN MOUNTAIN-LION (*Felis concolor*) is one of the largest predatory animals of the United States, sometimes weighing more than 200 pounds. Game conservationists recognize it as the greatest natural enemy of deer. Stockmen learn to their sorrow that when game is scarce the mountain-lion attacks young domestic stock, particularly colts, lambs, and kids, and even full-grown horses and cattle. In some western areas it is practically impossible to raise young colts or sheep on open stock ranges in the rough, rocky, and broken country that forms an ideal habitat for the mountain-lion.

The range of the mountain-lion, which is known also as cougar, panther, puma, and catamount, includes at present the large wilderness areas of the United States west of the one hundredth meridian. The heaviest infestation is in the Rocky Mountain States and southward through the desert mountain ranges of Arizona, Texas, and New Mexico. Farther westward mountain-lions are much less numerous, except in the coastal ranges of California, Oregon, and Washington, where they are somewhat abundant.

For the protection of domestic livestock and of large game in certain areas it is necessary to keep mountain-lions well under control. In spite of control measures, however, these predators will probably long continue to exist in the United States. There are many areas where normal hunting and the vicissitudes of the wild can be depended upon to keep their numbers within reasonable limits. There are also great stretches of wilderness areas that probably will never be touched by any mountain-lion-control campaigns.

This leaflet, intended to help stockmen and game protectors in local control of mountain-lions, is based on the experience of Biological Survey predatory-animal hunters. A similar publication (Leaflet No. 78) discusses control measures for such smaller members of the wild-cat family as the bobcat and the Canada lynx.

Mountain lions find most of their prey near the rougher and more inaccessible canyons, and in such places they live and breed with least disturbance. One of the most striking things about these animals is the distance to which they will go for food. Many have been known to travel 25 miles or more in a night, apparently without resting for any appreciable length of time. Because of their remarkable endurance, hunting them takes stamina and strength. Biological Survey hunters on the fresh track of a mountain-lion have trailed the animal for 10 consecutive hours or longer before treeing it.

Like the bobcat, the mountain-lion relies upon its senses of smell and sight in much of its foraging. Its smell is keener than that of the bobcat, though less so than in either wolf or coyote. It can see its prey for a long distance, but unquestionably it does much of its silent, cautious stalking by the sense of smell alone, taking advantage of every cover until within striking distance of its victim. Its sense of hearing also is acute.

In making a kill, the mountain-lion brings its victim to the ground with a stunning impact of its entire weight. It generally attacks at the throat and breast.

After making a kill and taking one meal, the mountain-lion will sometimes, though not always, bury the remainder of a carcass under leaves, litter, or other trash, to return for a later feast. Whether it will thus return depends to some extent upon weather conditions and on its ability to find prey elsewhere. Its killing and feeding habits vary in other ways also. In one instance, a lone lion attacked a herd of ewes and killed 192 in one night. Frequently more than one mountain-lion may feed on a single carcass. Near one cow carcass the writer once trapped six lions, of various sizes, evidently the parents and two litters of offspring.

The presence of a mountain-lion on a range may be indicated by its kill of deer or other game, even though domestic stock may not have been disturbed. If a kill is made in fall or winter, the meat may remain fresh for many weeks.

Where the control of mountain lions is essential, the principal means employed is the use of trained hounds.

Kentucky fox hounds and a cross between the Walker hound and the bloodhound have been found most satisfactory for trailing mountain-lions, though any good dog may tree one. The hunter must keep up with the pack, however, for a mountain lion that fights at bay instead of treeing, may kill all the dogs. When it chooses to fight, it uses teeth and claws, backed by powerful neck and shoulder muscles, in a telling way.

The use of poisons in mountain-lion control is not recommended. Hunting or trapping is more satisfactory, and it is unsafe to expose poisons on ranges where hunting dogs are being used.

## Text #2 Questions.

1) Scientific name for the American mountain lion is
   a) Felis concolor
   b) Puma concolor
   c) Felis nigripes
   d) Felis chaus

2) Which of the following names are not used for the mountain lion?
   a) Catamount
   b) Cougar
   c) Panther
   d) Lynx

3) In which US state are you most likely to find a mountain lion in his natural habitat?
   a) Arizona
   b) Connecticut
   c) California
   d) Washington

4) Why is it necessary to keep mountain lions well under control?
   a) To keep their population in check
   b) To protect human lives
   c) To protect domestic livestock

d) To keep them off the roads

5) Where do mountain lions find most of their prey?
a) Rough, rocky, and broken country
b) Inaccessible canyons
c) Desert mountain ranges
d) Coastal ranges

6) Arrange the strength of sense of smell in these animals in descending order. Pick the correct option.
a) Bobcat, mountain lion, coyote
b) Coyote, mountain lion, bobcat
c) Mountain lion, coyote, bobcat
d) Bobcat, coyote, mountain lion

7) Which of the following is not true about the hunting habits of mountain lion?
a) It travels great distance for its prey
b) It generally attacks throat or breast
c) It sometimes buries the carcass under leaves or trash
d) It never shares the prey with fellow mountain lions

8) Which of the following pair of adjectives most closely describes the mountain lion's hunting style?
a) Quiet and Cautious
b) Brash and Aggressive
c) Wild and Impetuous
d) None of the above

9) The principal means employed to control mountain lions is
a) Laying Traps
b) Trained Hounds
c) Poisoning
d) Hunting with crossbow

## Answers:

1) Scientific name for The American mountain lion is
**a) Felis concolor**

2) Which of the following names are not used for the mountain lion?
**d) Lynx**

3) In which US state are you most likely to find a mountain lion in his natural habitat?
**a) Arizona**

4) Why is it necessary to keep mountain lions well under control?
**c) To protect domestic livestock**

5) Where do mountain lions find most of their prey?
**b) Inaccessible canyons**

6) Arrange the strength of sense of smell in these animals in descending order. Pick the correct option.
**b) Coyote, mountain lion, bobcat**

7) Which of the following is not true about the hunting habits of mountain lion?
**d) It never shares the prey with fellow mountain lions**

8) Which of the following pair of adjectives most closely describes the mountain lion's hunting style?
**a) Quiet and Cautious**

9) The principal means employed to control mountain lions is
**b) Trained Hounds**

# TEXT #3

(Reference: The Project Gutenberg EBook of *Making Life Worth While*, by Douglas Fairbanks https://www.gutenberg.org/files/48565/48565-h/48565-h.htm)

Holding down a seat in the rocking chair fleet out on the shady piazza is most certainly not making the most out of life.

We all remember the line—"If wishes were fishes we'd have some fried." That is the answer to those who rock and dream, and hope for something to turn up instead of turning up something on their own account.

Of course, there is a time for everything, even the stealthy, creeping rocking chair—and that's about bedtime. In the estimation of an eminent neurologist there is no crime against nature in the home that cannot be traced to this monstrous thief of time, which, while apparently screeching and groaning under its load, is, in reality, shouting with joy at the job it is putting up on its occupant.

Taking the most out of life is the proper label for this old squeaker—breeder of idle contentment, day-dreams, inertia. Like everything else that saps the energy from mind and body, it counts its victims by the score, and throws them up on the sands of time.

Speaking of sand may serve to remind the reader of a well-known poem handed down from Grandmother days, which holds a lot of precious wisdom—probably more than any poem of its length—its breadth and depth being equal to the world in which we live. In childhood days this poem took my fancy, being short, to the point, and easy to remember. I was ready to recite it immediately and automatically upon request. I had no thought then as to its meaning, but as the years rolled by it tagged along in memory until now I find in it a sort of statement of fact upon which to build my theory of making life worth while. Here it is:

Little drops of water,
Little grains of sand,

Maketh the mighty ocean
And a pleasant land.

To those who adopt the idea of finding out just why little drops of water and little grains of sand accomplish so much, will come the greatest reward in the way of mental satisfaction—and, meanwhile, they'll keep busy.

There is unbounded happiness in the pursuit of knowledge; a wonderful satisfaction in building up one's treasure house of information. It's all so easy, requiring nothing more than a healthy, enquiring mind—and a zest for the sport.

Zest is a big word. It has to do with get up and git, which has been most appropriately boiled down into the word pep. Lazy people, mentally or bodily, seldom get anywhere. What they do get is either accidental or by absorption—if by the latter process, more likely through the pores than the brain. No use to talk to them about making life worth while.

The greatest of human possessions are a well-trained mind, a body to match, and a love of achievement, without which a man is old before his time. After that comes energy—the great propeller! What the brain directs the body will carry out—if the propeller is working. No hesitation—when the will commands the body acts. They synchronize—they are attuned, harmonious, fraternal, so to speak. And to hitch them together is just as easy as getting wet by standing bareheaded in the rain.

There is no intention of littering up this chapter with ways and means of putting one's upper story in fine working order—or the physical structure below. That is first-reader information. If we treat ourselves right, the brain will behave and the body will follow suit. Activity, mental and physical, is the meat in the cocoanut. Seeking knowledge leads along the sunlit paths of life where happiness abounds. The alternative is mental shiftlessness, leading from nowhere to nothing at all.

Cain killed Abel because, undoubtedly, of the shiftless life he led. Indolence and ignorance being the order of his day, he lacked the stamina with which to control his mind. His physical forces merely acted in consonance with his rage at

Abel's popularity. Cupidity led him on, but if Cain hadn't lost his head through lack of will to control himself the example of murder might never have been set before mankind.

## Text #3 Questions

1) "If wishes were fishes we'd have some fried" is the answer to those who

a) Make the most out of life
b) Rock and dream
c) Live in a shady Piazza
d) Turn up something on their own account

2) Taking the most out of life is the proper label for

a) A rocking chair
b) A crime against nature
c) Day dreaming
d) Breeder of idle contentment

3) According to the author, there is unbounded happiness in the pursuit of

a) Happiness
b) Day dreams
c) Knowledge
d) Mystery

4) Which qualities of mind are needed, according to the author, to live a more fulfilling life?

a) Healthy, Enquiring and Zesty
b) Satisfied, Healthy and Complacent
c) Content, Peppy and Active
d) Happy, Curious and Satisfied

5) Which kind of people get what they do by absorption?

a) Zesty
b) Active
c) Lazy
d) Curious

6) Which of the following is not one of the greatest of human possessions?

a) A well-trained mind
b) A body to match
c) A love of achievement
d) A passion for life

7) Provided there is energy, when does the body act?
a) When ideas synchronize
b) When the brain commands
c) When the muscles decide
d) When the propeller is working

8) The brain will behave and the body will follow suit if
a) We treat ourselves right
b) We treat others right
c) We eat more cocoanut
d) We seek knowledge

9) Why, according to the author did Cain kill Abel?
a) He was physically strong
b) Cupidity led him on
c) He lacked the stamina to control his brain
d) He wanted to set and example for the world

**Answers:**

1) "If wishes were fishes we'd have some fried" is the answer to those who

**b) Rock and dream**

2) Taking the most out of life is the proper label for

**a) A rocking chair**

3) According to the author, there is unbounded happiness in the pursuit of

**c) Knowledge**

4) Which qualities of mind are needed, according to the author, to live a more fulfilling life?

**a) Healthy, Enquiring and Zesty**

5) Which kind of people get what they do by absorption?

**c) Lazy**

6) Which of the following is not one of the greatest of human possessions?

**d) A passion for life**

7) Provided there is energy, when does the body act?

**b) When the brain commands**

8) The brain will behave and the body will follow suit if

**a) We treat ourselves right**

9) Why, according to the author did Cain kill Abel?

**c) He lacked the stamina to control his brain**

# TEXT #4

(Reference: The Project Gutenberg EBook of *My Life at Sea*, by W. Caius Crutchley
https://www.gutenberg.org/files/48582/48582-h/48582-h.htm)

Early in the year 1863 there was brought into the little harbour of Margate a vessel called the *Figaro* of Narbonne, a small craft with a cargo of wine. She had got into trouble on one of the many outlying sandbanks which make the entrance to the Thames a problem of considerable difficulty for any vessel not thoroughly qualified to meet any emergency that may arise through wind or weather. What the precise cause of this accident was escapes my memory, but whatever its origin, it was instrumental in sending me to sea, for it brought me into close contact with a London merchant, Mr. Trapp, who was interested in her cargo and who had come down to supervise her repairs. This merchant was also a shipowner, and had been at sea during the French wars in the early part of the century. He was good enough to tell me many stories relating to privateering and the customs of the sea, to all of which I listened greedily, for I was born with the sound of the sea in my ears and from my earliest recollections had made up my mind that the sailor's life was the only one worth living. Unfortunately this view was not shared either by my father or my mother, both of whom had set their minds upon making me a civil engineer. My head master was of the same opinion as myself as regards my future, but we reached the same conclusion by somewhat different roads, as will be seen.

I scarcely think I was tractable as a school-boy. I can distinctly remember that from the age of ten until4 I was fourteen I was always the "awful example," and my impression is that the cane was administered thrice daily with great regularity. At the age of fourteen there was a serious difference of opinion between the head master and myself; he suggested that my conduct in class was beyond his endurance, and I, considering his was also objectionable, expressed my view by launching a book at his head. When I turned to make my escape, there was no escape for me; I was headed off and cornered by masters lower down the room. And face downwards on a desk I both heard and felt the best arguments that can be used in such circumstances. When I got home, these arguments were only too palpable, and my indulgent parents brought my career at that school to a summary conclusion. Nevertheless, I bore the old boy no malice, for he was a good judge of a human boy's nature. When he asked me one day what I was going to be, I replied, "Civil engineer," to which he retorted, "A soldier or a sailor is all they will ever make of you," and it must be confessed that it was a fairly accurate forecast, though the prophecy was evidently not intended as a compliment to either army or navy.

After that episode it seemed to dawn upon my mind that it was time to learn something, and I was put as a private pupil with a man whose memory I shall always respect (afterwards Leetham of Thanet House), for he had the great gift of raising his pupil's enthusiasm for the subject he was teaching. We used to start quite early in the morning, before breakfast, take our time in the middle of the day for recreation, and again tackle the work in the evening. It was in one of the mid-day recreations that, happening to walk down the lower pier, I met my old friend the shipowner. I soon made up my mind that I must go to sea, and realised that here was5 the instrument by which my desire could be accomplished. A steady siege was at once commenced.

My dear old father would not listen to the scheme for a moment; salt water had no charms for him. Yet he himself had taught me the use of mathematical instruments and given me a fair grounding in plan drawing and similar matters. The shrine at which he worshipped, however, was that of Brunel and the great engineers who were then discovering the wonders of applied science. My mother, on the other hand, seeing that my mind was made up, offered no further opposition, and when the time arrived managed to give me the necessary assistance.

The scheme finally formulated was this. My friend Mr. Trapp had at that time a vessel in port of which he was part owner, and as she carried apprentices I was to take my place among them on her next voyage, but it was also stipulated that a premium was to be paid. How often, I wonder, have boys been jeered at by the old salts as being "blank gentlemen's sons that pay to go to sea," and when one considers in after life the hardships of a sailing-ship, such a custom certainly seems humorous.

Well, the appointed day arrived and my mother and I set out for London to carry out the necessary preliminaries. My father had provided funds in a surreptitious sort of manner, for when the die was cast he accepted the situation, though he never really acquiesced in it. Boys are heartless brutes as a rule where their inclinations are concerned, and set little store by the desires of those who have had the trouble of rearing them.

## Text #4 Questions

1) The vessel *Figaro of Narbonne* got into trouble while entering which river?

a) Thames
b) Volga
c) Rhine
d) Danube

2) Who came to oversee the cargo and repairs of the vessel?

a) Mr. Trapp
b) Mr. Leetham
c) Mr. Thanet
d) Mr. Brunel

3) The narrator considers which kind of life as worth living?

a) Pirate's
b) Captain's
c) Soldier's
d) Sailor's

4) How many times per day was the cane administered to discipline the young narrator?

a) Once

b) Twice
c) Thrice
d) Never

5) How did the adolescent narrator act when a difference of opinion arose between him and his head master?
a) The narrator slapped the headmaster
b) The narrator apologized to the headmaster
c) The narrator ran away from school
d) The narrator threw a book at the headmaster

6) Which professions did the headmaster opine as befitting the young narrator?
a) Civil Engineer or Architect
b) Soldier or Sailor
c) Doctor or Lawyer
d) Politician or Bureaucrat

7) Why does the narrator respect the memory of his private tutor?
a) He was a man of great wisdom and learning
b) He was someone who could discipline the narrator
c) He inspired enthusiasm in his pupils for the subject he taught
d) He was a great orator

8) Considering hardships of a sailing-ship, which custom seems humorous to the narrator?
a) The custom of paying a premium to become a sailor
b) The custom of becoming an apprentice on a vessel
c) The custom of initiation into the sailor's life
d) The custom of celebrating at the onset of a voyage

9) The narrator becomes a sailor with financial help from?
a) Mr. Trapp
b) His mother
c) His father
d) His headmaster

**Answers:**

1) The vessel *Figaro of Narbonne* got into trouble while entering which river?

**a) Thames**

2) Who came to oversee the cargo and repairs of the vessel?

**a) Mr. Trapp**

3) The narrator considers which kind of life as worth living?

**d) Sailor's**

4) How many times per day was the cane administered to discipline the young narrator?

**c) Thrice**

5) How did the adolescent narrator act when a difference of opinion arose between him and his head master?

**d) The narrator threw a book at the headmaster**

6) Which professions did the headmaster opine as befitting the young narrator?

**b) Soldier or Sailor**

7) Why does the narrator respect the memory of his private tutor?

**c) He inspired enthusiasm in his pupils for the subject he taught**

8) Considering hardships of a sailing-ship, which custom seems humorous to the narrator?

**a) The custom of paying a premium to become a sailor**

9) The narrator becomes a sailor with financial help from?

**c) His father**

# TEXT #5

(Reference: The Project Gutenberg EBook of *A General Introduction to Psychoanalysis*, by Sigmund Freud https://www.gutenberg.org/files/38219/38219-h/38219-h.htm)

I refer to the errors which an individual commits—as for example, errors of speech in which he wishes to say something and uses the wrong word; or those which happen to him in writing, and which he may or may not notice; or the case of misreading, in which one reads in the print or writing something different from what is actually there. A similar phenomenon occurs in those cases of mishearing what is said to one, where there is no question of an organic disturbance of the auditory function. Another series of such occurrences is based on forgetfulness—but on a forgetfulness which is not permanent, but temporary, as for instance when one cannot think of a name which one knows and always recognizes; or when one forgets to carry out a project at the proper time but which one remembers again later, and therefore has only forgotten for a certain interval. In a third class this characteristic of transience is lacking, as for example in mislaying things so that they cannot be found again, or in the analogous case of losing things. Here we are dealing with a kind of forgetfulness to which one reacts differently from the other cases, a forgetfulness at which one is surprised and annoyed, instead of considering it comprehensible. Allied with these phenomena is that of erroneous ideas—in which the element of transience is again prominent, inasmuch as for a while one believes something which, before and after that time, one knows to be untrue—and a number of similar phenomena of different designations.

These are all occurrences whose inner connection is expressed in the use of the same prefix of designation. They are almost all unimportant, generally temporary and without much significance in the life of the individual. It is only rarely that one of them, such as the phenomenon of losing things, attains to a certain practical importance. For that reason also they do not attract much attention, they arouse only weak affects.

It is, therefore, to these phenomena that I would now direct your attention. But you will object, with annoyance: "There are so many sublime riddles in the external world, just as there are in the narrower world of the psychic life, and so many wonders in the field of psychic disturbances which demand and deserve elucidation, that it really seems frivolous to waste labor and interest on such trifles. If you can explain to us how an individual with sound eyes and ears can, in broad daylight, see and hear things that do not exist, or why another individual suddenly believes himself persecuted by those whom up to that time he loved best, or defend, with the most ingenious arguments, delusions which must seem nonsense to any child, then we will be willing to consider psychoanalysis seriously. But if psychoanalysis can do nothing better than to occupy us with the question of why a speaker used the wrong word, or why a housekeeper mislaid her keys, or such trifles, then we know something better to do with our time and interest."

My reply is: "Patience, ladies and gentlemen. I think your criticism is not on the right track. It is true that psychoanalysis cannot boast that it has never occupied itself with trifles. On the contrary, the objects of its observations are generally those simple occurrences which the other sciences have thrown aside as much too insignificant, the waste products of the phenomenal world. But are you not confounding, in your criticism, the sublimity of the problems with the conspicuousness of their manifestations? Are there not very important things which under certain circumstances, and at certain times, can betray themselves only by very faint signs? I could easily cite a great many instances of this kind. From what vague signs, for instance, do the young gentlemen of this audience conclude that they have won the favor of a lady? Do you await an explicit declaration, an ardent embrace, or does not a glance, scarcely perceptible to others, a fleeting gesture, the prolonging of a hand-shake by one second, suffice? And if you are a criminal lawyer, and engaged in the investigation of a murder, do you actually expect the murderer to leave his photograph and address on the scene of the crime, or would you, of necessity, content yourself with fainter and less certain traces of that individual? Therefore, let us not undervalue small signs; perhaps by means of them we will succeed in getting on the track of greater things. I agree with you that the larger problems of the world and of science have the first claim on our interest. But it is generally of little avail to form the definite resolution to devote oneself to the investigation of this or that problem. Often one does not know in which direction to take the next step. In scientific research it is more fruitful to attempt what happens to be before one at the moment and for whose investigation there is a discoverable method. If one does that thoroughly without prejudice or predisposition, one may, with good fortune, and by virtue of the connection which links each thing to every other (hence also the small to the great) discover even from such modest research a point of approach to the study of the big problems."

## Text #5 Questions

1) Which kind of errors are not mentioned in the text?
   a) Errors in speech
   b) Errors of thought
   c) Errors in reading
   d) Errors in hearing

2) Allied to the phenomenon of behavioral errors and forgetfulness is that of
   a) Erroneous ideas
   b) Remembering at inopportune moments
   c) Weak memory
   d) Slips of tongue

3) How often, according to the text, docs the phenomenon of losing things attain practical importance?
   a) Frequently
   b) Very Frequently
   c) Rarely
   d) Never

4) Why, according to the text, is psychoanalysis important?

a) It studies phenomenon considered too insignificant by the sciences

b) It explains psychic disturbances as frivolous

c) It decodes optical illusions

d) It helps people cope with delusions

5) Why is the criticism of psychoanalysis termed "not on the right track"?

a) It really seems frivolous to waste labor and interest on such trifles

b) It confuses the sublimity of the problems with the conspicuousness of their manifestations

c) Psychoanalysis cannot boast that it has never occupied itself with trifles

d) Its observations are generally simple occurrences

6) The author compares the working of psychoanalysis with

a) Winning the favor of a lady

b) The investigation of a murder case by a criminal lawyer

c) Both A and B

d) None of the above

7) Which, according to the author is sign that you have won the favor of a lady?

a) An ardent embrace

b) An explicit declaration

c) A prolonged handshake

d) A passionate kiss

8) What should we not undervalue in the course of psychoanalytic investigation?

a) Dreams

b) Small Signs

c) Scientific method

d) Good fortune

9) While conducting scientific research one must not have

a) Predisposition
b) Premonitions
c) Definite resolutions
d) Modesty

**Answers:**

1) Which kind of errors are not mentioned in the text?
**b) Errors of thought**

2) Allied to the phenomenon of behavioral errors and forgetfulness is that of
**a) Erroneous ideas**

3) How often, according to the text, does the phenomenon of losing things attain practical importance?
**c) Rarely**

4) Why, according to the text, is psychoanalysis important?
**a) It studies phenomenon considered too insignificant by the sciences**

5) Why is the criticism of psychoanalysis termed "not on the right track"?
**b) It confuses the sublimity of the problems with the conspicuousness of their manifestations**

6) The author compares the working of psychoanalysis with?
**c) Both A and B**

7) Which, according to the author is sign that you have won the favor of a lady?
**c) A prolonged handshake**

8) What should we not undervalue in the course of psychoanalytic investigation?
**b) Small Signs**

9) While conducting scientific research one must not have
**a) Predisposition**

# Text #6

(Reference: http://wikitravel.org/en/Casablanca)

Casablanca, almost universally referred to as 'Casa', may be the cosmopolitan, industrial and economic heart of Morocco (and its largest city), but it is one of the less endearing in the country.

With a small, unassuming *medina* and a traffic-congested *ville nouvelle*, travellers arriving via Casablanca may be tempted to find the first train out to nearby Rabat. The awe-inspiring Hassan II Mosque and happening nightlife, however, are worth at least a day of your Moroccan itinerary.

The modern city of Casablanca was founded by Berber fishermen in the 10th Century BC and was subsequently used by the Phoenicians, Romans, and the Merenids as a strategic port called Anfa. The Portuguese destroyed it and rebuilt it under the name *Casa Branca*, only to abandon it after an earthquake in 1755. The Moroccan sultan rebuilt the city as Daru l-Badya and it was given its current name of Casablanca by Spanish traders who established trading bases there. The French occupied the city in 1907, establishing it as a protectorate in 1912 and starting construction of the *ville nouvelle*, however it gained independence with the rest of the country in 1956.

Casablanca is now Morocco's largest city with a population of almost 4 million and also boasts the world's largest artificial port but no ferry service of any kind . Casablanca is also the most liberal and progressive of Morocco's cities. Young men flirt brazenly with scantily-clad women, designer labels are the norm in the chic, beachfront neighbourhood of 'Ain Diab and many young Moroccans speak to each other exclusively in French.

But not everyone is living the Casablancan dream. Tens of thousands of rural Moroccans who fled the drought-ravaged interior to find work in the city are struggling under high unemployment rates and expensive housing. The poverty, prevalent in slums on the city's outskirts, has led to high rates of crime, drug use and prostitution

Mohammed V International Airport (IATA: CMN) is the busiest gateway to the country and is well-connected to Europe. Royal Air Maroc flies to New York JFK, Canada, many cities in Europe, and has connecting flights to all northern and many other African countries such as Nigeria, Central African Republic, Senegal.

To get from the airport into Casablanca or vice versa, take the train to/from Casa Voyageurs station which is on the outskirts of the central city and then a fairly long walk or petit taxi (circa 10DH) into the centre. A second class ticket from the airport to Casa Voyages was 40 dirhams as at May 2014. Trains depart hourly and the last one leaves the airport at 10:00pm. Maps are available at the Train Chief's office. Casa Voyageurs is the 3rd stop from the airport.

On arrival at Casa Voyageurs you should expect to be besieged by touts and taxi drivers offering outrageous fares and refusing to use their meters. Even if they say they will use the meter, they will subsequently announce a 10 dirham surcharge per person or per bag applies. For destinations in the central city you will be lucky to get the fare below 30 dirhams - two to three times its likely true value.

If your luggage is not heavy, simply ignore them all and walk away from the station where you are far more likely to find an honest driver who will use his meter. Alternatively, if you know the tram runs close to your accommodation, it is only 7 dirham to buy a rechargeable ticket at the stop immediately in front of the station.

Buses to the center leave regularly.

The most convenient way to reach major Moroccan cities is by train. The downtown station Casa Port only has a couple of trains, while all others pass through Casa-Voyageurs station, which serves trains to Meknes/Fes/Oujda, Marrakech or Tangier with stops in between. The trains are comfortable, the stations easy to navigate, and boards display the time of departure/arrival. Be sure to check the schedule for express trains; for instance, the train that leaves Casablanca at 7:05AM daily takes 3 hours to reach Fes, as opposed to the normal 5 hour journey. Trains for Rabat leave half-hourly.

Trains are divided into first and second-class compartments; the first-class ones generally cost an extra

50%, but have more room and guarantee a seat. Boarding second-class compartments during peak hours may mean that you have to stand until a seat is free.

CTM coaches (intercity buses) and various private lines run services to most notable Moroccan towns as well as a number of European cities. These run from the Gare Routière on Rue Léon l'Africain in downtown Casablanca.

The main Gare Routière (Ouled Ziane) is in the outskirts of the city and serves the same (and more) destinations as CTM. This is definitely not the best place to be around at night (as most train/bus stations in the world), but no one will try to bother you once you get inside the station. The fares are slightly cheaper and busses tend to leave more frequently, however their quality might be lower and some do take longer for the trip (always ask if they take the highway (autoroute) if available on your route). Most busses don't leave according to a fixed schedule, but when all the places in the bus are sold out. If buying a ticket there, make sure you don't pay anyone until you see the bus and you are sure there is a place for you to sit on.

A government department puts out an exhaustive map of Casablanca in book form called Carte Guide de Casablanca that you can find in bookstores or online; in all likelihood, though, it isn't necessary. Other than that, Casablanca is like any other European city: the streets (mostly) have signs, and passersby are extremely helpful in French or Arabic and, more rarely, Spanish or English. The Medina can be hard to navigate, but it's so small that no matter how blindly you wander into it, you're never more than ten minutes from an exit.

## Text #6 Questions

1) Which of the following is not a characteristic of the city of Casablanca?

a) Cosmopolitan
b) Economic heart
c) Industrial
d) Endearing

2) Modern city of Casablanca was founded by?
a) Ottoman Turks
b) Berber fishermen
c) The Romans
d) The Portuguese

3) In which century was the modern city of Casablanca founded?
a) 10th
b) 11th
c) 12th
d) 13th

4) What event of significance took place in the year 1755 in Casablanca?
a) A fire destroyed it
b) Portuguese destroyed it
c) An earthquake destroyed it
d) Berber Fishermen destroyed it

5) Who gave Casablanca its modern name?
a) Spanish
b) French
c) Portuguese
d) Dutch

6) Which is not a sign of liberal traditions present in Casablanca?
a) People talk to each other in French
b) Men flirt openly with scantily clad women
c) Designer labels are a norm in certain places
d) Financial markets are deregulated

7) Distress migration from the interior has brought which of the following to Casablanca?
a) Poverty
b) Unemployment
c) Disease
d) Prostitution

8) For 40 Dirhams, you can get to the Casa-Voyageurs station from?

a) Ville nouvelle
b) Mohammed V International Airport
c) Beachfront neighbourhood of 'Ain Diab
d) Meknes/Fes/Oujda

9) Which language are you least likely to get help in, within Casablanca?

a) English
b) Arabic
c) French
d) Spanish

## Answers:

1) Which of the following is not a characteristic of the city of Casablanca?

2) Modern city of Casablanca was founded by?
**b) Berber fishermen**

3) In which century was the modern city of Casablanca founded?
**a) 10th**

4) What event of significance took place in the year 1755 in Casablanca?
**c) An earthquake destroyed it**

5) Who gave Casablanca its modern name?
**a) Spanish**

6) Which is not a sign of liberal traditions present in Casablanca?
**d) Financial markets are deregulated**

7) Distress migration from the interior has brought which of the following to Casablanca?
**c) Disease**

8) For 40 Dirhams, you can get to the Casa-Voyageurs station from?
**b) Mohammed V International Airport**

9) Which language are you least likely to get help in, within Casablanca?
**a) English**

# Text #7

(Reference: http://www.bartleby.com/60/124.html)

Though most of us acknowledge that Milton dwells on the heights of English poetry, we are likely, because of his very sublimity, to look up to him with awe, as unapproachable. The charm of the minor poems of his youth may be felt without difficulty; but the obstacles to loving intimacy with his most important works, those into which he poured "the precious lifeblood of a master spirit," seem many and forbidding. We remember that Byron sneered at his angels and archangels joining in quibbles, and we apprehend that his theology must be dull or perplexing. We open "Paradise Lost" at almost any page, and meet with phrases and allusions that are unfamiliar. Habituated by our contemporary literature and journalism to receive an easy delight from the shocking, the bizarre, and the exceptional, we are not immediately attracted by an art whose characteristics are dignity and restraint. In Dr. Johnson's words, "we desert our master and seek for companions." As if to encourage our truancy, there arise those who question whether, after all, Milton is a master. The chief of a prominent American library refuses to advise the reading of "Paradise Lost," an ultra-modern critic professes to have discovered "new literary valuations" which at last destroy the poet's long-established reputation, and respectable literary journals actually find it necessary to defend a fame that had seemed imperishable.

**The Sources of Milton's Greatness**: The serious-minded who, despite such babbling, conclude that he to whom every great man of letters from Dryden to Meredith has granted the crowning laurel must surely be one whom it is an honourable privilege to know, may be assured that the obstacles to familiarity with Milton are not at all insuperable. From three sources especially does his greatness arise—the strength of his imagination, the harmony of his verse, and the truth of his thought. Each of these will become more clearly apparent to the reader if he will accept certain practical suggestions. To grow aware of the astounding imaginative power of Milton in "Paradise Lost," "Paradise Regained,"

"Samson Agonistes," and even the "Nativity Ode," one should before turning to those works read the biblical passages, in each case brief, which gave the poet the outlines of his themes. It need hardly be said that such a story as that of Adam and Eve has in the Bible a simple and poignant beauty which is perfect in its way; but when one turns from the few chapters that contain it and follows the course of the great epic, one begins to realize how sublimely Milton's imagination enlarges our conceptions of the past, the distant, and the unseen. Nor is it only realms, forces, and spirits unvisited and unknown that he reveals. Read the short account of Samson, or of the temptation of Christ; observe how few, though graphic, are the strokes of characterization; and you will thereupon in "Samson Agonistes" and "Paradise Regained" recognize with what vision Milton has penetrated into the hearts of hero and Lord and devil.

The mistake which prevents a full enjoyment of the musical beauty of Milton's blank verse is to read it silently—a sure way to make it seem like prose curiously printed. Aloud the blind poet uttered the most and the best of it; and aloud it should be read. Only thus can the artistic sense that slumbers within us be aroused to feel responsively the grandest rhythm and resonance that ever proceeded from an English tongue. Like ocean breakers, in varying lengths and with tireless energy, it beats and surges upon our emotions; and presently we are ready to receive those elevated thoughts it is marvelously designed to instill, because the sound has lifted us into a mood exalted above our ordinary state. He who thus comes to feel the artistic powers of Milton has taken a decisive step toward literary culture: he will thenceforth not easily be imposed upon by whatever is imaginatively weak or fantastic; and his ear, once attuned to the "grand style" of the master, will no longer delight in verse that is thin or harsh.

**Milton as a prophet**: But Milton did not use his poetical powers for the mere pleasure of exercising them. In him, as in Isaiah, the great artist is embodied in the greater prophet. This is a commonplace, yet many approach Milton as if it were untrue. In the case of "Paradise Lost," admittedly the fullest expression of his message, the first two books are mistakenly recommended as typical. In them, to be sure, are superbly displayed his artistic powers, but certainly not his dominant thought. In fact, to confine oneself to them has proved a direct way to misunderstand him. Because they deal with the fallen angels, we have arising the persistent error that Satan is the hero of "Paradise Lost," and that the arch-rebel preoccupied the poet's interest. The result in our day, when belief in a personal devil is faint, is the impression that Milton devotes his genius to themes that, however picturesque, possess for us slight moral significance. And so we have the pitiable result that the mere artist is admired, but the prophet not hearkened to. Yet his message, grasped as a whole, comes home to our very hearts.

**The theme of "Paradise Lost"**: The theme of Milton is not primarily Satan, nor even God and angels, but humanity. Not only do the opening lines of "Paradise Lost" proclaim the subject "man's disobedience," but throughout the epic it is the fate of man that is made the issue of every event in the universal creation. Thus Milton begins his story, not when Satan is conspiring against God, but when the defeated devil turns his revengeful thought toward the future inhabitants of the earth. Of that new world man is solemnly made the lord, God himself descending to breathe into him a spiritual life. It is to warn man against his fall that the rebellion in heaven is related; and in the central books it is the glory and the weakness of human nature that we see displayed. Finally, the future history of the world is communicated to Adam, not so much to manifest the absolute power of God or the futility of Satan's hate, as to assure the children of God of his eternal love toward them. In short, the subject is not theology but religion—not the nature of God and of Satan, but the relation of the powers of good and of evil to ourselves. Could a poet deal with a problem of more compelling and everlasting interest to us? The reader who focuses his attention upon the human beings in "Paradise Lost" will do what the poet did, and will, though accidental details may elude him, follow Milton's essential thought. The descriptions of heaven and hell, which may not correspond precisely to the reader's notions of the states of bliss and of misery, will recede into the background, where they belong;

and gradually there will rise before him Milton's idea of the true meaning of human life.

## Text #7 Questions

1) Why might Milton become unapproachable to a general audience?

a) Because he is sublime
b) Because he dwells on the heights of English poetry
c) Because he is self-indulgent
d) Because his works are too complex

2) The theme of Milton's "Paradise Lost" is?

a) Satan
b) Angels
c) God
d) Humanity

3) Where does Milton begin his story of "Paradise Lost?"

a) When Satan is conspiring against God
b) When the future history of the world is communicated to Adam
c) When the defeated devil turns his revengeful thought toward future earthlings
d) When weakness of human nature is displayed

4) Which mistake prevents a full enjoyment of the musical beauty of Milton's blank verse?

a) Reading it aloud
b) Reading it silently
c) Singing it
d) Not reading it

5) Which of the following is not a source of Milton's greatness?

a) The strength of his imagination
b) The harmony of his verse
c) The truth of his thought
d) The outlines of his themes

6) Which of the following do not belong to those who question whether, after all, Milton is a master?

a) Dr. Johnson
b) The chief of a prominent American library
c) An ultra-modern critic
d) Literary journals

7) He who thus comes to feel the artistic powers of Milton has taken a decisive step toward?

a) Teaching English as a language
b) Literary culture
c) Literary critique
d) Understanding Milton the prophet

8) Which of the following books is not written by Milton?

a) Naivety Ode
b) Samson Agonistes
c) Paradise Regained
d) Paradise Lost

9) Why is the future history of the world communicated to Adam?

a) To manifest the absolute power of God
b) To manifest the futility of Satan's hate
c) To assure the children of God of His eternal love toward them
d) To assure the children of God of His eternal forgiveness

**Answers:**

1) Why might Milton become unapproachable to a general audience?

**a) Because he is sublime**

2) The theme of Milton's "Paradise Lost" is?

**d) Humanity**

3) Where does Milton begin his story of "Paradise Lost?"

**c) When the defeated devil turns his revengeful thought toward future earthlings**

4) Which mistake prevents a full enjoyment of the musical beauty of Milton's blank verse?

**b) Reading it silently**

5) Which of the following is not a source of Milton's greatness

**d) The outlines of his themes**

6) Which of the following do not belong to those who question whether, after all, Milton is a master?

**a) Dr. Johnson**

7) He who thus comes to feel the artistic powers of Milton has taken a decisive step toward?

**b) Literary culture**

8) Which of the following books is not written by Milton?

**a) Naivety Ode**

9) Why is the future history of the world communicated to Adam?

**c) To assure the children of God of His eternal love toward them**

# Text #8

(Reference: *Why Bitcoin is and isn't like the Internet* http://joi.ito.com/weblog/2015/01/23/why-bitcoin-is-.html)

I'm fundamentally an Internet person -- my real business life started around the dawn of the Internet and for most of my adult life, I've been involved in building layers and pieces of the Internet, from helping start the first commercial Internet service provider in Japan to investing in Twitter and helping bring it to Japan. I've also served on the boards of the Open Source Initiative, the Internet Corporation for Names and Numbers (ICANN), The Mozilla Foundation, Public Knowledge, Electronic Privacy Information Center (EPIC), and been the CEO of Creative Commons. Given my experiences in the early days of the net, it's possible that I'm biased and everything new looks like the Internet.

Having said that, I believe that there are many parallels between the Internet and Bitcoin and there are many lessons from the Internet that can help provide guidance in thinking about Bitcoin and its future, but there are also some important differences.

The similarity is that Bitcoin is a transportation infrastructure that is decentralized, efficient and based on an open protocol. Instead of transferring packets of data over a dynamic network in contrast to the circuits and leased lines that preceded the Internet, Bitcoin's protocol, the blockchain, allows trust to be established between mutually distrusting parties in an efficient and decentralized way. Although you could argue that the ledger is "centralized," it's created through mechanical decentralized consensus.

The Internet has a root -- in other words, just because you use the Internet Protocol doesn't mean that you're necessarily part of the Internet. To be part of THE Internet, you have to agree to the names and numbers protocol and root servers that are administered by ICANN and its consensus process. You can use the Internet Protocol and make your own network, using your own rules for names and numbers, but then you're just a network and not The Internet.

Similarly, you can use the blockchain protocol to create alternative bitcoins or alt.coins. This allows you to innovate and use many of the technological benefits of Bitcoin, but you are no longer technically interoperable with Bitcoin and do not benefit from the network effect or the trust that Bitcoin has.

Also like the beginning of the Internet, there are competing ideas at each of the levels. AOL created a dialup network and really helped to popularize email. It eventually dumped its dialup network, its core business, but survived as an Internet service. Many people still have AOL email accounts.

With crypto-currencies, there are coins that don't connect to the "genesis block" of Bitcoin -- alt.coins that use fundamentally the same technology. There are alt.coins that use slightly different protocols and some that are fundamentally different.

On top of the coin layer, there are various services such as wallets, exchanges, service providers with varying levels of vertical integration -- some agnostic to whichever cryptocurrency ends up "winning" and some tightly linked. There are technologies and services being built on top of the infrastructure that use the network for fundamentally different things than transacting units of value, just as voice over IP used the same network in a very different way.

In the early days of the Internet, most online services were a combination of dialup and x.25 a competing packet switching protocol developed by Comité Consultatif International Téléphonique et Télégraphique, (CCITT), the predecessor to the International Telecom Union (ITU), a standards body that hangs off of the United Nations. Many services like The Source or CompuServe used x.25 before they started offering their services over the Internet.

I believe the first killer app for the Internet was email. On most of the early online services, you could only send email to other people on the same service. When Internet email came to these services, suddenly you could send email to anyone.

This was quite amazing and notably, email is still one of the most important applications on the Internet.

As the Internet proliferated, the TCP/IP stack, free software that anyone could download for free and install on their computer to connect it to the Internet, was further developed and deployed. This allowed applications that ran on your computer to use the Internet to talk to other programs running on other computers. This created the machine-to-machine network. It was no longer just about typing text into a terminal window. The file transfer protocol (FTP) and later Gopher, a text-based browsing and downloading service popular before the web was invented, allowed you to download music and images and create a world wide web of content. Eventually, permission-less innovation on top of this open architecture gave birth to the World Wide Web, Napster, Amazon, eBay, Google and Skype.

I remember twenty years ago, giving a talk to advertising agencies, media companies and banks explaining how important and disruptive the Internet would be. Back then, there were satellite photos of the earth and a webcam pointing at a coffee pot on the Internet. Most people didn't have the imagination to see how the Internet would fundamentally disrupt commerce and media, because Amazon, eBay and Google hadn't been invented -- just email and Usenet-news. No one in these big companies believed that they had to learn anything about the Internet or that the Internet would affect their business -- I mostly got blank stares or snores.

Similarly, I believe that Bitcoin is the first "killer app" of The Blockchain as email was the killer app for the beginning of the Internet. We are in the process of inventing eBay, Amazon and Google. My hunch is that The Blockchain will be to banking, law and accountancy as The Internet was to media, commerce and advertising. It will lower costs, disintermediate many layers of business and reduce friction. As we know, one person's friction is another person's revenue.

One of the main things we worked on when I was on the board of ICANN was trying to keep the Internet from forking. There were many organizations that didn't agree with ICANN's policies or didn't like the US's excessive influence over the Internet. Our job was to listen to everyone and create an inclusive and consensus-based process so that people felt that the benefits of the network effect outweighed the energy and cost of dealing with this process. In general we succeeded. It helped that almost all of the founders and key technical minds and technical standards organizations that designed and ran the Internet worked together with ICANN. This interface between the policy makers and the technologists -- however painful -- was viewed as something that wasn't great but worked better than any of the other alternatives.

## Text #8 Questions

1) On the board of which of the following has the author not served?

a) Open Source Initiative

b) Internet Corporation for Names and Numbers (ICANN)

c) The Mozilla Foundation

d) Common Knowledge

2) The author is of the opinion that the Internet and Bitcoin are?

a) Somewhat alike
b) Not alike
c) Exactly alike
d) Unrelated

3) Bitcoin is a transportation infrastructure that is

a) Decentralized
b) Efficient
c) Based on open protocol
d) All of the above

4) Bitcoin's protocol is called the?

a) Keychain
b) Blockchain
c) Keyblock
d) Open protocol

5) To be part of THE Internet, you have to agree to the names and numbers protocol and root servers that are administered by?

a) IEEE
b) ICANN
c) Creative Commons
d) Mozilla Corporation

6) According to the author, the first killer app of the Internet was?

a) Chatroom
b) Browser
c) Email
d) File sharing

7) Gopher succeeded which Internet protocol?

a) TCP/IP
b) BGP
c) ITU
d) FTP

8) Bitcoin and its protocol will revolutionize which fields of human endeavor?

a) Banking, Law and Accountancy
b) Media, Commerce and Advertising
c) Medicine, Health and Wellness
d) Teaching, Training and Education

9) The interface between the policy makers and the technologists?

a) Wasn't great but worked
b) Was painful and didn't work
c) Was responsible for forking the internet
d) Was a liability

**Answers:**

1) On the board of which of the following has the author not served?

**d) Common Knowledge**

2) The author is of the opinion that the Internet and Bitcoin are?

**a) Somewhat alike**

3) Bitcoin is a transportation infrastructure that is?

**d) All of the above**

4) Bitcoin's protocol is called the

**b) Blockchain**

5) To be part of THE Internet, you have to agree to the names and numbers protocol and root servers that are administered by?

**b) ICANN**

6) According to the author, the first killer app of the Internet was?

**c) Email**

7) Gopher succeeded which Internet protocol?

**d) FTP**

8) Bitcoin and its protocol will revolutionize which fields of human endeavor?

a) **Banking, Law and Accountancy**

9) The interface between the policy makers and the technologists?

**a) Wasn't great but worked**

# Text #9

(Reference: http://www.bartleby.com/60/132.html)

Astronomy was destined to liberate the modern intellect from the bondage of the Middle Ages, and by teaching man that the earth is not the fixed center of the universe, but a satellite of one among many stars, to shake the confidence with which he had long regarded the universe as made for him, the earth for his abode, the heavens for his enjoyment. This is the great contribution of astronomy to thought; to civilization it has also contributed some of the most important advances, such as an accurate calendar, the standard of time, and the exact measure of time, sound methods of navigation and geography; and commencing earlier than all the other sciences, it has built up one of the most admirable structures of scientific knowledge.

Astronomy was long the leader among the sciences, and as such gave to the world trigonometry, in part logarithms, and Newton's dynamics. But though astronomical progress has by no means ceased, the accelerated growth of other sciences—first physics, then chemistry, and of late biology—has rendered it less conspicuous. The continued importance of astronomy is, however, well illustrated by the marvellous results of spectrum analysis, while to-day the study of nebulae and of the physics of the sun possesses the highest interest.

**Hipparchus And The Ptolemaic System**: The principal results of ancient astronomy go by the name of Ptolemy (the Ptolemaic system), but are mainly due to the labors of Hipparchus. Hipparchus knew the latitude and longitude of 150 fixed stars within a fraction of a degree, when, in the year 134 B. C., a new star of the first magnitude suddenly appeared. Encouraged by this extraordinary event, he applied himself diligently to astronomical measurements, establishing the position of more than 1,000 fixed stars. It was no doubt this sound basis of accurate quantitative data, and the familiarity with his subject which such work provided, that led to his great achievements. He discovered the precession of the equinoxes, and measured it with considerable accuracy; he measured the length of the day with an error of but six minutes; but his great achievement was a mathematical device whereby the position of the sun and, with less accuracy, the positions of the moon and planets could be calculated.

The essential features of this device consisted in imagining the sun to move in a circle of which the earth was not quite the center; this is the exocentric of ancient astronomy. Another more difficult idea was that of epicycles. These two mathematical ideas did very good service in the work of Hipparchus, for the practical purposes of the calendar. But later, in the hands of Ptolemy, and in the succeeding centuries, they ceased to be arbitrary assumptions, or even mere theories, and in the Middle Ages became dogmas which were held most tenaciously and blindly. As astronomical knowledge slowly increased, it became necessary to make the theory more and more complex in order to fit the facts, and, long before the work of Copernicus, astronomical theories had reached a degree of absurdity that could not have endured in any other age. Yet more than one of the astronomers of antiquity had believed that the earth moves, either rotating on its axis, or revolving round the sun, or both.

**The Copernican Theory**: Copernicus was born at Thorn in Poland (1473) of a German mother. Educated first in medicine, he studied astronomy in Vienna, and he was later in Italy (1495-1505) at the height of the Renaissance. When he returned home, his uncle, the bishop of Ermeland, presented him with a clerical position at Frauenburg. Here for forty years he labored to bring astronomical calculations and observations into harmony, and finally, long after he had become convinced of the soundness of the heliocentric view, published the work which marks the first great step in modern science, a work which he saw for the first time on his deathbed in 1543.

Copernicus showed that all the difficulties which the movements of the planets present would become very much less if the moon were left the only satellite of the earth, and the earth itself and all the planets were assumed to move around the sun. He did not prove—in truth being wise and realizing his own limitations, he did not seek to prove—this hypothesis, but only to present the reasons why it must appear the most probable explanation of the principal astronomical phenomena.

The new doctrine made converts slowly. At first it was opposed by the professional astronomers, with whose time-honored habits it interfered, and who were, for the most part, not competent to understand it. Later the opposition of the great Tycho Brahe worked against it for many years. Still later the opposition of theologians effectually cut off many converts, most notably Descartes. But the discovery of Kepler's laws completely destroyed the Ptolemaic system, and must have convinced nearly all reasonable men of the correctness of that of Copernicus. These famous laws are as follows: The line joining the sun with a planet sweeps over equal areas in equal periods of time. Every planet moves in an ellipse with the sun at one focus. The squares of the times of the revolution of any two planets are in the same ratio as the cubes of their mean distances from the sun.

**Galileo And Newton**: The next important step in the growth of knowledge of the solar system was Galileo's study of the laws of fall and the composition of two kinds of motion, like fall and projection, as in the case of a projectile. This was followed by Newton's magnificent extension of gravity from the earth to the whole of space, with the assumption and proof that the intensity of gravitational attraction varies inversely as the square of the distance.

These ideas, combined with Kepler's laws, led at once to the theory of planetary motion and its proof, in Newton's "*Principia*." The motion of the planets appeared as the resultant of their tendency to go on in the direction in which they were moving (inertia), and their tendency to fall to the sun (gravitation). The problem yielded completely, so far as two bodies are concerned, to the mathematical genius of Newton.

Still the revolution of the earth about the sun was not, by many astronomers, considered to be proved, while some even denied it. For if the earth really revolved about the sun, the relative positions of the stars ought not to appear the same to us from different parts of the orbit. Yet no difference in their places at the two solstices could be detected, although the stands of the observer were separated by a hundred and eighty million miles in the two instances.

James Bradley was the first person to obtain important results from the investigation of this problem of parallax. He found, not, to be sure, a periodic change of the apparent position of the stars that could be explained as parallax, but a different change of position, quite unexpected. This he called aberration, and recognized that it was due to a composition of the motion of the earth and of the light from the star itself, which is analogous to the entry of rain falling straight down, yet into the open front of a moving carriage. Here, nevertheless, was a proof, the more valuable because unexpected, of the earth's motion. It was not until 1837 that Bessel finally measured the parallax of a fixed star, and this finally ended the problem. The whole difficulty had been due merely to the enormous distance which separates us from the nearest of the stars.

**Spectrum Analysis**: A new period in the history of astronomy followed upon the discovery of spectrum analysis by Bunsen and Kirchhoff. At the outset the chemical composition of the sun revealed itself. Later that of the stars became known; still later it became possible to classify the stars on the basis of their spectra, and at length it has become evident that variations in spectra are at least largely due to differences in the age of suns (the length of time during which cooling has gone on), that all stars are probably very much alike both chemically and physically, and that our sun is probably very much like all other stars. The geological doctrine of uniformity has been extended to astronomy.

## Text #9 Questions

1) Which of the following is not a contribution of astronomy to civilization?

a) Standard of time
b) Exact measure of time
c) Sound methods of navigation
d) Liberation from the dark ages

2) Astronomy has become less conspicuous because of?

a) Economic growth
b) Popularity of social sciences
c) Growth in other sciences
d) Popularity of Newton's dynamics

3) The principal results of ancient astronomy go by the name of?
a) Ptolemy
b) Hipparchus
c) Copernicus
d) Tycho Brahe

4) Who discovered the precession of the equinoxes?
a) Galileo
b) Hipparchus
c) Newton
d) Copernicus

5) Continued importance of astronomy is illustrated by the results of?
a) Spectrum Analysis
b) Trigonometry
c) The Copernican Theory
d) Ptolemaic system

6) Which discovery completely destroyed the Ptolemaic system?
a) Copernican Theory
b) Kepler's laws
c) Newton's dynamics
d) Newton's "Principia"

7) Who was the first person to obtain important results from the investigation of the problem of parallax?
a) Bradley
b) Bunsen
c) Kirchhoff
d) Bessel

8) The motion of the planets appeared as the resultant of their tendency to move?

a) About the sun
b) Relative positions of the stars
c) In the direction in which they were moving
d) Towards the sun

9) Which of the following is not one of Kepler's Laws?

a) The line joining the sun with a planet sweeps over equal areas in equal periods of time

b) Every planet moves in an ellipse with the sun at one focus

c) All the planets move around the sun

d) The squares of the times of the revolution of any two planets are in the same ratio as the cubes of their mean distances from the sun

**Answers:**

1) Which of the following is not a contribution of astronomy to civilization?
**d) Liberation from the dark ages**

2) Astronomy has become less conspicuous because of?
**d) Popularity of Newton's dynamics**

3) The principal results of ancient astronomy go by the name of?
**a) Ptolemy**

4) Who discovered the precession of the equinoxes?
**b) Hipparchus**

5) Continued importance of astronomy is illustrated by the results of?
**a) Spectrum Analysis**

6) Which discovery completely destroyed the Ptolemaic system?
**b) Kepler's laws**

7) Who was the first person to obtain important results from the investigation of the problem of parallax?
**a) Bradley**

8) The motion of the planets appeared as the resultant of their tendency to move?
**c) In the direction in which** they **were moving**

9) Which of the following is not one of Kepler's Laws?
**c) All the planets move around the sun**

# Text #10

(Reference: http://en.wikisource.org/wiki/Mary_(1631-1660)_(DNB00))

MARY, Princess Royal of England and Princess of Orange (1631–1660), born at St. James's Palace on 4 Nov. 1631, and baptised on the same day by Laud, then bishop of London, was eldest daughter of Charles I and Queen Henrietta Maria. She was brought up under the tuition of the Countess of Roxburghe, and became celebrated for her grace, beauty, and intelligence. In the lighter accomplishments, such as dancing, she excelled, but her general education was defective.

In January 1640 a proposed marriage between Mary and William, a lad of fifteen, the son of Frederick Henry, prince of Orange, was rejected by her father, who wished to marry her to the son of Philip IV of Spain. Subsequent events, however, compelled him to agree to William's offer. On 10 Feb. 1641 he announced to parliament that his daughter's marriage treaty had been brought to a conclusion, and that it only remained to consider the terms of a political alliance between England and the Dutch republic (Lords' Journals, iv. 157). Charles privately believed that, in case of extremity, Frederick Henry would assist him in the maintenance of his authority in England. The marriage was celebrated at Whitehall on Sunday, 2 May 1641. There was little ceremony. Henrietta Maria disliked the match; the elector palatine, Charles Lewis, who had desired to marry Mary himself, refused to attend the banquet. According to the marriage treaty Mary was to remain in England till she had reached her twelfth year; her husband was to allow her 1,500£ a year for pocket-money, and her dower in case of his death was to be 10,000£ a year, with two residences. Henrietta Maria, on quitting England in February 1642, took Mary to Holland, where, in February 1644, she was fully installed in her conjugal position. She gave audiences, received foreign ambassadors, and fulfilled all functions of state with a gravity and decorum remarkable for her years. The following month she mingled in a series of court festivities on the occasion of a recent alliance between France and Holland, and presided over an entertainment given by her husband to the French envoys. With the struggles of her father against the parliament she warmly sympathised. In December 1646 a Dutch man-of-war nut in at Newcastle-upon-Tyne, where the King then was, bringing him a letter from Mary ; she urged him to take the opportunity of escaping to Holland. With her aunt, Elizabeth, queen of Bohemia, Mary lived on terms of warm friendship; but with her mother-in-law, Amelia, her relations were never cordial.

Prince William at his father s death, on 14 March 1647, was elected stadt holder, and in 1648 welcomed to Holland his brothers-in-law, Charles, prince of Wales, and James, duke of York. In 1650 he was foiled in an attempt to seize Amsterdam in order to make himself absolute, and he died on 6 Nov. in the same year, leaving his widow pregnant of a son, afterwards William III, king of England, who was born on 14 Nov. following. The Princess-dowager Amelia, grandmother of the infant prince, wished to become his guardian, on the plea that Mary was still in her minority ; but by a decree signed on 15 Aug. 1651 it was settled that Mary should be tutrix of the person of her son, and should dispose of all vacant offices about him and in his possession ; while his grandmother and the elector of Brandenburg, his uncle, should be joint inspectors of his property. The States, however, refused to reinstate the prince in the honours enjoyed by his father, and, by contrivance of the princess-dowager, Count Dona was confirmed in his office as governor of the town of Orange by the States-General, although he had taken solemn oath to Mary's husband to maintain the place for her in case of his death, and to obey no orders but hers.

Mary's chief confidants were Catherine, lady Stanhope, who had accompanied her to Holland as governess, and who remained with her as chief lady of honour, and Lady Stanhope's Dutch husband, Heenvliet, who held the post of superintendent of the princess's household. M. de Beverweert, a Dutch counsellor, swayed her opinions in political matters. She was always unpopular in Holland, and did not trouble to learn Dutch. She disliked the people on account of their general sympathy with Cromwell, and declined to employ any Hollander in her son's service. In conjunction with the Duke of York and the queen of Bohemia, Mary sought to celebrate the first anniversary of her father's death (30 Jan. 1650) as a solemn fast, but the proceeding was prohibited by the States of Holland as being offensive to the English parliament. A little later, when ambassadors from the English parliament were received by the States-General, she retired to her dower residence at Breda, but to the influence of her party was attributed the failure of the envoys to conclude an alliance with Holland. In October 1651 Charles II landed at Helvoetsluys, and Mary secretly domiciled him in one of her country houses at Teyling, until he left for Paris. Her readiness to assist her brothers liberally from her own resources, and to bestow money or office on their adherents, roused the jealousy of the States, who at length forbade her receiving her relatives in Holland at all. Mary's court and that of the queen of Bohemia, it was reported by their opponents, were nests of vipers, in which were hatched all plots, not only against Dutch freedom, but also against that of England ; and schemes for the assassination of Cromwell were rumoured to originate there (Thurloe, State Papers, ii. 319, 344). The outbreak of war between England and Holland in May 1652 led to a reaction in favour of the house of Orange in many of the states of the Dutch republic. Mary's son, William, was formally elected stadtholder by Zealand and several of the northern provinces, but De Witt, the republican leader, succeeded in excluding him from the state of Holland, and Cromwell, upon negotiating a treaty of peace with the Dutch commissioners, insisted that William should be declared incapable of succeeding to his father's military dignities, and that all enemies of England should be expelled from Holland. Mary passionately declaimed against these proposals, and drew up a remonstrance. But De Witt stood firm, although the country was divided and civil war seemed to threaten it; the treaty of peace containing the offending clauses was signed on 27 May 1654.

Mary's health suffered under the growing anxieties of her position. To save expense in the interests of her brothers, she announced her intention of resigning two of her palaces, retaining only Breda and Honslardyke (ib. ii. 284). In July 1654 she set out for Spa, and passed several weeks there; she afterwards moved to Aix-la-Chapelle, and subsequently visited Charles II at Cologne. She returned to Teyling in October, but again visited Charles at Cologne in July 1655, and took a trip incognito to Frankfort fair, setting out on her journey home on 15 Nov. In January 1656 she visited Paris, where she was royally received.

Mary had not been without suitors in Holland, and George Villiers, second duke of Buckingham (q.v.), bad been dismissed her court there on account of the unbecoming importunity of his appeals to her. Unfounded rumours of a liaison with Henry Jerinyn, first baron Dover (q. v.), were at onetime in circulation. At Paris Charles Emmanuel II, duke of Savoy, Ernest Augustus of Brunswick-Luneburg, and George William, duke of Brunswick, were said to have offered her marriage, while Cardinal Mazarin showed her especial favour. She left Paris on 21 Nov., and after staying at Bruges for two months at the court of Charles II, she returned to the Hague on 2 Feb. 1657, after nearly a year's absence. The Dutch still credited her with political aims in behalf of her son and brother. A proposal secretly made to Charles by Amelia, the princess-dowager, that he should marry her daughter Henrietta, was discovered and warmly resented by Mary. A temporary reconciliation took place when brother and sister met at Breda in October 1659. Next month, when she and the Princess-dowager Amelia took the young Prince of Orange to Leyden to commence his studies there, they were accorded an enthusiastic welcome. The new year (1060) was initiated by the performance in his honour of a tragi-comedy, entitled 'The Amorous Fantasm,' written by Sir William Lower (q. v.), and dedicated in flattering terms to the princess royal.

Meanwhile, in August 1608, Mary, who had attained her full majority, twenty-five years of age, in November 1657, had been acknowledged by the parliament of Orange sole regent for her son, according to the terms of her husband's will. Count Dona, nephew of the Princess-dowager Amelia, who was governor of the town of Orange, warmly opposed this formal recognition of Mary, and threatened to dissolve the parliament of the province by force. The Princess Amelia and the elector of Brandenburg sided with Dona, but Mary firmly asserted her rights (November 1658), and obtained through

Queen Henrietta Maria assurances of support from Cardinal Mazarin and Louis XIV. The French king sent a war frigate to cruise in the Rhine to prevent Dona from levying tolls due to Mary on vessels passing down the river, and Dona fitted out gunboats to chase the frigate. Amid these disorders, Mary laid before the States-General a long statement of her claims, to which the Princess Amelia prepared a reply, and Mary another rejoinder. At length, in October 1659, the States-General addressed a remonstrance to Louis XIV, complaining of Mary's action, and requesting that Louis would appoint judges who should compose the strife. To a request that she should accept an accommodation Mary returned an evasive answer. But Louis's suggestion that Dona should deliver Orange into his hands, coupled with the threats of her opponents in Orange to deprive her of her dower, reduced her to a more compliant mood. She made an offer (although she afterwards refused to confirm it) of fifty thousand florins to Dona if he would relinquish the government of Orange, and undertook to send a special messenger to induce Louis to desist from his projected attack. She was too late. The citadel capitulated to Louis's forces on 25 March 16(K). Mary tried hard to justify herself in having called in French interference, and laid the blame on Dona.

## Text #10 Questions

1) Who was the mother of Princess Mary?
   a) Catherine
   b) Countess of Roxburghe
   c) Henrietta Maria
   d) Lady Stanhope

2) Which of the following qualities was princess Mary not celebrated for possessing?
   a) Beauty
   b) Intelligence
   c) Grace
   d) Charm

3) Which of the following is true about Mary's marriage with William?

a) It was celebrated at Whitehall on Sunday, 2 May 1641
b) There was a big ceremony
c) Mary's mother was in favor of the marriage
d) Charles Lewis attended the banquet

4) Which activity did Mary not perform in her conjugal position?
a) She gave audiences
b) Received foreign ambassadors
c) Mingled in a series of church festivities
d) Presided over an entertainment given by her husband to the French envoys

5) Who among the following cannot be said to be close to Mary?
a) Oliver Cromwell
b) Catherine
c) Heenvliet
d) M. de Beverweert

6) To which destination did Mary take an incognito trip?
a) Holland
b) Paris
c) Frankfurt
d) Berlin

7) Which one of the following was not one of Mary's suitors in Holland?
a) George Villiers
b) George Jerinyn
c) Charles Emmanuel II
d) George William

8) The tragic-comic play 'The Amorous Fantasm,' was written by?
a) William Shakespeare
b) Geoffrey Chaucer
c) William Lower
d) None of the above

9) Why did the French king send a war frigate to cruise in the Rhine?

a) To dissolve the parliament of the province by force
b) To prevent Dona from levying tolls
c) To deprive Mary of her dower
d) To induce Louis to desist from his projected attack

## Answers:

1) Who was the mother of Princess Mary?
**c) Henrietta Maria**

2) Which of the following qualities was princess Mary not celebrated for possessing?
**d) Charm**

3) Which of the following is true about Mary's marriage with William?
**a) It was celebrated at Whitehall on Sunday, 2 May 1641**

4) Which activity did Mary not perform in her conjugal position?
**c) Mingled in a series of church festivities**

5) Who among the following cannot be said to be close to Mary?
**a) Oliver Cromwell**

6) To which destination did Mary take an incognito trip?
**c) Frankfurt**

7) Which one of the following was not one of Mary's suitors in Holland?
**b) George Jerinyn**

8) The tragic-comic play 'The Amorous Fantasm,' was written by
**c) William Lower**

9) Why did the French king send a war frigate to cruise in the Rhine?
**b) To prevent Dona from levying tolls**

# APPENDIX B - GLOSSARY

***A Priori* Knowledge:** The knowledge we gained from previous experience or learning, not the knowledge that appears in current text.

**Anchor Marker:** Answers some fundamental question allowing you to retrieve information in the future. Other markers just connect to anchors to generate further details and linking to additional information. The anchor marker helps you remember both the question and the answer. In a mind map, the anchor is the place from where you access your whole mind map

**Chunking:** Grouping several pieces of information, visual markers, mind maps or other mnemonic structures a according to common criteria.

**Clarity**: Clarity is simply the determining the purpose of the text from its title and deriving certainty from it.

**Coloring the Text:** To keep track of various perspectives "color" the text according to the dominant perspective of each paragraph. Try to follow the "colors" in the visualization themes and try to reproduce the article photographically with "color" to improve navigation when re-examining the article. The most important tip here is keeping the colors consistent with the article, not your own thoughts.

**Compare**: Compare your measurements against your requirements. Does this process save time? Does it take too much time? Does it accomplish the desired result?

**Convergent Thinking**: Focusing and reducing the number of hypothesis/ideas to the best hypothesis for the next learning or processing stage.

**Creative Connections:** Different from logical thinking; allowing the strangest, out of the box, unrelated connections to surface by continually asking the same questions and coming up with different solutions each time.

**Critical thinking:** Clear, reasoned thinking involving critique.

**Divergent Thinking:** Involves producing multiple or alternative perspectives from available information.

**Domain of Knowledge:** An area of learning or human endeavor, a discipline requiring specific set of skills. For example, medicine, math, programming, history, music. Since most of our activities are interdisciplinary, the knowledge we acquired that is relevant to what we are learning may be called "domain knowledge." We can build our new understandings on top of what we already know.

**Dual Coding:** There are many ways information is processed in our brain. Some ways are independent, like audio and visual processing. Other senses could be used, faces of people or personal emotions as different and almost independent non-verbal cognitive abilities. By perceiving information through several independent cognitive abilities, the chance of retrieving the information from the memory is multiplied when the time comes.

**Dual Coding Theory:** A theory of cognition; dual-coding theory postulates that both visual and verbal information is used to represent information.

**Eidetic or photographic memory**: Typically lasts for several seconds, not more. A person with eidetic memory can read a section or maybe a couple of pages and recollect the text from visual memory.

**Encoding:** Adding meaning to the information by converting it into something we understand: acoustic, semantic (meaning), or visual information.

**Eye Span:** Focusing on one spot and seeing words on either side, i.e., seeing 5 words while focusing on the central word of a phrase.

**Innovate**: Search for new, better ways to do the same work or achieve the same result. Look for smarter, more efficient routes to the same end-goal that boosts productivity.

**Intention**: Intention is reading with a purpose and ensuring the reading is conscious, intentional and not careless.

**KeyToStudy**: A new path-breaking methodology for faster learning, better retention and efficient information processing for everyone. The KeyToStudy System is laid out and explained at www.KeyToStudy.com.

**Main Branches**: In a mind map, the main branches are allocated for main ideas springing from the trunk. Typically, you have three to six main branches per mind map, which correspond to sections within an article.

**Major System:** A mnemonic technique used to aid in memorizing numbers.

**Marker:** Mental images that have been created and imbued with details, which are used to represent specific information

**Measure**: Examine whether the process is efficient using quantifiable data, like time to complete, hours spent, etc.

**Memorization:** The process of committing something to memory. The act of memorization is often a deliberate mental process undertaken in order to store in memory for later recall items such as experiences, names, appointments, addresses, telephone numbers, lists, stories, poems, pictures, maps, diagrams, facts, music or other visual, auditory, or tactical information.

**Mental model:** A set of assumptions and facts that form a perspective, a way to see things.

**Metacognition:** "Cognition about cognition," or "knowing about knowing." It comes from the root word "meta," meaning beyond. Metacognition can take many forms;

it includes knowledge about when and how to use particular strategies for learning or for problem-solving. There are generally two components of metacognition: knowledge about cognition, and regulation of cognition.

**Metaguiding:** Using a finger/card while reading in order to increase reading speed

**Mindfulness**: Keep the title of the text in mind and read with a certain presence of mind.

**Mnemonic or mnemonic device:** Any learning technique that aids information retention. Mnemonics aim to translate information into a form that the brain can retain better than its original form.

**Neurons**: Electrically excitable cells that transmit information using electrochemical signals

**Ontology**: A formal naming and definition of the types, properties, and interrelationships of the entities that really or fundamentally exist for a particular domain of discourse. It is thus a practical application of philosophical ontology, with a taxonomy. An ontology compartmentalizes the variables needed for some set of computations and establishes the relationships between them

**PAO (Person-Action-Object) System:** A popular method for memorizing long random numbers and decks of playing cards. The most common form of the PAO system is for every 2-digit number to convert into a series of three visual images: a person, an action, and an object.

**Personal Marker Dictionary:** Markers for names and places are hard to create, but once we create them, we can reuse them in all the text we read as a personal marker dictionary. We do not need to recreate the name and place markers each time we see them, we just reuse readily available imagery from our personal dictionary.

**Polyglot:** (noun) A person who speaks, writes, or reads a number of languages

**Pomodoro:** A time management method developed by Francesco Cirillo in the late 1980s. The technique uses a timer to break down work into intervals traditionally 25 minutes in length, separated by short breaks. These intervals are known as "pomodori," the plural of the Italian word *pomodoro* for "tomato." The method is based on the idea that frequent breaks can improve mental agility.

**Prediction/Correction:** in context of speedreading, predict what the author will say by maintaining an inner dialog of questions, but then correct it by what is actually said.

**Preread-Read-Analyze Cycle:** A cycle of skimming/scanning, reading and pausing to analyze what we just read.

**Prereading:** Encoding all names, dates and other dense material within a paragraph and the relevant markers are available to be used.

**Priming**: Asking creative and logical questions to tune the brain to retain more material within a text. Questions generate the context for details and logical structures to build upon and themes for marker creation.

**Repeat**: Go back to step one and start again.

**Reread**: In speedreading, it is not recommended to reread single words, but rather whole paragraphs and sections to understand better the text and remember the details.

**Retrieval:** Accessing the newly stored information, thereby solidifying its neural connections and integrity

**Retrieval Marker:** These markers are created *AFTER* reading the article and are used as triggers to remember the root node from as many perspectives as the article supports.

**Rhythm:** A movement marked by the regulated succession of strong and weak elements, or of opposite or different conditions. This general meaning of regular recurrence or pattern in time can apply to a wide variety of cyclical natural phenomena, i.e., music, dancing, clapping hands, steady turning of pages, etc.

**Saccade:** (noun) A rapid movement of the eye between fixation points

**Saccadic Masking:** A physiological phenomenon that actually blinds a person between columns. The 0.01 second "blind time" is used to generate markers and details.

**Scanning:** Look *only* for a specific fact or piece of information without reading everything

**Skill et:** A set of skills that form our personal toolbox, which allows us to reach our goals and work effectively.

**Skimming:** Looking *only* for the general or main ideas

**Socratic Method**: Named after the classical Greek philosopher Socrates; form of inquiry and discussion between individuals, based on asking and answering questions to stimulate critical thinking and to illuminate ideas.

**SQ3R**: A reading comprehension method named for its five steps: survey, question, read, recite, and review.

**Standardize**: Come up with a process for a specific activity that is repeatable and organized.

**Storage:** Transferring the encoded information from working memory to short term memory and (hopefully) to long term memory

**SuperLearner:** (noun) One who is repeatedly able to synthesize, understand, and retain vast amounts of information in abnormally short periods of time. A SuperLearner is a person who desires to take learning to the next level by acquiring skills that enhance reading speed, comprehension, and memory

**Synapse:** These electrically excitable cells process and transmit information using electrochemical signals. These signals are called synapses. Synapses are specialized connections between the cells.

**Synesthesia:** A neurological phenomenon in which stimulation of one sensory or cognitive pathway leads to automatic, involuntary experiences in a second sensory or cognitive pathway. The system works by converting numbers into consonant sounds, then into words by adding vowels. The system works on the principle that images can be remembered more easily than numbers.

**Synectics**: A problem-solving methodology that stimulates thought processes of which the subject may be unaware.

**Tachistoscope**: A device that displays an image for a specific amount of time. It can be used to increase recognition speed, to show something too fast to be consciously recognized, or to test which elements of an image are memorable.

**Thinking Hats:** A book by Edward de Bono which describes a tool for group discussion and individual thinking involving six colored hats.

**Working Memory:** A part of our brain associated with short-term memory. The system responsible for the transient holding and processing of new and already stored information. Working memory is an important process for reasoning, comprehension, learning and memory updating.

# ABOUT THE AUTHORS

# Dr. Lev Goldentouch, Lifehacker And Technology Guru

Dr. Lev Goldentouch earned his PhD in machine learning and information theory when he was 27 years old. Understanding the similarities of machine learning and human super-learning allowed Lev to learn immense amounts of knowledge in many technological and cognitive subjects. Lev opened a consulting company, which offers its services to highly skilled individuals, agile startups and technological giants like Samsung. Lev is an active lifehacker, holds a number of patents, and is constantly looking for new and better ways to do things. He takes great pride in sharing his unique knowledge and experience with others.

Lev is also a prolific writer. Lev published several books and articles on various technical and cognitive subjects, creativity and languages. Lev's blog www.KeyToStudy.com holds a large number of insightful advices, training exercises and useful resources. The super-learning tools developed by Lev allow ordinary people to learn at 10 times the speed of their colleagues, and enable machines to solve extremely complex problems.

# Prof. Anna Goldentouch, Education Guru

Prof. Anna Goldentouch started teaching super-learning skills when she was 17 years old. Anna developed the super-learning abilities as a tool to deal with personal dyslexia, after taking several courses on super-learning. After finishing advanced degrees in education and sociology, Anna started to teach in Bar Ilan and Ben Gurion Universities in Israel. Anna's courses on speedreading, memory development and didactic techniques are extremely popular with students. Anna also provides consulting services and training for various large companies and government services.

Anna made it her mission to teach people how to learn in a better, more efficient and fulfilling way.

Anna offers 1:1 Skype sessions for students all over the world, seminars for institutions, webinars and training days for corporate bodies and government organizations. Anna's ability to create extremely effective custom-tailored learning strategies saved countless hours to tens of thousands on

Anna's students. Anyone in need of Anna's advice can write to info@KeyToStudy.com.

# Suraj Sharma, Writer

Suraj is a writer from Chandigarh, India. Suraj has a wide range of interests ranging from behavioral psychology to public diplomacy. Being autodidact, he uses his skills as a communicator to make sure the message behind KeyToStudy remains easy to understand and accessible by all readers.

# INDEX

## A



## B



## C

**N**



**O**



**P**

## R



## S

**T**



**V**



**W**

6138071R00252

Printed in Germany
by Amazon Distribution
GmbH, Leipzig